Something That Matters

A Theology for Critical Believers

David R. Mason

PRAEGER

AN IMPRINT OF ABC-CLIO, LLC
Santa Barbara, California • Denver, Colorado • Oxford, England

BT
77
.M29
2011

Copyright 2011 by David R. Mason

All rights reserved. No part of this publication may be reproduced, stored in a retrieval system, or transmitted, in any form or by any means, electronic, mechanical, photocopying, recording, or otherwise, except for the inclusion of brief quotations in a review, without prior permission in writing from the publisher.

Library of Congress Cataloging-in-Publication Data

Mason, David R.
   Something that matters : a theology for critical believers / David R. Mason.
      p. cm.
   Includes bibliographical references and index.
   ISBN 978–0–313–38742–5 (cloth : alk. paper) — ISBN 978–0–313–38743–2 (ebook)
   1. Theology, Doctrinal—Popular works. 2. Ogden, Schubert Miles, 1928– I. Title.
BT77.M29   2011
230—dc22   2011011999

ISBN: 978–0–313–38742–5
EISBN: 978–0–313–38743–2

15 14 13 12 11   1 2 3 4 5

This book is also available on the World Wide Web as an eBook.
Visit www.abc-clio.com for details.

Praeger
An Imprint of ABC-CLIO, LLC

ABC-CLIO, LLC
130 Cremona Drive, P.O. Box 1911
Santa Barbara, California 93116-1911

This book is printed on acid-free paper ∞

Manufactured in the United States of America

For Margaret

Contents

Preface

The thesis of this book, and a theme that runs through its various chapters, is that to be human at all is to live with an unshakable confidence in the meaning and worth of life. This is the ineradicable confidence that we all make a difference in the life of God, that we are "something that matters." This common faith is what all religions, in one way or another, express. Christianity gives voice to this claim by witnessing to Jesus as the decisive re-presentation of the God who is the ground of this confidence. That is, the One who is known to be always already present to all creatures, interacting with them, is worshiped "through Jesus Christ." Whitehead's insight that to be anything at all is to be something that matters for oneself, for others, and for the Whole serves as a prism that sheds light on significant Christian beliefs about God, Christ, and the world; about faith that runs deeper than the sense of meaninglessness that some experience, and yet is cognizant of massive evil and sin and suffering in the world; about religion and Christianity and the need for theology; about Christianity and other religions; about what it means to be human; about prayer and the ethical life; and, finally, about our ultimate destiny.

The philosophers I have learned from most are Alfred North Whitehead and Charles Hartshorne. Not only is Whitehead the one who coined the sentence, "Have a care—here is something that matters," his entire metaphysics, and that of Hartshorne, underlies and energizes all my thought. The theologian who has guided me is Schubert M. Ogden. I have often declared to my students, and occasionally to a congregation of Episcopalians, that Ogden is "the greatest theologian of our day." I am aware, however, that his precise and demanding theology is often thought to be too recondite, and so I have tried to present his theology in a simplified or popular form. I hope that, in doing so, I have not misconstrued or bowdlerized a critical theology. The aim, as with Whitehead and Hartshorne, is to make important ideas accessible to a broad spectrum of intelligent persons.

Although their names appear only rarely in this work, I am indebted to the work of John B. Cobb Jr. and David Ray Griffin among the growing army of "process thinkers." I am indebted, also, to my colleagues in the Theology and Religious Studies department of John Carroll and, in particular, to Joseph F. Kelly and John R. Spencer for their critical assessment of my thought. Also, I am indebted to an old friend, Richard A. Ball, a sociologist at Penn State, for reading and reacting to some of my work.

The material, in one form or another, has shown up in many of my courses, and students have helped me to clarify and rework my ideas. Many should be thanked, but I will single out only a few: Tony Palermo, Chris Robichaud, and Sheela Pawar from years past; Jimmy Menkhaus, Jim Madrzak, Joan Carney, and Vince Mudd more recently. I am grateful to all of these persons.

I am grateful to three journals for permission to reuse material originally published with them: to *Encounter* at The Christian Theological Seminary, for permission to reuse "Reflections on 'Prayer' From a Process Perspective" as Chapter 9, "A Theology of Prayer"; to the *Journal of Ecumenical Studies* for permission to reuse "A Christian Alternative to (Christian) Racism and Antisemitism" in Chapter 7, "Christianity and Other Religions"; and to *Dialog: A Journal of Theology* for permission to reuse "A Christology of Universal Redemptive Love" as Chapter 5, "A Christology of Universal Redemptive Love."

A work of this sort could not see the light of day without the help of many persons. I would like to thank my agent, Brian Romer, for getting this to the publisher, and Michael Wilt, Senior Acquisitions Editor at ABC-CLIO, for shepherding the work through the process. And I thank Kathy Merhar, the department secretary at John Carroll, for help with the computer. Above all, I thank my wife, Margaret, to whom this book is dedicated. Margaret is the light of my life, the love of my life.

1

Faith, Religion, and Theology

This chapter raises, clarifies, and answers the question: "What is the point of doing theology, and in particular, what difference does it make to the church and to the secular world?" This question requires that we come to terms with two other more basic terms: faith *and* religion. *Theology, then, is the conscious effort to make explicit the meaning and significance of the implicit faith of humanity that every being is "something that matters," and it does so in the terms of a particular religion, in this case, Christianity. Several questions for my understanding of theology are raised and answered: (1) Does it undermine the faith of believers? (2) Is theology too abstract or wordy? (3) Is theology already biased? Do we not have to have faith to do theology? (4) Is theology too academic and inattentive to the needs of oppressed groups?*

The general perception of the worth of "theology" is at a low ebb these days. This is so, in part, because many of its traditional doctrines are at odds with our daily experience and with ideas we take for granted. But a deeper reason is that many people simply don't see any point to it. They regard theology as some sort of utopian speculation that is, at best, idle and, at worst, perverse. Consider, for example, the understanding of theology that is taken for granted by one very bright and influential public intellectual: In an op-ed column in the *New York Times*, Thomas Friedman speaks of the Bush administration that came into office bearing Republican theological positions on tax cuts, the environment, and missile defense—positions that were hatched in conservative think tanks and chanted with religious devotion, but were never tempered by the real world as it has evolved over the last eight years. Again, with reference to tax cuts, Friedman speaks of the Republican theology that all problems can be solved by slashing taxes. A third time, speaking of an ideology that would press for a Star Wars missile shield irrespective of whether it is needed or can work, he says that such is realism lost in theology.[1] One need not disagree with Friedman's main point to see that he simply uses "theology" or "theological" as shorthand for doctrinaire opinions that are utterly untested and detached from real-world facts.

It is not only public intellectuals who think of theology as useless speculation. Friends and clergy alike seem to want to dismiss theology as pointless. For instance, recently my wife and I had dinner with an intelligent and devoted parishioner, a woman with a PhD in art history who kindly asked what I was up to these days. When I replied, perhaps too enthusiastically, that I was teaching an introductory course in *systematic theology*, an instant expression of pained incomprehension crossed her face. "What is *that*?" she groaned. I suppose I replied something like the following: Well, it's a "deliberate, methodical, and reasoned [examination of] the meaning and truth of the Christian witness of faith."[2] "What difference does that make?" put a quick end to this conversation, and we immediately switched to casual chitchat.

The next morning a popular homilist began (in feigned gravitas): "Recently, I have been studying the works of the *great theologians*. And the greatest of these is a man called . . . *Dr. Seuss*!" The relief among the congregation was palpable. I should say that the preacher's homily was not bad. As I recall he made much of *Horton Hears a Who*, saying that Horton took seriously all the little folk, and he applied this to Christ. What I gathered from the homily and from the congregation's response, however, was that theology might be disregarded as irrelevant.

The attitudes laid bare here—and the examples might be multiplied a thousand times—expose a serious problem. They tell us that theology is widely perceived to be purely academic, without any practical use. Whereas people see clearly how *being* religious makes a real difference in their lives, they fail to see how discussing ideas *about* religion can do anything more than amuse those few who relish outmoded concepts. Years ago Alfred North Whitehead warned educators of the danger of "inert ideas," ones "that are merely received into the mind without being utilised, or tested, or thrown into fresh combinations."[3] He observed that to traffic in such inert ideas can only produce a kind of "mental dryrot" in both teacher and learner. The same warning is clearly evident in the attitudes exhibited above and the questions put to me. They constitute a demand that the work of theology not be undertaken in vain, and that its ideas be shown to have important consequences for how we order our lives.

The first thing we need to get straight is that ideas inevitably *do* have consequences, whether or not the connection is explicitly recognized and acknowledged. For instance, the Enlightenment idea that autonomy is fundamental to being fully human helped spawn the rise of Western democracies. And Thomas Jefferson's well-known words in the Declaration of Independence, "that all men are created equal, that they are endowed by their Creator with certain unalienable Rights, that among these are Life, Liberty, and the Pursuit of Happiness,"[4] express that idea and enable us to see the connection between the idea and its practical effect.

Similarly, Marx's view that the history of the world is the "history of class struggle," and that, therefore, what is called for is the abolition of private property and the creation of a classless society—"an association in which the free development of each is the condition for the free development of all"[5]—clearly has had a tremendous impact on the lives of millions of humans, for good or ill, as the history of the twentieth century attests.

Another example that illustrates that ideas have real consequences is the ultimate reality or God that people accept and live by. To be sure, this idea is often only vaguely or loosely held, being a kind of inherited presupposition. Even so, different ideas of ultimate reality have different consequences. For instance, insofar as ultimate reality is conceived as Nirvana or Emptiness, believers are not likely to petition for help, because Nirvana is not understood to be responsive or, in any sense, personal. They are much more likely to engage in meditation. Moreover, their ethical principles lead them to try to extinguish all desires or acts that promote the individual self at the expense of fellow creatures or to sharpen definite personality traits in any way. By contrast, believers in a personal deity ask God for things and expect divine activity in the world in response to that petition. And despite the fact that, at its best, such theism requires the faithful to love their neighbors as themselves, it nonetheless promotes selfhood more than nontheistic beliefs do. It also encourages activity designed to influence other humans and to change or redesign the natural environment.

Thus the ideas of God or of ultimate reality that lie at the base of various religions insinuate themselves into the cultures influenced by these religions and help to mold the ethical perspective and the behavior of the people of that culture.

As these examples show, it is never really a matter of *whether* ideas have consequences, but only of *what* the consequences of particular ideas are likely to be. The issue at stake, then, is how to be as clear and precise as possible about what the basic ideas are so that we can see their inevitable implications for other correlative ideas and their likely practical effect. As regards the ideas consciously entertained or presupposed by a religion, it is of the utmost importance to be clear about what they are, what they mean, and what they entail. Failing to reflect on such fundamental ideas or the meaning of the originating events of that religion is likely to make one captive to the interpretations given by a previous generation, and merely to parrot the theology of the past. And the surest way to produce *bad* theology and an inadequate religious response is to reproduce thoughtlessly the theology of a bygone day.[6]

It is just that pitfall that I hope to avoid in this work. I aim generally to demonstrate how a clear grasp of certain fundamental Christian doctrines makes a difference in the lives of believers. This entails being clear, not only about what ideas are fundamental to Christianity but also what these ideas mean for us today, and in what sense they can be taken to be true; it also entails showing the difference these ideas make in the lives of those who hold them and so in the world at large. In this way theology can justify faith and its religious expressions both rationally and practically.

More specifically, I aim to use the insights and concepts of process theology to unpack the meaning of the Christian message for us today and to show that it is not only credible but also relevant to our lives in practical ways. Process theology has the capacity to resolve or avoid the many intellectual difficulties that traditional theology notoriously falls prey to, dilemmas such as the following: What sense does it make to say, "God loves the world, but is utterly unaffected by it" (as no lover would ever be)? Or, what is the point of praying to a being who is unmoved and immutable? Why try to affect a being who cannot change? Or, what sense does it make to assert that God is both all-good and all-powerful at the same time that we acknowledge the obvious, that evil exists in the world? For, as the philosopher David Hume and others have convincingly argued, if God were all-good, God would desire that creatures suffer no evil, and if God were all-powerful, God would form creation so that no evil cropped up; yet evil persists.

This last dilemma discloses a genuinely moral dimension to be addressed: Is God thus responsible for the massive evil in the world? Or, if God is both omnipotent and omniscient, in the sense of knowing all future acts and events in their particularity, what is left to human freedom and responsibility? The theology that follows, which utilizes the insights and concepts of process philosophy, addresses these and other issues in ways that the traditional theology seems incapable of doing; at the same time it strives always to represent adequately the heart of the Christian message.

To realize these aims we must take the first step, which is to try to be clear about what "theology" really is and just what a theologian does. To accomplish this, however, we must distinguish what we mean by "theology" from what we mean by "faith" and "religion." Regrettably, the terms *faith*, *religion*, and *theology* are often used carelessly as if they were interchangeable or merely synonymous. Even those who ought to know better sometimes mistake the disciplined study that is "theology" for the practice of "religion."[7] Sometimes we speak of both religion and theology as "irrational" or "non-rational" when the point we're struggling to make is that the prior *faith* on which both religion and theology are grounded is itself not based on rationality.

For the sake of clarity it is helpful to differentiate the three terms. To be sure, they are bound together, but they should not be confused or used as equivalents. Each stands for a distinct dimension of existence: Briefly, *faith* stands for a fundamental disposition that everyone has irrespective of how to conceptualize it; *religion* stands for a particular historical expression of the underlying faith—for example, Christianity or Judaism; and *theology* stands for the more or less reasoned effort to make sense of the claims of a religion. The clearer we are about the distinctions, the better able we will be to understand what theology is, why theologians do the things they do, and what difference it makes. The following three sections, therefore, will aim to shed light on these terms, drawing out their distinct meanings and showing their connections.

FAITH

I begin with the term that is most often misunderstood and is, perhaps, the most difficult to comprehend, namely, *faith*. It is the term we use for that attitude or orientation that lies at the base of religion and theology. One reason why it is so difficult to get the meaning of faith straight is that throughout our history the word has been used in several different ways. For instance, in the New Testament we find the apostle Paul and the author of the Letter of James apparently at loggerheads with each other over the indispensability of faith to the life of the believer. Paul declares that "a person is justified by faith apart from works prescribed by the law" (Romans 3:28). James, as if to refute Paul, insists that "a person is justified by works and not by faith alone," so that "faith without works is also dead" (James 2:24, 26).

Taken at face value, the two assertions clearly contradict each other. Yet I suggest that each author is working with such an utterly different understanding of faith as to be making a wholly different point. According to the understanding that James apparently takes for granted, faith is a matter of giving intellectual assent to a proposition: to have faith, in this sense, is to entertain a belief *about* something, in this case about God or about some religious claim. If this is the idea of faith that James assumes, it follows that the belief must be followed by appropriate deeds; otherwise, it is "dead." Like inert ideas, beliefs about God or religious matters that do not issue in right behavior are so much mental and spiritual dry rot.

But is this the understanding of faith that Paul has? I do not think so. For Paul, faith is an orientation of the whole person, rather than merely the mind, which has God or Jesus Christ as the center of gravity toward which we are inevitably drawn, the be-all and end-all of existence. Thus faith is not at all a belief *about* God, but it is belief *in* God in the sense of being an utter trust in God's steadfast love no matter what may occur to us in this life. It is an orientation such that, no matter what the legitimate concerns of life may be, one's "ultimate concern," to use Paul Tillich's phrase, is focused on God.[8] And, as Tillich also saw clearly, this understanding of faith is concretely expressed in the words of the great commandment: "You shall love the Lord your God with all your heart, and with all your soul, and with all your might" (Deuteronomy 6:5). We can see from this expression that faith includes an emotional component (heart), a spiritual or intellectual one (soul), and an active component (might) but is not identified with any one of them. Rather, as deeper and more inclusive, faith inevitably gives rise to a thoughtful explication of the basic orientation, and it necessarily issues in activity—"faith working through love" (Galatians 5:6)—but it is distinguished from both intellect and works.

I believe that the understanding of faith that I have attributed to the apostle Paul is sounder than the one that I suspect James held. James views faith as a species of knowledge. But, because it is regarded as no ordinary kind of knowledge, the normal warrants for supporting claims to truth are waived. Thus faith becomes a belief about matters for which either no explanation is given or else one that is strained or preposterous. In the best of cases, then, the grounds for faith are obscure. In the worst of cases faith is treated as something utterly senseless, a mindset expressed by the schoolboy who said, "Faith is when you believe something you know ain't true."[9] That is, faith, as a belief *about* divine things, runs counter to everything we have good reason to believe.

Paul, too, understands that faith is not rational. But this is because, as an orientation of the entire being toward God in trust, faith lies beneath the level of reason. It is not, however, anti-rational. In fact, it is the condition for any sort of reasoning. In that sense, it is "pre-rational." As the wellspring of every element of human personality faith gives rise to the human quest for meaning. It is, as Anselm put it, "faith seeking understanding."[10] Paul's view is the one I believe to be the best. But before expounding its meaning further, there is one other point I wish to emphasize:

Properly speaking, the object of faith is *God* and nothing less. Whether we take faith to be a "belief about" or "belief in," it is always directed toward God and not toward this-worldly beings. To be sure, there are attitudes or states analogous to faith that are directed toward objects much less than God. For instance, we believe that the world is round or that water is composed of two parts hydrogen and one part oxygen. Moreover, we trust other humans; we are dedicated to them and loyal to their cause. But, strictly speaking, faith is not given to objects or persons in this world. It is only given to the ultimate ground and end of all being—God.

Having made that point I return to consider more about the understanding of faith as an orientation of the whole person, the orientation that lies at the base of knowledge and of activity. There are two distinct senses contained within the one major understanding, and we should be clear about them.

First, there is an implicit faith that is an attitude fundamental to the act of being human. Many persons would not wish to affirm belief in God explicitly, and some would positively deny it. And yet all of us, I believe, would affirm what may be called the common faith of humanity: every act and every experience, no matter how small or unnoticed, is, in Whitehead's telling phrase, "something that matters."[11] Thus, given with human existence itself is the conviction that everything we do or undergo makes a difference somewhere in the world. It is proverbial that the stone, dropped in the pond, sends ripples across to the farther edge or that a typhoon in the western Pacific alters the weather patterns in California. What is even more important is that this same cause-effect relation lies at the heart of human life. Our most private thoughts, as well as our public acts, have their effects and make a difference in our continuing lives and those of the people we interact with.

For instance, my response to the report of a colleague's promotion and increase in salary, whether it be jealousy, happiness at her good fortune, a lurking fear that it says something about my own inadequacy, a resolve to improve my work habits, or some combination of these, will surely affect my subsequent behavior and thus have a ripple effect among my coworkers. Similarly, the attitude I take toward the news that I have a terminal illness, whether it be terror, anger, resignation, resolve to make the most of my remaining time and to endure the pain with grace, a sense of peace, or gratitude for the life and love I've already had, will make a difference in the quality of my remaining life and in the lives of loved ones looking after me.

Thus, no thought or occurrence is too small, private, or seemingly isolated to be of no effect; every thought, word, or deed makes a difference in ourselves and has an impact in the world around us. This being so, and being, as I believe, central to our deepest conviction, it takes only a little reflection to conclude that no act or experience, having once registered itself in the world, can vanish into sheer nothingness. Every act or experience, having occurred, has established itself as a value for all times. This means that every thought, deed, and experience makes an *abiding* difference in the universe. Put otherwise, to be is to be "something that matters," and to be something that matters everlastingly.

This perspective is critical to the understanding of faith that is implicit in every act of living. It is, I believe, this "deeper faith" that Schubert Ogden declares to be "logically prior to every particular religious assertion," namely, "an original confidence in the meaning and worth of life" or, alternatively, "our ineradicable confidence in the final worth of our existence."[12] Every human shares this implicit faith. It is not reserved to the pious, nor is it an eccentric view held only by a few optimistic believers. Consider what Albert Camus, supposedly a champion of the absurd or of nihilism, writes. In making the point that "the absurd can be considered only as a point of departure," and that "a literature of despair is a contradiction in terms," he asks: "How can one limit oneself to the idea that nothing has sense and that we must despair of everything?" This is a serious question for one who has wrestled deeply with the issue, and his answer is revealing:

> Without going to the bottom of the matter, one can at least observe that, in the same way that there is no absolute materialism, since merely in order to fashion this word it is already necessary to say that there is in the world something more than matter, there is no total nihilism. From the moment one says that all is nonsense, one expresses something which has sense.[13]

If this insight carries any force—and it seems clear to me that it does—the same logic tells us that to act in any fashion, whether creative or destructive or even suicidal, is to act *as if* that act had meaning and value beyond itself in the universe. It is to "express something which has sense." To exist at all is to affirm one's abiding worth—for good or ill. As Whitehead says: "Our enjoyment of actuality is a realization of worth, good or bad. It is a value experience. Its basic expression is— Have a care, here is something that matters!"[14]

I recognize that to insist on our inescapable trust in the meaning and worth of all our actions and experiences is to raise the suspicion of merely ignoring the dark side of life. Such a faith may appear to be nothing but the irrepressible optimism of a Pollyanna. It is not. It well knows tragedy, sorrow, and acute suffering. Yet, in the teeth of all of life's ills, this faith also knows that such experiences are not in vain, for it affirms that what is done cannot be undone; what happens is etched indelibly into the face of the universe. Hence, each deed, no matter how seemingly trivial or apparently wasted, is of unfading importance; each experience, no matter how drenched in suffering, is seen to matter infinitely.

My conviction, and that of generations before me, is that this common faith, when fully understood, entails explicit faith in God. Although clearly not everyone will agree, I believe that the idea of a personal God who not only creates but redeems all creation is the one that most adequately makes sense of the implicit faith of humanity.

This brings us to the other sense in which we speak of faith as an orientation of the total personality: the explicit faith in, or utter reliance on, God. To be sure, we should never confuse claims of having faith with actually living a faithful life. We all know persons (perhaps ourselves) who profess faith in God yet live as if some lesser idol (e.g., money, power, intelligence, youth) held sway. The genuinely faithful person may confess that faith explicitly, but the confession itself does not guarantee the genuine article. As Jesus says: "Not everyone who says to me, 'Lord, Lord,' will enter the kingdom of heaven, but only the one who does the will of my Father in heaven" (Matthew 7:21).

In fact, there is no human way to measure the degree of faith in the strictest sense, because, as an inner orientation of the whole person, faith is invisible to all but God. As Paul says to the people of Corinth: "But with me it is a very small thing that I should be judged by you or by any human court. I do not even judge myself. . . . It is the Lord who judges me" (I Corinthians 4:3–4).

Even so, although we can never measure the genuineness of faith in others or in ourselves, we can specify the distinguishing features of such a radical trust in God, and we can see what such trust comes to.

To the extent that we actually live faithfully, we place our ultimate confidence in God's steadfast love rather than relying on our own resources and those of our fellow creatures. Such explicit faith does not force us to withdraw from this-worldly endeavors; the world is, after all, God's. But it allows us to place all our efforts in the proper perspective. By relying on God's love as the final justification for our worth, we are enabled to dismiss certain kinds of fear. We are released from the anxiety that our activities are meaningless, that no one cares, that we are utterly alone in the world, and that our efforts do not make any difference. Also, we are released from the poisonous attitude that insists that for something to be of worth it must be *mine*. It is a great boon to be free enough to rejoice when others have talents, possessions, or good fortune that we do not, and perhaps cannot, have. Being thus *freed from* the stultifying preoccupation with self or from idolatrous reliance on merely temporal goods, relations, or structures as the ultimate object of our trust, we are actually *freed for* responsible and productive living, for loving service to this world—to this world as itself the object of God's love.

RELIGION

Let us now pass on to a brief explanation of the second, historically conditioned dimension of existence, religion. By *religion* I mean a particular cultural expression of a group's underlying faith that gives order to the members' lives according to the precepts of the faith as thus formulated. Religion is a complex cultural phenomenon comprising many elements, among which are ritual, myth, emotion, belief, a code of behavior, and an organizational structure. All of these elements are bound together by a rich set of symbols. I know of no better short, comprehensive definition of religion than that of the anthropologist Clifford Geertz: "A religion is a system of symbols which acts to establish powerful, pervasive, and long-lasting moods and motivations . . . by formulating conceptions of a general order of existence and clothing these conceptions with such an aura of factuality that the moods and motivations seem uniquely realistic."[15]

This anthropological definition may seem unduly abstruse because it is compact and uses terms in an unfamiliar way. But its point is that any religion must be seen as a complex cultural expression of a fundamental worldview. It expresses this worldview concretely in terms of symbols, rites, stories, dogmas, and the like. And it is these concrete expressions that lend to each religion its particular ethos—its ethical norms and aesthetic preferences.

Seen in this light, religion is both a product of culture and a producer of culture. One example will suffice to illustrate the claim that it is a product. The language in which the stories of a religion are told and its beliefs expressed is culturally rooted. This language clearly shapes the ideas and forms of the particular religion. To understand this is to see that all religions are, in part, products of the culture in which they arise and that they represent and serve. Most of us easily recognize this truth with respect to other religions. It is the beginning of wisdom, however, to acknowledge the truth with respect to our own. To admit the cultural relativity of our own religion, to see it as simply a special expression of the "one, true faith," and at the same time to recognize that there is a common faith at the base of all religions is to eschew the idolatry of equating our religion with God and to take a step toward trusting the one God who creates and redeems all.

But this is not the whole story. Although any religion is built up out of many cultural expressions, it is not merely one more cultural institution alongside others such as family, work, government, schools, or the military. Nor is it *only* a product of culture. Religion occupies a unique and indispensable place in the life of any culture. It is the most comprehensive of all the cultural institutions because it touches every aspect of human life. For this reason it is the treasure house of that culture's living symbols and the agency for celebrating its deepest values. But more than this, religion raises and addresses the primary human question, the question of the meaning and worth of life, which is the issue of faith. Therefore, a religion is the chief instrument for expressing and promulgating that culture's fundamental worldview, and in doing so it creates new cultural expressions.

Finally, each religion articulates the principles that coordinate the basic elements of the worldview with the practical lives—public as well as private—of the members of its culture; it fuses worldview and ethos by grounding our "ought" in a fundamental "is." For example, if God not only is, but is the loving creator and redeemer of all, it follows that our response to God should be to love as much of God's creation as we can: "You shall love the Lord your God with all your heart, and with all your soul, and with all your mind, and with all your strength [and] . . . you shall love your neighbor as yourself" (Mark 12:30–31, summarizing the Law and citing Deuteronomy 6:5 and Leviticus 19:18). Thus religion brings together and synthesizes the various disparate elements of a living people, and so stamps their history as a particular culture. It is a producer as well as a product.

If the foregoing links religion and culture, whether as product or producer, we need also to see that living religions transcend their cultures. For, even as a religion gathers together the diverse elements into one unified cultural expression, it also seeks to give expression to that invariant faith that lies beneath all cultures. As Whitehead says:

> Religion is the vision of something which stands beyond, behind, and within the passing flux of immediate things; something which is real, and yet waiting to be realized; something which is a remote possibility, and yet the greatest of present facts; something that gives meaning to all that passes, and yet eludes apprehension; something whose possession is the final good, and yet is beyond all reach; something which is the ultimate ideal, and the hopeless quest. . . . Apart from [the religious vision] human life is a flash of occasional enjoyments, lighting up a mass of pain and misery, a bagatelle of transient experience.[16]

As expressive of that which utterly transcends all culture, religion is bound to come into conflict with culture. There is always an element of judgment when the universal touches the particular. So religion contains the prophetic as well as the priestly; it convicts as well as completes. But whether religion celebrates or challenges, it is the one fundamental sacrament, since it is the "outward and visible sign of an inward and spiritual grace" given by God to humanity.

THEOLOGY

Let us now turn to the task of theology. Religion has many dimensions, but one of them is the inherent demand to examine, clarify, codify, and communicate the faith as expressed by the stories, symbols, preaching, and practice of that religion. Just as religion is a particular way of incarnating the more elemental faith, so one of the demands of that same faith is that it be made intelligible. As Anselm saw clearly, faith must seek understanding. Theology is that part of religion with the special task of making the underlying faith understandable. In doing so, it also makes it more accessible.

Strictly speaking, "theology" is *logos* about *theos*, or rational discourse about God. But such discourse never occurs in a cultural vacuum. There are no statements about God wholly detached from their historical moorings. Therefore, theology undertakes its task by examining, appraising, and interpreting the witness of faith as passed down to us in the writings, worship, and practice of a specific religion, and doing so critically.

This means, in the first place, that theology is always the theology of a particular religion (e.g., "Christian theology," "Jewish theology,"

"Muslim theology"). There is no non-historical or absolute theology. But to affirm this does not, at all, license theology to become an ideology. The task of theology is not merely to rationalize and defend a position already taken. This is the point of insisting that it be critical. Although theology takes as its point of departure the culturally relativized *witness* of faith, it seeks to unpack the meaning of that faith itself, and to do so in ways that are fully public, fully accessible to impartial scrutiny. Theology should never make its appeal to some special authority that is unavailable to other intelligent and interested seekers after truth. Insofar as it has done so, and regrettably it sometimes has, theology has failed.

But it need not fail. We may define theology as the deliberate, critical, and systematic reflection on the underlying faith, the basic claims, and the full range of activities of a particular religion. To be adequate it must critically examine the religion's tradition, especially its earliest witness where the tradition is closest to the originating genius of that religion. Also, and just as important, theology must try to establish the meaning and truth of that religion's claims as measured against the best available sources for expressing human understanding.

These sources will inevitably include philosophy, the time-honored discipline for evaluating the meaning and truth of various claims. They should also include the humanities and the social sciences, because these help us to understand the many ways of being human. Where relevant they should include the natural sciences, which also help us to understand what it means to be human. No one can hope to have mastered several—much less all—of these fields. But all theologians must be attentive to what they teach us about the world and about methods for evaluating claims.

The point is that theology must never simply assume that the claims of its religion are true, so that all it has to do is uncover their meaning and communicate that meaning effectively. It must test the meaning and truth of this witness of faith against the best available criteria of meaning and truth. Thus theology is the intellectual or rational arm of religion, which itself re-presents (presents again) in a culturally conditioned way the common faith of humanity.

SOME ISSUES FOR THIS VIEW OF THEOLOGY ADDRESSED

Having put the matter this way, it remains for me to address a few issues raised by some who disagree with my understanding of theology. I am aware of four related, but distinct, criticisms. In responding to these I shall try to show that theology, as I understand it, is of immense practical significance.

The first criticism is that the study of theology often undermines the faith of the college student or seminarian. This criticism betrays the fact that, for some, the problem is not that theology makes *no* difference; rather, it is believed to make *too much* difference, but of a pernicious sort. More than once I have heard the complaint that a young person went off to college or seminary on fire with zeal for the Lord's work only to encounter nonbelieving teachers. Under their spell, the complaint goes, the student either turned away from theology or, worse, fell into their snare and lost his or her faith.

This is a serious charge, and it must be answered. I suspect that the first response should be to paraphrase Socrates and say, "An unexamined faith is not worth having." Any so-called faith incapable of withstanding careful scrutiny is not as strong or deep as was supposed. Genuine faith is always prepared to be examined in the clear light of day and discussed objectively free from the emotional supports of a strictly religious context.

What sometimes is paraded before us as faith, however, may be closer to idolatry: an emotional attachment to, and reliance on, certain forms of religious expression that at one time had the power to convey the deeper faith. But faith in *God*, utter reliance on God's creative and redemptive love, should never be equated with belief in the literal veracity of particular expressions of that faith. For example, the Gospels are replete with miraculous stories about Jesus. The purpose of these stories is to proclaim that the loving God, who is always energizing our lives by urging us toward our highest potentiality and receiving us into God's own life, is dramatically and decisively re-presented in Jesus. The claim, also, is that this has made all the difference in the lives of those testifying.

Whether the stories are literally true or not is beside the point, except insofar as the demand to accept them literally is made the test of faith. When that occurs, idolatry has triumphed. Faith in God must never be reduced to a literal acceptance of that which can be verified empirically, because "God"—whatever we may decide about the full meaning of that term—can never denote an object of empirical investigation. This concern lays bare one of the pitfalls of the intellectualist approach to the meaning of faith.

More than this, if my earlier discussion of faith is to the point, we cannot literally "lose our faith," since at its deepest level faith is ineradicable. Those who are said to have lost their faith more than likely have either broken down the barriers to a more genuine faith or have shifted their allegiance from a religious set of idols to a more secular set. The move away from religion may, in fact, be an important step in a person's development in faith. The psychiatrist Scott Peck has shown that in certain cases it is actually necessary to help patients cast off a religion that has shackled them to promote spiritual growth even when the prospects for replacing the old with a new, more helpful, religion are dim. "It is indeed possible," he claims, "for us to mature out of a belief in God." To be sure, Peck's deeper conviction is that neither atheism nor agnosticism attains the highest level of human wisdom as does the best sort of theism. "There is reason to believe," he continues, "that behind spurious notions and false concepts of God there lies a reality that is God. This is what Paul Tillich meant when he referred to the 'god beyond God.' "[17]

In Peck's mind, therefore, as well as my own, the rejection of an inadequate and often harmful religious view does not entail the rejection of God. In fact, as I understand it, no one can wholly escape an encounter with God, the One who is re-presented by the Christ proclaimed by the Christian witness. This God is experienced by all as their creative ground and their redemptive end whether or not they see Christ as the decisive revelation of God or even whether or not they believe that God exists. Critical theology makes this clear, and so plays a vital role in the life of faith and the lives of those who witness to it.

A second criticism is that theology is too abstract, too wordy, or doesn't make any sense and so is irrelevant to my life. I am sympathetic with this criticism, but it is not one that is unique to theology. Every academic discipline that I know of, once it enters deeply into its subject matter, is forced to develop precise and technical language. There is good reason for this. Things are never as simple as they seem at first blush. What reason is there to suppose that rational discourse about the author and finisher of all creation, together with an analysis of the entire range of religious symbols and activities, would be any less complex than, say, physics? To treat this complex topic with care and integrity requires the ability to make distinctions and to use precise and technical language with some subtlety.

I am aware of the criticism that systems restrict and technical language deadens thought. But clear, consistent, and systematic language does not necessarily handcuff thought or imprison the imagination. On the contrary, the use of precise language can set our minds free to examine our assumptions and discover what the effects of modifying those assumptions might be. It enables us to make clear the meaning of our basic assertions and to see clearly what their consequences are or what conclusions we should draw from them. What is more, language that is too colloquial does not wear well from generation to generation; frankly, the more abstract and systematic language does. Therefore, if a particular theological offering is to be more than a passing fad, it is bound to use precise and technical—but, one hopes, clear—language.

Because theology is felt to be of vital importance to many who are not professional theologians, there is a demand to transpose the technical language into one that is intelligible to laypeople. This task, too, requires special skills. It requires a mastery of a large, complex, and growing field, together with an understanding of the mind of the people at a particular time, and the literary craft to bridge the two. This is no small task. Some of us are trying, but I beg the reader to be patient if we do not measure up to the standards set by the great masters of the past.

A third criticism stems from the view that we cannot do theology at all unless we "have faith" or "stand within the circle of faith." What this usually means is that the theologian must acknowledge his or her prior commitment to the content of the witness of faith. Therefore, the theologian need never even address the truth claims of the witness of faith. According to this view theology has a prior commitment to the truth of that witness, and so only has to unfold its meaning. I repeat the position taken earlier in this chapter: the task of the theologian is not merely to rationalize and defend a position already taken. The theologian who is not free to *assess* the truth of the community's claims is unable to *assert* them as true.

Those who would require a theologian to profess a particular expression of faith confuse "religion" with "faith." To be sure, one cannot theologize apart from faith; as I have understood the matter, we cannot even live as humans apart from faith. But this does not mean that a particular, culturally relativized expression of the underlying faith—one religion—is inevitably true in all of its claims. The claims of a religion remain to be argued for, tested, reasoned about. It is the business of theology to do just that, making use of the best available criteria for evaluating those claims.

If theology undertakes its work by uncritically assuming the truth of all the religious declarations, it inevitably sinks into the pit of dogmatic assurance and complacency that have been the bane of all healthy religions. If, on the other hand, theology deliberately, critically, and systematically reflects on the fundamental assumptions and assertions of a particular religion, it enables that religion to tap the power of its originating event and to gain access to truth, beauty, and goodness in its contemporary setting. Nor should we be misled by the demand to be systematic. Systems do not have to be "closed systems." They can be open to modification or even to their own demise. The point about being systematic is that rationality requires that basic principles be coordinated so that they are not at odds with one another.

Finally, it should be said forthrightly that even the truth of the central or fundamental doctrine (e.g., for theistic religions, the belief that "God" is the object and ground of faith) must be subject to critical testing. Any theology worth its salt will insist that the criteria for testing truth claims about God are never empirical, but are properly metaphysical. What I mean is that, since God is never properly conceived as one object among others in the natural world but is, rather, to be understood as the ground of all things that come to be, the method of observing by noting differences (the empirical method) is wholly beside the point. We must seek to establish what is unavoidably present when anything exists and then show that only God, properly understood, makes sense of this. Thus theology, conceived along the lines I have suggested, is far more valuable to religion than theology narrowly conceived.

The fourth, and last, criticism to respond to is that voiced by theologians who ground their theology in the experience of oppressed people. Seeing the task of theology as working for the liberation of such groups as the poor of Latin America and other Third World countries, blacks in the United States, and women in America and Europe, these "liberation theologians" sometimes claim that academic theology is irrelevant to the real work of God's people. That work is the liberation of all oppressed people. Theology, they say, must serve the real life of the church, and any theology (academic theology by implication) that does not do this ought to be disregarded or thrown out.

I am in sympathy with much that this important recent work has taught us, and I hope I have learned that the church and theology can never retreat from the issues that liberation theology has raised for us. But the issue here is, "What is the role of theology?" The liberation theologians are right that theology exists to serve the church. That is never in doubt, although it is also true that it exists to serve all humanity as well. The only issue is *how* theology can best serve the church or the work of God's people in the world.

As I said in responding to the previous point, theology can never sufficiently perform its task by assuming without question the truth of a religion's claim and then merely trying to render the expressions of a former age in meaningful language for the present. Many theologians often seem not to have considered this point. Moreover,

I suggest that theology will never fulfill its promise by simply identify-ing particular demands for political, economic, or social liberation with the liberation that the Bible proclaims as intrinsic to salvation. I hasten to add that I am convinced that the freedom proclaimed in scripture as arising from faith in God does, in fact, translate into politi-cal, economic, and social liberation. But the point is that theology cannot perform its service to religion either by uncritically accepting that religion's claims or by equating present-day concerns with the fundamental witness of faith. Either of these moves inevitably turns theology into the servant of special-interest groups.

My conviction, then, is that if theology did not undertake the diffi-cult task of examining, evaluating, systematizing, and articulating the beliefs of a religion, that religion would never survive from one gener-ation to another; it would dissipate into hazy emotional attachments. The systematic and critical work of theology forms, as Whitehead says, "the ark within which the Church floats safely down the flood-tide of history." But as Whitehead also warns, "the Church will perish unless it opens its windows and lets out the dove to search for an olive branch."[18] That olive branch, which signals sure footing, is the critical, dispassionate, objective quest for truth.

2

Process Thought: Its Background and Basic Ideas

Since "process philosophy" is not a household term, it is helpful to demystify it by uncovering some of its background and laying bare some of its basic ideas and terms. Those parts of the background that are uncovered are basic ideas of Whitehead and Hartshorne. The fundamental ideas, including that all actualities are inevitably temporal, dynamic, and interrelated, are seen to be distillations from common secular experience. When understood and properly applied to God and religious beliefs they are more appropriate for making the biblical story compelling and intelligible than are the ideas and terms of classical theology.

The specific form of thinking that underlies this work is often called *process philosophy*. Because this is not a household term, it is useful to explain how the word *process* is understood and used here. In general, it points to the insight that change is built into the nature of things. More specifically, this means that to be actual at all is to be *temporal* (always having a past and always facing potentiality), *dynamic*, and *interrelated* with other actualities. Not only is the universe itself viewed as a process made up of innumerable processes; God, too, because seen as an actual entity and not a mere abstraction, is understood to be similarly temporal, dynamic, and interrelated with all others.

I will elaborate this intuition more fully in Chapters 3 and 4, where I hope to show many of its implications for our idea of God. First, however, it seems helpful to show how the insight was gained, and how the two philosophers most influential in laying the groundwork for process thought arrived at their views of God. Then, still in this chapter, I will return to a more thorough airing of the word *process* and will offer some additional comments aimed at connecting the discussion with our ordinary experience.

BACKGROUND

The philosophy that forms the backbone of process theology is worked out most extensively and thoroughly in the writings of two philosophers, Alfred North Whitehead (1861–1947) and Charles Hartshorne (1897–2000).

Whitehead, the son of an Anglican clergyman, first distinguished himself as a mathematician at Trinity College, Cambridge University. This part of his career was capped with the production of *Principia Mathematica* in collaboration with Bertrand Russell, his former pupil. In 1910 he moved to London, a year later joining the faculty of the University of London. At this time he developed a novel and sophisticated philosophy of science and, in a series of essays, a philosophy of education. In 1924, at the age of 63, he came to America to join the philosophy faculty at Harvard. And for the next dozen years or so he produced some of the twentieth century's richest, most comprehensive, and most influential metaphysics. Between 1925 and 1938 Whitehead turned out seven books, the most systematic and comprehensive—and also the most difficult—of which is *Process and Reality*. In addition to these important works, he wrote a number of quite readable essays and was recorded in conversation by Lucien Price, an editor for the *Boston Globe*.

Even so, his thought does not form a closed system. We can discern considerable development—even some radically new departures— within this period. Whitehead's mind was fertile and expansive, even adventurous; and although he always tried to coordinate his ideas, he was equally suspicious of any hint of dogmatic finality or closure. "We must be systematic," he writes, "but we should keep our systems open."[1]

Such a development in his thought can be observed in his understanding of God. When, in *Science and the Modern World*, Whitehead was elaborating the idea of the world as a web of events ceaselessly coming into being, it became more and more clear to him that such a world required a "Principle of Concretion" or "principle of limitation." Without some limitation on the potentially infinite sea of possibilities, all would be chaos. Without an overarching principle of order, there could be no world of actual events at all. This principle, he realized, was what religions worship as God. Nevertheless, he was uneasy with the idea of God as a mere "principle." He understood that principles could not really order anything, because ordering is an activity; it is an *act*, and every act requires an *actuality* at its source. So, when he wrote *Religion in the Making*, he treated God as an actual entity rather than an abstract principle.

Within a few years, when working out *Process and Reality*, Whitehead developed the idea of God further, making what many believe to be his most significant contribution to philosophical theology: Since God was now conceived as an actual entity, and not merely the principle of limitation, God was seen to exemplify the metaphysical principles that apply to *all* actualities. To be sure, God was understood to be the primary and indispensable exemplification of these principles rather than simply one more instance of actuality. Even so, God could not be conceived as contrary to every other actual being. This meant for Whitehead that God is dipolar, analogous to all individual units of actuality in the world. That is, in addition to being an actor or a creator, God is acted on. And, in addition to having an internal life of reflection independent of temporality, God has real temporal relations with the finite actualities that constitute the world. These relations make a real difference in the ongoing life of God.

Whitehead, therefore, developed the concept of God as comprising two fundamental aspects or poles. In the one, God is seen as eternal and both the ground of order for the world and a continuous urge toward actualizing new experiences. In this respect God is "creator," although God's creative activity is regarded as continuous rather than as a once-for-all act. In the other aspect, God is seen as temporally related to all other entities as their "redeemer." By virtue of the fact that God alone experiences all finite actualities as they become determinate, they are saved and so immortalized in the ongoing life of God. God is thus both Alpha and Omega, and is both eternal in some respects and temporal in others. Yet it is only as temporal, as genuinely interactive with temporal entities, that God is fully actual and fully conscious. Just as God is immanent in the world, the world is immanent in God and is, thereby, something that matters.

Since God could thus be understood philosophically as interactive with the world, and as both creator and redeemer, Whitehead was justified in portraying God as "the poet of the world, with tender patience leading it by his vision of truth, beauty, and goodness," and as "the great companion—the fellow-sufferer who understands," and, finally, as judge of the world who treasures the world's gifts with "a tender care that nothing be lost."[2] These metaphors carry a heavy freight of emotion, but they also reflect accurately the meaning inherent in the more technical discussion.

And yet, despite his use of such dramatic personal images as "poet," "companion," "fellow-sufferer," and "judge," and despite his additional intuition that the "Galilean origin of Christianity" held a clue to the nature of deity,[3] Whitehead was loath to speak of God as a "person." Apparently, he was convinced that the personal images that had dominated traditional Western thought about God were images of a "ruling Caesar" or a "ruthless moralist" for which he had nothing but contempt. Also, for him the soul, or mind, and the body were inextricably bound together to constitute the "one human being" with personal identity.[4] But he could not see clearly how to build up the soul-body interplay as the basis for an analogy of the God-world relation. Whitehead was breaking new ground, and his intuitions were outrunning his ability to systematize them. It was left to Charles Hartshorne to develop the idea of God as the personal whole of reality interactive with its parts, and to do so with rigor and imagination.

Hartshorne, an American philosopher educated at Haverford and Harvard, is most justly famous as the twentieth century's chief defender and interpreter of the so-called ontological argument for the existence of God. This argument was put in its classical form by St. Anselm in the eleventh century, but Anselm has frequently been misunderstood. Hartshorne saw early on that the nub of Anselm's reasoning was not to argue from the idea of *any* being to its reality, as so many had supposed. Rather, Anselm's point was that the concept of *God*, as "a being than which nothing greater can be conceived," entails the idea that it is "a being which cannot be conceived not to exist" (which is today called having "necessary existence").[5] Anselm simply tried to make clear the implications of this insight. Therefore, the criticism, popular since the philosopher Kant, which says that the argument is fallacious because "existence" is not a distinguishing feature of God but is always assumed whenever we discuss *anything*, is itself beside the point. This criticism does not address the issue of "necessary existence," which is at stake when "God" is the subject of discussion. Here is what Hartshorne (and Anselm before him) saw that Kant and others missed:

Even though mere "existence" may not distinguish any particular type of being, the *mode* of a being's existence does distinguish it, and this is crucial. All ordinary or finite beings can be said to exist, but they hold in common the fact that they might not have existed at all or might fail to exist. Philosophers call this having "contingent existence." "Necessary existence" is of a wholly different order. It is the type of existence that applies to whatever cannot, under any circumstances, fail to exist. And this is said to be the type of existence that God has.

Hartshorne saw that Anselm's basic intuition in framing the argument originally was to exclude, as wholly wide of the mark, all references to contingent existence when treating *Gods* existence. Some opponents of the ontological argument used examples such as "perfect islands" or "unreal dollars" to argue that we cannot get from the idea of a thing to its reality. But by using examples from mere contingent existence, they showed that they missed the point and were not prepared to deal with the central issue.

In an early publication[6] Hartshorne laid out in some detail why the argument is unique and has to do only with necessary existence and not with contingent or ordinary existence. Anselm's argument makes the point that if we understand clearly what "God" means, we will see that the being to whom the name applies necessarily exists—it cannot fail to exist. Yet Hartshorne, unlike Anselm, does not simply *assume* that such a being is legitimately conceivable. He tries to make a good case for the idea of God, but in doing this, he finds it essential to clear away some previously cherished beliefs.

He shows that the idea of God taken for granted and expressed in much traditional theology contains incompatible elements that make it impossible to accept no matter how we argue. Take, for example, the claim that God is wholly eternal and utterly absolute and yet knows all temporal facts and occurrences. The first half of the claim asserts that God is wholly changeless and has no relation to temporality. The second half clearly asserts that God *is* temporal, since to know temporal things intimately is to know them as they come to be. It is impossible for any being to know *as actual* what is still in the future, since the future consists solely of possibilities, but not actualities. And to know which particular possibilities get actualized, as they are actualized, is to know occurrences through time. In addition to this line of thought we can see that to know anything is to take it into account, and so to be affected by it; and when we are affected we undergo a change. In every respect, then, to know temporal matters is to be temporal and to change. God cannot be both wholly eternal and know temporal facts and occurrences.

Similarly, the claim that God is wholly "impassible" (i.e., incapable of suffering or of undergoing any change) and yet has compassion for the creatures is a contradiction, since it can be shown that to have compassion entails "suffering with" and so to be affected. There are many other contradictions contained in the idea of God as this was held by traditional theologians.

Are we to conclude, then, that God does not exist? When an idea is shown to be self-contradictory, the reality it purports to mirror could

not possibly exist. Like a "round square," for example, it is an impossibility. And so the idea of God cherished by traditional theology
implies that God could not exist.

Hartshorne, however, does not allow the matter to rest here. He
clears away a particular idea of God—one that actually fuels the atheists' argument—to re-appropriate a deeper religious intuition and to
bring it forward in an intelligible way. The idea of God fundamental
to biblical religion (as distinct from traditional theology) is that of a
personal being who is utterly worthy of our worship. This being was
said by Anselm and others to be one "than which nothing greater can
be conceived" or to be "perfect." As true as this may be, some of what
was thought about perfection does not follow. Unfortunately, the
entire theological and philosophical tradition took it for granted that
to be perfect meant to be complete, such that nothing need be, or even
could be, added to it. This is the source of the problem.

If, however, we take as our starting point the biblical model of God
as supremely personal, loving, and just, we are led to a different understanding of what it means to be perfect. A perfect being, one who is
utterly worthy of worship by all other beings, is the one who loves all
others and is worthy and capable of receiving their love in return.
And this means that the perfect being is utterly reliable and trustwor-
thy, but is always being affected by those it loves. To love and to be
loved is to enter into a relationship of mutuality, and this means that
the perfect being, who is inevitably present (who exists, as the Bible
says, "from everlasting to everlasting"), is also constantly changing.

Here is where a little-noticed insight by Hartshorne pays big divi-
dends. By making clear the idea that divine perfection must be modeled
on love, he enables us to see that the idea of God as the perfect being
does *not* mean that God must be viewed as complete in every respect,
incapable of having new experiences, as most of traditional theology
assumed. It *does* mean that no other being could possibly rival or surpass
God in any way. And this realization allows Hartshorne to redefine
God, the perfect one, as the "self-surpassing surpasser of all."[7] Thus it
makes good sense to say that God, in different states of existence, could
surpass in richness of content or experience God in previous states of
existence even though God could never cease being God and no other
being could possibly rival God in any way.

The question lingers, however, whether by understanding God as
temporal and changing, Hartshorne has not eliminated everything that
is essential to our concept of God: absoluteness, eternity, immutability, and the like. Briefly, the answer is no, but to make this answer stick
we need to exercise some care. To make sense of an idea that both

adequately represents the God of the Bible and, at the same time, does justice to all that the traditional theologians held dear, we must keep in mind an important distinction: we need to distinguish between a being's bare *existence* and its full, concrete *actuality*.

This distinction is one we habitually make when we are dealing with ourselves or other persons. We think of a person as maintaining the same existence throughout his or her lifetime, whereas obviously the states of existence of that person change from moment to moment. For instance, I look at a picture taken of "me" when I was six. My memory, the name written on the back, and all sorts of other evidence tell me that I am the same person. Yet, how much I have changed over the years, not only physically but also mentally and in terms of my experience. This is often easier to notice in others. We meet a friend after an absence of 15 or 20 years and we think (even if delicacy dictates that we not say): "My, how you've changed!" There is some identifiable "you" that remains the same, but what leaps out at us is the change—not merely in bodily appearance, but in mind, experience, and attitude.

Precisely this distinction is crucial with respect to God. God's *existence*, which the ontological argument is concerned with, is literally unchanging. We can properly say that it is necessary, absolute, eternal, immutable, etc. What the sum total of all of these claims comes to is that God cannot fail to exist no matter what occurs. Or we might say that God is necessarily actualized in some state or other. But the claim for necessary existence does not exhaust what may be said about God. It does not mean that God does not change at all or that God is unrelated to temporal events. For God's fuller, concrete *actuality* or, as we might say, the particular "state" of God's existence—God at this time or God at that time—is contingent and relative to the things of the world. Thus *God*, as distinct from God's bare existence, is supremely temporal and mutable. This means that the contents of God's life might have been otherwise than they are, but that no matter what occurs God's life is constantly enriched by interaction with all the creatures. Thus God always has a past and always has a future, and so is everlasting.

This distinction between the "existence" and the "actuality" of God reinforces the credibility of the ontological argument by making clear that necessary existence is only one fundamental attribute of the fuller, more concrete, actual individual, God. At the same time the distinction lends rational underpinning to the biblical picture of a personal God.

Hartshorne's contribution to the process philosophy of God is not limited to understanding the implications of the ontological argument. He is probably as knowledgeable about Whitehead's thought as anyone. And, although Whitehead himself could not see his way clear to develop the idea of God as a person, he did provide a clue for such a development. In *Modes of Thought*, Whitehead sets forth an argument that all facts are of "intrinsic importance" for themselves, for others, and for the whole. Yet, it is only as they are "embraced in the unity of the whole" that they are finally "something that matters." The "whole" or "totality" is God in the role of ultimate redeemer.[8] Hartshorne takes up this insight and develops it as the centerpiece of his doctrine of God.

For Hartshorne the whole is the *personal whole of reality* interactive with its parts. He utilizes the soul-body or the mind-brain relation as the best model for conceiving the God-world relation. God is understood as the world soul that has the universe as its body. This model, which is currently enjoying some favor among theologians, should not be dismissed as either a fad or a reprise of discredited ideas borrowed from the ancient Stoics. But it needs careful exposition. Hartshorne regards the soul as entirely social and temporal. That is to say it is a complex and dynamic entity that receives and synthesizes data from its own past and that of its environment and, in turn, acts in subsequent experiences. The soul is neither a spiritual substance wholly unrelated to matter nor a wispy part of a greater body. Rather it is understood to be that personal whole that sums up all the parts of the body and is interactive with them in an ongoing intercourse. The soul is that which gives definition to the individual, making it an individual rather than a mere conglomeration of parts.

I shall have more to say on these matters, which are critical to process theology, in Chapters 3, 4, and 8. Many of these ideas took root and began to flower at the University of Chicago, where Hartshorne taught philosophy from 1928 to 1955 and where, from 1943, he held a joint appointment in the Divinity School. The dean of the Divinity School, Bernard Loomer, extended the influence of process thought, and it is not by chance that the two greatest process theologians of the last third of the twentieth century—John Cobb and Schubert Ogden—were educated at the Divinity School of the University of Chicago. Thanks to them, and to numerous others, process modes of thought continue to make a significant contribution to theology in our day. Let us, therefore, take a look at some more general ideas that are woven together to make up process thought.

THE HEART OF THE MATTER IN PROCESS THOUGHT

The term "process philosophy" was apparently coined by Bernard Loomer at Chicago. Whitehead called his metaphysics the "Philosophy of Organism,"[9] although clearly the idea of process is central to *Process and Reality* and to all his thought. It is helpful to consider both key terms, process and organism, to get a firm grasp on this view of the world.

Sometimes, when people first hear about process philosophy or process theology, the image that comes to mind is of processed foods. Another image is of an activity as distinct from an outcome. For instance, psychologists and sociologists often examine the dynamics of group interaction rather than what the group finally does or decides, and this understanding naturally leaps to mind. For a few, "process" suggests the sayings attributed to Heraclitus: "All things flow" or "No one steps into the same river twice." While all of these images contribute something to an understanding of the process perspective on the world, each one distorts the picture. To not produce a caricature, we need to exercise great care.

For example, the image of processed foods correctly suggests that the synthesizing of several ingredients into some new product is deeply descriptive of all actuality. Process thinkers often assert that each instance of actuality is a "creative synthesis." Yet the image also carries with it the unfortunate suggestion that this mode of thought is concerned only with superficialities, products of no lasting value. This is far from the case. Process thought is concerned with analyzing the fundamental characteristics of all reality, but also with showing that all facts are of abiding value.

Similarly, the idea that process thought is concerned only with the process, but never with the product, is a distortion. To be sure, it takes seriously the insight that the fundamental units of actuality are events, or micro-processes, which come into being. Therefore, it demands that we examine carefully the process of coming-to-be, the creative synthesis. Even so, it never forgets for one minute that what comes to be is a product, a stubborn fact that affects the course of all subsequent events. And so it analyzes just as carefully how stubborn fact conditions the creative process.

Finally, the truth embedded in the Heraclitean sayings is that reality is inherently dynamic or temporal. The distortion comes about by assuming that *nothing* abides, or that *everything* is flux. The modern process thinkers understand that events cannot merely come into being in a moment and then de-become, or vanish into nothingness. As stubborn facts that have come into being, they make their mark in the universe and so abide everlastingly. Another unfortunate idea connected with the river image is that time should be understood as some substrate that carries along the moving bits of matter that are themselves inert or unchanging.

All these distortions of the basic ideas of process thought can be partially corrected by keeping in mind that what comes to be and passes into the being of others is, itself, an organism. Each event that comes to be is a complex unity conditioned by others, and yet is partially self-created out of the many data given to it. Thus, rather than being an isolated and self-contained bit of matter, what comes to be is always organically related to its environment. That environment is the entire past world of actualities out of which it takes its rise and the future into which the entity projects itself.

More light can be shed on this position, I believe, by inspecting its point of departure and the method by which process philosophy arrives at its conclusions about the world and God. We begin with an analysis of the invariant features of any human experience—those that are present under all conditions. The problem with most ways of analyzing human experience is that they take clear consciousness and instances of precise sense perception as the models for *all* human experience. Types of experience such as holding an idea firmly in mind and comparing it with another, similar one, or figuring out the likely consequences of an act, or seeing the chair before me clearly and distinguishing it from the wall behind, are thought to provide the clue to all human experience. But they do not. They are examples of the pinnacle of human experience intermittently reached, but by no means do they exhaust our total human experience.

Everyone has experiences in which consciousness is dim or absent. We all know of experiences for which the sensory data are vague but powerful. For instance, we have all experienced ourselves in a reverie, and we are convinced that we have experiences when we are asleep. If we should awake suddenly from a bad dream, we carry the residue of those experiences which *we* had, while unconscious or semiconscious, into our waking consciousness. What is more, while awake, we feel emotions. The feeling of such emotions is internal to us and only indirectly, if at all, related to sensory impressions. In fact, in retrospect we realize that we had experienced emotions welling up within us although we were unaware of them at the time. And we experience ourselves as living from moment to moment, out of the immediate past and into the immediate future. If someone should challenge this, asking, "How can you be sure that you are the same person who was present a few moments ago?" we reply: "I *remember* my past experiences and I *feel* the continuity of my past operative in my present existence." We also experience both eager hope and vague, but compelling, apprehensions regarding our future. In all these cases the sense data are unclear or even missing, and consciousness is, at best, faint.

In fact, when we reflect on our actual living, apart from the prejudicial philosophical model, we see that highly conscious experiences are fleeting and constitute only a small part of the millions of experiences that a human undergoes each day. Clear-cut sense experience fares but little better. This insight led Whitehead to say, "Consciousness flickers; and even at its brightest, there is a small focal region of clear illumination, and a large penumbral region of experience which tells of intense experience in dim apprehension. The simplicity of clear consciousness is no measure of the complexity of complete experience. . . . [C]onsciousness is the crown of experience, only occasionally attained, not its necessary base."[10]

What, then, is the "necessary base" of experience? What do all experiences have in common if not consciousness? When we inspect our experiences free of the dogma that all genuine experiences must be conscious or highlight precise sense impressions, we find several significant things: we notice, first, that every experience seems to grow out of the immediately past environment with which it is intimately connected and apart from which it could not be understood in its concreteness. But this is not all. No experience is ever exhaustively explained in terms of its conditioning past, its causes. Each experience has a novel perspective on the universe. It is *this* experience rather than *that* one, and however much like another experience, it is distinctive. When we penetrate to the heart of any experience, it seems that it is partially a result of the conditioning causes that constitute its past, but also contains some novel element. This novel element appears as a decision to actualize certain definite possibilities from among those available to it and to synthesize itself in a definite way as this experience.

Now, in view of the fact that I have rejected consciousness as basic to all subjective experiences, I need to justify the last claim: that decision is intrinsic to every experience. Again, I think we can appeal to common experiences in which consciousness is focused elsewhere, or is dimmed or even absent, and yet in which, on subsequent reflection, we realize we had made decisions: for example, the decision to swerve the car to avoid hitting an animal that has dashed into our path; the decision to get back to work from a deep reverie; the decision to scratch an itch while concentrating on a lecture or a piece of music; a spur-of-the-moment decision to take a walk. From the outside such actions may appear arbitrary or random or, perhaps, wholly determined by subconscious causes. But, from the inside they are experienced as decisions, as the cutting off or eliminating of various genuine possibilities while actualizing one such possibility. Perhaps the only decision is how to respond to and synthesize the various data that are the indispensable background for the particular occasion of experience. In many cases, though, the kind of clarity and concentration on detail that is the hallmark of consciousness is missing. Thus there appears to be something like decision even when conscious-ness is absent.

There is, I believe, another element to every experience. In addition to growing out of its past and to being a unique experience, a value for itself, there is inevitably the sense of making a difference to others, or of being something that matters in the universe beyond this present experience. Otherwise we would be caught in what Whitehead, follow-ing the philosopher Santayana, calls "the solipsism of the present moment."[11] Just as no experience is isolated at its inception, wherein it receives from its past, so none is isolated at its outcome, when it gives itself to its successors.

Process thought believes that by starting from human subjective experiences that we know best, we have the basis for grasping the invariant elements of any experience whatever. To be sure, we must lay aside or ignore those elements, such as consciousness and clear-cut sense perception, which distinguish high-grade and human experi-ences from others. But if our experience is carefully attended to, we are prepared to move beyond the specifically human experiences. The method is that of "descriptive generalization" or "imaginative gener-alization" controlled by the rigid requirements of coherence and logic, adequacy and applicability.[12]

We begin from an analysis of what we are most intimately acquainted with to see how, and to what extent, its constituent parts are descrip-tive of other aspects of the universe. This is a variant of the method of uniformity of explanation that is so important to natural science, although it is employed with a much wider scope. Whitehead makes use of the simile of the flight of an airplane to elucidate the method of discovery of what is common to all experience: "It starts from the ground of particular observation; it makes a flight in the thin air of imaginative generalization; and it again lands for renewed observation rendered acute by rational interpretation."[13] He notes that whereas empiricism—"the method of difference"—fails to discern those elements that are constantly present, imaginative thought disciplined by the demands of logic and coherence may penetrate to this common core. The results must be applied to various types of experience and tested for adequacy.

The upshot, so far as process thought can be trusted, is that every actuality is analogous to a momentary human subjective experience: all actualities are events or units of becoming; each one is a unique experience; all are organically related units of creative synthesis. If we attend closely to what we have found, we may highlight several points from the foregoing.

1. Although every actuality or experience grows out of, and so is conditioned by, its immediate past, no experience is wholly determined by past causes. Every experience includes both possibilities and the decision to actualize certain of these possibilities. Here we have the ground both of natural causation and of freedom that are so critical to the natural and social sciences. This is well put by Schubert Ogden:

> [W]hat the process philosophers . . . mean when they use the concept "process" is simply the process of creative synthesis, or self-creation, whereby whatever becomes actual does so only by freely synthesizing the free self-creations of others. . . . [T]o be anything actual at all is to be a free response to other freedom—or, more exactly, to the results of other freedoms in the form of the many other things themselves already actual.[14]

2. Our analysis has suggested that every event, every experience, is a subject organizing its own concrete realization. To speak of "subjects" as being related to "objects" is a useful way to understand the world. And to organize our thought into a subject-object scheme can shed considerable light on the nature of reality. But the distinction is not what ordinary beliefs, reinforced by the conventions of language, often suggest: the division between conscious beings who can have experiences, on the one hand, and inert matter that cannot have experiences but can only be moved about or somehow be experienced, on the other. The distinction is, rather, a perspectival or temporal one applying to every instance of actuality: subjectivity refers to the act of synthesizing the many data into one present, unified actual occasion of experience; objectivity refers to being a datum for a subject, whether as a past, determinate actuality or as a possibility. Thus subjectivity refers to the present fact, whereas objectivity refers to objects-for-this-subject in its past or future. We should keep this temporal or perspectival distinction in mind when contemplating the process point of view.

3. Another point to note is that every actuality, in becoming determinate, also becomes significant beyond itself; in becoming a value for self, it is a value for others. The process does not stop. Events do not de-become or evaporate. Although each experience, each event or unit of actuality, is ultimately unique and determinate so that nothing more can be added to it, nevertheless it adds itself to the ongoing universe by acting in subsequent occasions and becoming part of their experience. Process thought, however, will not let us stop with the value for

other finite actualities. Each experience, it sees, is not only something that matters for itself and for others; it is something that matters for the whole. *This* is the intuition that forms the energizing force at the base of religion. In other words, each experience is something that matters in the ongoing life of God.

4. A point implicit in all that I have said is that actuality is inevitably temporal. We should be careful, however, not to picture this temporality that lies at the heart of all things as an "ever-rolling stream" *on which* actualities bob along like flotsam. Nor should we conceive a momentary experience, or a present subject, as an instant devoid of temporality, dividing the future from the past. Such would be, in Whitehead's words, "an intellectual theory of time as a moving knife-edge, exhibiting present fact without temporal extension."[15] What is meant by temporality in process thought is that each event, each occasion of experience, becomes out of the data that are its *past*, together with those (the possibilities) that constitute its *future*. The act of synthesis, the subjective experience, is its *present*. Every present fact is an irreducible occasion of experience that, on becoming determinate, hurls itself forth as an object for supervening subjects, and the process begins again: "The many become one, and are increased by one."[16]

5. Another point to be made explicit is that each experience is not only a recipient of its data but an *agent*. As we have seen, every event acts to synthesize the data given it; it decides and organizes for itself. But the event also acts in subsequent occasions; it lays a claim on all that succeed it. Ultimately, we cannot separate being from doing.

6. Finally, all this analysis of actuality applies supremely to God. God is actual, but not pure actuality, for God always faces possibilities. God is eminently social, being internally related to all other actualities, which is to say that God is affected by them as they actualize themselves. God is the supreme agent, acting in all other actualities. (How this is conceived so as to ennoble the idea of divine power without eliminating the essential creaturely freedom is worked out in Chapters 3 and 4.) God is temporal, having at all times a past and a future and, at each moment, being the supreme present that synthesizes everything—God is temporal, but everlasting. And yet, as the concrete and supremely temporal being, God alone contains an eternal, or necessary, pole.

SOME FINAL REFLECTIONS ON EXPERIENCE

In one way or another, the above points underlie, and are embodied in, all that follows. I am acutely aware that much of the foregoing will have an air of unreality about it and may seem foreign to many readers.

Partly this is because the account has been so abbreviated as to appear abstract. It is a bare-bones account to which the following chapters attempt to give flesh.

Partly, too, the difficulty lies in the fact that many people unreflectively carry assumptions about what constitutes our primary experiences, which run counter to this account. Common sense, reinforced by ordinary language, seems to tell us that primary experiences are of the sort that can be expressed as "I see that red figure at this instant" or "I have this precise thought right now." Both types of so-called primary experience, however, abstract from the complexities that inevitably are present and penetrate the primary experience: the situation of the red figure; the transmission of the image from the retina to that part of the brain that registers it; the hidden background and feeling tones that accompany the reception of this red image or the meditation on that particular thought; the entertainment of alternative possibilities (e.g., slightly orange rather than pure red) or the implications of this idea, etc. No such experiences are isolated; all are situated, take time, and have consequences. We miss their richness and concreteness if we abstract from these and concentrate on details (which, admittedly, we must do for certain purposes such as scientific research or getting on with the quotidian round).

If Whitehead and I have failed to convince you that your basic experience is one of living from moment to moment, out of your immediate bodily past and into the next embodiment of your selfhood—and not the clear-cut sense perception or moments of lucid consciousness that differentiate human experiences from others—you are not likely to resonate to the rest of process thought. And if you, the reader, remain unconvinced that such a present experience—vague, heavy with emotion, and essentially temporal—is the clue to understanding all actuality, then Whitehead and I are like intrusive telemarketers, and you will probably hang up. I hope, however, to have gotten your attention.

One more difficulty may be uncovered in hopes of persuading you to take these ideas seriously. What I have been trying to get at is the common denominator of all experience, what all actuality has in common. Habitually, we attend to things by noting differences: When I look out the window and see the car across the street, I distinguish it from the house behind it and from the "empty" spaces before and behind it; when I notice the clicking of heels on the sidewalk below, I distinguish these sounds from "silence" or from the general hum of cars, birds chirping, the rustling of leaves, and the chatter of schoolchildren in the street. But it takes a great effort to search for the invariant elements of all experiences, what every experience shares with every other experience no matter how divergent. Yet this is what is required if we are to get straight our fundamental ideas about God and the world, the meaning of God-for-us in Christ, who we are, the nature of religion, faith, prayer, what constitutes behavior commensurate with our faith, and our hope for everlasting significance.

It is the task of metaphysics to disclose and examine the common factors of all experience—the fundamental elements constitutive of all actuality. However difficult that task may be, it is not to be avoided or dismissed if we are to think theologically. As Ogden has said: "[T]he only alternative to a good metaphysics, when one undertakes to explicate the beliefs about God implicit in the Christian witness, is bad metaphysics; and one of the ways of virtually insuring that one's metaphysics will be bad is to take it over incidentally and uncritically instead of deliberately and reflectively."[17]

I have tried to be deliberate, reflective, adequate, and candid. I may simply be wrong! More likely, I will have been inattentive to the richness of experience or the truth embodied in divergent views. But this can best be tested by proceeding to particular doctrines and seeing how process theology, as I understand it, works them out.

3

The God We Worship

The proper understanding of worship as "love of God with all our heart, soul, mind, and strength" with the corollary, "love of neighbor as self," gives us the clue to understanding God as the being supremely worthy of worship. God is the ultimate lover and the final recipient of all acts, a personal being who is the ground and end of our significance. God's transcendence is understood in terms of God's necessary existence and universal interactivity.

As the arguments and examples in Chapter 1 made plain, ideas have real consequences for how we live. What we think about reality or any part of it inevitably guides our behavior. Chief among the ideas that have dominated the human imagination is the idea of God.

Certainly, for Christians, there is nothing more fundamental than the worship of God, and all worship, like all faith, carries with it certain convictions about the nature of God: What kind of deity is being worshiped? Who is this God who elicits our faith? All that we say and do depends on this. Thus the litmus test for any viable theology, and indeed any ethics, is the idea of God that lies at its base.

SOME PROBLEMS WITH THE TRADITIONAL IDEAS ABOUT GOD

What exactly is the Christian idea of God? Down through the centuries a great body of doctrine developed that constitutes the major tradition in theology. This tradition attempted to develop and make sense of the biblical imagery of God, but in doing so it imported

certain Greek philosophical concepts that are at odds with the fundamental intuition about God at the heart of the Christian faith.

Of the attributes of God that were incorporated into the theological
mainstream, perhaps the overarching one is that God is wholly *absolute*, being utterly unaffected and unconditioned by the relations that
God has with the world. Another way to put this is to say that God is
in every respect *necessary*, and so without the possibility of different
and new experiences or contingent states of existence. In this tradition,
Aristotle's idea of God as the "unmoved mover" is taken for granted.
God is thought to act in or on the world, but in such a way as to be
immune to the creatures' reactions being entirely unaffected by them.
Thus God is said to be *immutable*. Moreover, God in this tradition is
often said to be strictly *eternal* in the sense that God is a "standing
now" or a static present without any past or future. Therefore, strictly
speaking, God would see everything that we take to be future possibility as already actual. A corollary to this is that God is said to be *pure act*
without any possibilities or potentiality, since possibility or potentiality constitutes the future for temporal beings. Therefore, when God
in this tradition is said to be "infinite," it means that God comprehends
all being at once rather than that God is everlasting, ongoing, and able
to face unending possibilities. So God is also said to be *simple*, being
without any parts or composition.[1]

The theological tradition that elaborated these attributes has had such
a widespread and powerful influence that many people simply assume
that they are intrinsic to the biblical-Christian idea of God. We must,
however, challenge this assumption. In the first place, consider whether
the idea of God worked out by the major theological tradition genuinely
reflects the portrait of God given in the Bible. There we find God as the
active and compassionate lord, judge, creator, and redeemer of history
who is inevitably a living person and is seen in the New Testament as
the Father of Jesus, the One to whom we can pray and make a difference;
in fact, the New Testament portrays Jesus himself as the signal disclosure of this God. Second, consider whether the God of the theological
tradition can be treated as genuinely actual by a world that regards actual
beings as interactive and not wholly unconditioned. Briefly, the questions are whether the traditional theological view is adequately biblical
and whether it makes sense or is credible.

To both questions, the answer from many quarters is no. The conviction has grown among biblical scholars and theologians that many
of the inherited theological concepts are utterly at odds with the picture of God given in the Bible. For instance, it is extremely difficult
to square the idea of God as the unmoved mover of all, the absolute

creator and omnipotent ruler who knows the outcome of everything beforehand and who cannot be affected by anything, with the picture of the compassionate God of the Bible who leads along the Israelites, who chastises and welcomes them back when they go astray, who is moved by their prayers, and whose deepest being is most clearly revealed on the cross.

In addition to being at odds with the biblical portrait of God, the traditional idea runs counter to our modern view of what is real and of worth. For to insist that God, as the ground of all being, is wholly self-contained and utterly timeless, devoid of potentiality, lacking any complexity, and impervious to change means that God is the *exception* to the principles that are exemplified by all actual individuals. The most penetrating analyses of the last 150 years agree that to be an actual individual at all is to become in relation to others; that is, all actual beings are, in some sense, relative and temporal. But if these qualities are declared inapplicable to God, it is hard to see what sense it could make to think of God as actual. What is more, and possibly more damaging to the traditional theological concept of God, our deepest conviction is that all our efforts, decisions, acts, and relationships really do make a difference in the world, and so are of abiding worth. But if we can never make a difference to God, if nothing we do matters finally, because it cannot affect or change God in any way, then this conviction becomes hollow.

Also, the typical theological claim that God foreknows every detail of our lives (which, in effect, is to foreordain them) offends our sense of integrity and makes a mockery of the growing awareness of freedom in human decisions and the presence of potentiality in all real individuals even at the atomic level. Most people who have thought about the matter are led to reject any notion of divine—or human or natural, for that matter—determination and control of the concrete details of our lives as contrary to our experience of freedom and the conviction that what we do is of infinite worth. This-worldly value is real value; our accomplishments or failures cannot be written off as merely elements in the unfolding of the divine scheme. Thus the idea of an absolute divine determiner is repugnant to both our sense of freedom and our sense of individual worth.

These are not the only problems that the traditional theological idea of God has generated. The difficulties spring up like weeds. For instance, with the rise of science and its increasing ability to explain natural phenomena in terms of natural cause-effect relations, supernaturalistic explanations of the same things in terms of "miracles," conceived as God's suspension of the laws of nature, have lost their power to convince. In fact, they are regarded by increasing numbers of people as simply incredible. What used to be taken to be literal accounts of divine intervention in the course of the world in the Bible and other ancient scriptures are now understood to be profound myths or stories whose point is to address the inner meaning of our lives before God rather than to give an objective account of historical or natural events. A religious or theological objection to the notion that divine acts can be observed and measured empirically is that it treats God as one more finite cause. Claims that intended to pay God compliments actually reduce God to the status of a natural object.[2]

Finally, the "problem of evil" raises insuperable difficulties for the traditional notion that God is absolute, omnipotent, and possesses exact foreknowledge of everything to the crack of doom: namely, how could there be such massive natural and moral evil in the world if God is all-powerful and all-good? In other words, Why do "bad things happen to good people" if God is benevolent and in control?[3]

All these problems and contradictions call into question much of what the main theological tradition has said about God. And, if that tradition exhausted the options we have for belief in God, one could hardly fail to be an atheist on both intellectual and moral grounds. Yet it is *not* the only option. We have at hand other options that enable us to represent the personal God of the Bible both adequately and reasonably. I am convinced that the careful application of the concepts of process philosophy to God enables us to accomplish the best of what the tradition desired without dragging along its baggage of contradiction, inferior morality, and anti-biblicism.

THE MEANING AND IMPLICATION OF WORSHIP

Perhaps we can launch a new beginning by thinking about the working definition of God given by one of the greatest of the traditional theologians. St. Anselm initiated his argument for the existence of God with this definition: God is "a being than which nothing greater can be conceived."[4] Now, excellent as this definition is, it is not wholly foolproof, because it admits of two quite different interpretations. Much of our trouble stems from the habit of taking it in the least biblical way, which is, also, least in accord with our view of what any individual must be.

That is, for most of our history Anselm's fairly abstract definition has been taken to mean that no individual whatever, including God, could be ever greater than God is at present. Clearly, this interpretation prejudices the definition in favor of a static, nonbiblical idea of God.

It assumes a God with no past or future and no ability to experience anything new.

The other interpretation is actually more surefooted. To say that God is "a being than which nothing greater can be conceived" should be read to say that no being *other than* God could possibly rival God in any way. But this allows us to see that God could surpass former states of God's own being in certain important ways. It is with this insight in mind that Charles Hartshorne says we can properly speak of God as "the self-surpassing being that positively surpasses all others."[5] This way of interpreting the definition of the perfect being enables us to retain the fundamental concept of God as the greatest conceivable *individual*, the one who is supremely worthy of worship by all other individuals, and at the same time make the point that such an individual can surpass former states of its being as it interacts with lesser individuals. That is, by interacting with every creature, God has ever-new experiences, and so surpasses former states of God's being. This interpretation is much more in line with the dynamic, personal God of the biblical witness. It, also, enables us to make sense of God as an individual who is both relative and temporal as all individuals must be.

We can shed more light on this second interpretation of Anselm's definition of God by examining the meaning and implications of worship. Clearly, only the greatest conceivable being would be worthy of worship by all others. But what is it to worship? To answer this I suggest that we can do no better than to turn to Jesus's own penetration to the heart of biblical religion, the Summary of the Law. He said, "The first [commandment] is 'Hear O Israel: The Lord our God, the Lord is one; and you shall love the Lord your God with all your heart, and with all your soul, and with all your mind, and with all your strength.' The second is this, 'You shall love your neighbor as yourself.' There is no other commandment greater than these" (Mark 12:29–31). The Summary of the Law makes the point that genuine religion, or worship, consists in utter devotion to God. It is love of God with every facet of our being: heart, soul, mind, and strength. And, as a necessary corollary, worship demands the same sort of love of our neighbors and ourselves.

Now let us inspect this familiar passage more closely. If to worship God means to love God with the totality of our being, it clearly implies that we do, in fact, make a difference to God, since this is part of what it is to love; we contribute something to the enrichment of the divine life. However many and various the forms of love may be, all of them require that we enter into a relationship of mutuality with the one loved. This is a relationship of give-and-take in which we both affect and are affected by the one loved. At the least, to love another means to be deeply concerned for the well-being of the other through life's changing circumstances and to act to promote that well-being. But the initial concern means being attuned to the needs of the other and so being receptive of that being's influence; our loving response has its effect in the life of the other. In short, love is a relationship of inter-action or reciprocity.

This insistence on mutuality or reciprocity as intrinsic to the love relationship need not mean that both sides give and receive in equal measure. For example, in a normal parent-child relationship, espe-cially when the child is young and immature, the parent unavoidably gives more and the child receives more: the parent provides food and security, teaches the child how to approach different experiences, nurtures, establishes principles of value, sympathizes, etc. But every loving parent knows the immeasurable richness that is added to his or her life by the presence of the child. And the influence of the child on the parent grows as the child grows.

Similarly, even among adults there are some whose capacity to give of themselves is greater than that of others. Significantly, it seems that those with the greater capacity to give are precisely the ones with the greater capacity to receive many and diverse influences, and so to grow. Perhaps this is one meaning of the biblical dictum: "To every-one who has more will be given" (Luke 19:26). Whatever the point of the parable of the severe king, however, there are those among us who manifest the power both to give of themselves without being diminished and to receive and coordinate influences from a wide vari-ety of sources. Such persons are sometimes said to be "great souls," for they are the great exemplars of love. To love, in every instance, means to act on and influence others and also to be open to and receptive of the action and influence of others.

If this principle applies to *any* loving being, surely it applies to God. So if God is the being who is worthy of the worship of every other being, and if to worship means to love, then inasmuch as we worship God we enter into a loving relationship with God. We influence, enrich, and *change* God in the same relationship in which we are open-ing ourselves to God's subtle influence in our own lives. And, if God is the one who can be worshiped by *every* creature, then God is not only present to all and active in all, but is acted on and affected by every-thing that comes into existence.

The early Christian theologians, eager to establish God's "perfection," thought that it was necessary to insulate God from any change at all.

They thought it was incompatible with God's nature to be acted on or to suffer in any fashion. And so they insisted that God be conceived as immutable and impassible, incapable of changing and suffering. We can surely sympathize with their intention. No doubt their aim was to present God as steadfast, utterly reliable, imperishable, and incapable of being diminished by our deeds and misdeeds. Yet, important as these qualities are, they in no way require that God be treated as wholly incapable of change or suffering. Rather, they require only that God's *existence* (but not God) be immutable and that God always steadfastly desire the good and be consistent in applying the principles of justice. The additional claim that such a steadfast God be incapable of enrichment, or of sharing the sufferings of the creatures, or of giving different content to the consistent principles of justice in changing circumstances, is wholly unwarranted.

In fact, the God who is perfect, in the sense of being supremely worthy of worship, is the one who is, thereby, loved and affected by all. This is the one who is capable of *infinite* change. This God, moreover, is capable of suffering with all who in any way suffer. If the cross is central to the Christian revelation, one wonders how theologians can have failed to draw this conclusion. But it was left largely to the twentieth century to grasp the point clearly and make it forcefully. Thus, writing from prison in 1944, Dietrich Bonhoeffer said, "Man's religiosity makes him look in distress to the power of God in the world: God is the *Deus ex machina*. The Bible directs man to God's powerlessness and suffering; only the suffering God can help."[6] Bonhoeffer's insight had taken shape only under considerable duress. But 15 years earlier, in less dramatic circumstances but with more systematic and rational underpinning, Whitehead had declared, "God is the great companion—the fellow-sufferer who understands."[7] From differing starting points, the theologian and the philosopher were both returning to a New Testament, and in some respects a prophetic, idea of God.

Another point uncovered by a close inspection of the Summary of the Law is that, although we are admonished to devote 100 percent of our mental, physical, and emotional love to God, we are by no means required to direct our concerns away from this world. In fact, as Jesus consistently makes clear, in loving God we are to love our neighbors and ourselves. The genuine worship of God, who is the universal person, is never regarded as an activity that points us away from God's world; rather, it forces us to look at the things of this world in a new light. This is attested everywhere in the Bible but is most powerfully set forth in the parable of the last judgment in Matthew. Here the King says both to the righteous and to the accursed: "I was hungry . . . I was sick . . . I was in prison," and either they did or did not respond and minister to him. And to the queries as to when they had had opportunities to minister to him, the King responds: "Truly, I tell you, just as you did it [did not do it] to one of the least of these who are members of my family, you did it [did not do it] to me" (Matthew 25:34–45).

The implication of the parable is clear: If we disregard or fail to attend to the needs of anyone in this world we are turning our backs on God; we cannot devote ourselves to God by ignoring the little ones who are all members of God's family. The first letter of John puts this point bluntly: "Those who say, 'I love God,' and hate their brothers and sisters, are liars. . . . The commandment we have from him is this: those who love God must love their brothers and sisters also" (I John 4:20–21).

This intuition, that the worship of God entails love of our human neighbors, can and should be extended. Love, as a fundamental principle of all existence, demands more than concern for our fellow humans; it requires a concern for the well-being of all of God's creation, a point that had been made subtly at the end of Jonah. And just as the love of persons entails a concern for their well-being and a response to their needs, but also a respect for their integrity and an active knowledge of their inner being, so the love of God promotes a concern and responsibility for, and respect and knowledge of, as much of God's creation as is given into our stewardship. Genuine worship requires that we value even the nonhuman part of the world, and that we take with utmost seriousness knowledge of the laws of nature and of human institutions, that we promote freedom and integrity for all individuals, and that we cultivate good in the world at every level of existence.

A third point, implicit in all that I have said, but that should be made explicit, is that God, who is supremely worthy of the love of all and able to receive that love, is supremely loving. John says several times that "God is love" (I John 4:8,16). John's clear meaning is not that the term "God" is merely a nominal symbol for human love, but that God is the *source* of all love; God is the supremely loving being: "We love because he first loved us" (I John 4:19). One of the clear implications of our original definition of God, understood as the Bible understands it, is that the one who is supremely worthy of worship is the preeminent lover of the universe. And, as I have insisted all along, to love means not merely to act but also to be susceptible to the actions of others. To have compassion necessitates having passion; it is the capacity to be affected, to be acted on, to suffer. To be supremely compassionate means to be affected by everything that occurs, to feel the sufferings of every creature.

To see this clearly, however, is to see that it poses a great problem for the tradition that insisted that God, as wholly absolute, must be regarded as immune to suffering and be unaffected in any way. In fact, St. Anselm actually saw this problem and expressed it candidly: "How art thou compassionate, and at the same time, passionless?" he asks. "For, if thou are passionless, thou dost not feel sympathy; . . . but this it is to be compassionate. But if thou art not compassionate, whence cometh so great consolation to the wretched?" Having put the question so sharply, however, Anselm wavers in his answer. At first he seems to resolve the difficulty by denying that God is truly compassionate. But then he equivocates by affirming that God is both "compassionate" and "not compassionate":

> Truly thou art [compassionate] in terms of our experience, but thou art not so in terms of thine own. For, when thou beholdest us in our wretchedness, we experience the effect of compassion, but thou dost not experience the feeling. Therefore, thou art both compassionate, because thou dost save the wretched, and spare those who sin against thee; and not compassionate, because thou art affected by no sympathy for wretchedness.[8]

As honest as Anselm is in raising the question, his attempted resolution exposes the poverty of this tradition in theology. The kindest interpretation we can give this statement is to say it means that, even though we experience something like love in its effects, we do not really experience love, because God is not compassionate. A less friendly critic might insist that this is but a verbal solution masking nonsense. If words are used consistently God cannot be said to be both compassionate and not compassionate.

Many defenders of traditional theology have resorted to the line that human concepts, such as love, knowledge, and the like, do not apply literally to God who transcends human categories absolutely. They often appeal to such biblical statements as this: "For my thoughts are not your thoughts, nor are your ways my ways, says the Lord. For as the heavens are higher than the earth, so are my ways higher than your ways and my thoughts than your thoughts" (Isaiah 55:8–9).

I am fully aware that there is an infinite difference between God and anything else. Divine transcendence, however, should never be defended by uttering contradictions or by depriving God of the essential quality of love. And there is a proper way to affirm divine transcendence without resorting to contradiction or reducing God to an abstraction. The infinite difference between God and the creatures can be accounted for both in terms of the types of existence appropriate to each and the capability (or incapability) of *universal* interaction. All creatures, by their nature, are *contingent* in every respect: they might never have existed; they are dependent on others for their existence as well as their states of existence; they are finite and fragmentary; and not only do they come to an end, every creature can interact with only a limited group of beings in a lifetime. God, on the other hand, exists *necessarily*; God could not fail to exist. And, unlike creatures, God is infinite, universally interactive, and thus inclusive of all that comes to be. These all-important differences between God and anything else establish divine transcendence firmly. Yet, in no way do they imply that God, who necessarily exists and interacts with everything, should be thought of as nonrelative, immutable, and static. Nor do they mean that there is a kind of divine love unlike any other love in that it is unilateral, independent, unaffected by anything, and immutable. Such customary claims are unbiblical and do not make any sense.

There is, to be sure, a difference between divine love and creaturely love commensurate with the difference between divine and creaturely existence and actuality. Whereas human love is finite, fragmentary, and shortsighted, and suffers from a lack of openness and insensitivity to all the demands placed on it, divine love is infinite, whole, all-seeing, and supremely sensitive to every need as it arises. Divine love is capable of balancing its response in accordance with the requirements of the given situation, the needs of all individuals at that moment, and God's own vision of truth, beauty, and goodness. The mark of divine love, therefore, is not inflexibility, but infinite flexibility. It is not the ability to act unilaterally for our good, but the inexhaustible compassion that understands all because it is affected by all and suffers with all.

HOLDING THE CENTER; EXPANDING THE HORIZON

If all of this, then, follows from the biblical view of God and if it fits our religious sensibilities and our demands for intelligibility, how could traditional theologians have set forth such opposing views? How could those who were entrusted with the intellectual articulation and justification of our faith have developed concepts of God that are both non-biblical and nonsensical? Perhaps I have been too heavy-handed with this tradition. After all, the theologians had real concerns that required careful treatment. Let us take another look at the problems they faced and the perspective they brought to bear on them, and then see how we may treat the same problems so as to retain the biblical view of God and simultaneously make sense.

The early church theologians were culturally and intellectually rooted in the Greek tradition, which typically regarded change or mutability as a sign of inferiority. That which endures, they believed, is superior to that which comes into existence, remains for but a while, and perishes. Moreover, they reasoned that, if a thing changes for the better, it must not have been as perfect as it could have been. And, if it changes at all, who is to say that it must change for the better? Often things change for the worse, and then clearly they are not perfect specimens. The theologians correctly saw that anyone who could not be trusted to remain true to his or her principles is not to be highly esteemed. Certainly the person who vacillates and is "blown about with every vain wind of doctrine," or who is partial to this selfish concern or ready to give preferential treatment to that special-interest group, is not the one to be entrusted with power, much less the power to govern the universe. Finally, the theologians believed that to undergo suffering or to be subject to outside influence of any sort is a defect. They cherished steadfastness and constancy that, unfortunately, they confused with being nonrelative, independent, non-temporal, and immutable.

Let us inspect this point of view carefully. First, it is true that if a thing can perish, it cannot, in the long run, be relied on; a perfect being must continue in existence. Also, it is a virtue to remain true to one's principles, provided that these principles strengthen the quest for the greatest good, beauty, and truth. If they are unsound, however, being anchored to a set of values that are shortsighted or selfish, to stick to them come what may would be considered mulish, stupid, insensitive, or even brutal. More than this, to remain constant to the principles of love and justice for all does not mean that God, or any being, must be unyielding or utterly fixed in the concrete application of these principles. An ideal or principle is one thing; its application to specific instances in a concrete and changing world is another. The ideal—say, to love come what may—can remain constant. Its application, however, will inevitably be different in each particular case. Good decisions, right actions, loving responses must take account of the specific needs of particular persons in changing circumstances. Thus, to be dependable, to remain steadfast in the pursuit of truth, beauty, and goodness, requires both an unchanging ideal and the ability to apply the ideal differently by taking account of contingencies and adjusting accordingly.

For example, every responsible parent quickly learns the importance of adjusting his or her ideas of what constitutes love or fairness to the shifting needs of the growing child. We do not treat each child alike; yet the different treatment is not a function of inconstancy in our love. Rather, different personalities and circumstances demand different applications of the one ideal. It would be monstrous to offer the same advice to an 18-year-old that we gave to the child of three. There is wisdom in the words of James Russell Lowell: "New occasions teach new duties; time makes ancient good uncouth."[9] No matter that the language is quaint; the point is clear. It is not that principles or ideals should change; it is, rather, that what was a good decision in one context cannot simply be repeated in all contexts with no changes made to adapt to differing circumstances, differing personalities, differing needs. Moreover, the advent of nuclear power and incredible technologies to prolong life have taught us that we must learn to make wise and careful decisions about matters that did not even exist in former times.

Every capable political leader soon learns that to pursue a fixed course, no matter how ideal, without taking into account the diverse needs of a varied constituency is, at best, counterproductive and, at worst, evil. No leader can satisfy all the conflicting demands being made, but a wise leader will weigh as many as possible against one another and against the ideal before taking action.

More generally, the superior person will cast his or her net wide. I think this point was well put by Hartshorne when he said, "A 'good' man is not, compared to a bad or inferior one, any less relative or contingent, but rather, he is more adequately related to other things and richer and more harmonious in his accidental qualities." Hartshorne acknowledges that it is not good to be partial to one part of the environment. But to remain indifferent or unaffected is no remedy. "Balanced appropriateness in one's relativity to other things or persons," he continues, "not non-relativity is the mark of wisdom and goodness. The non-relative or merely inflexible person, who will not be influenced, who will not or cannot adjust to the actual situation sensitively and quickly, need not be especially admired."[10]

I think that everything that I have said can be applied appropriately to God. Remember that qualities such as love, wisdom, and justice are themselves ideals or principles that can remain unchanged *because* they are ideals. But their concrete application in particular cases—a loving response, a wise decision, a just act—will inevitably be relative to different situations, and the one who makes the response will experience change. Our theological predecessors were not especially subtle in this matter. They praised immutability and sheer independence absolutely without observing that these qualities apply to ideals rather than to specific responses and acts. Then, without taking into account the important distinction between an ideal and its concrete application, they insisted that God be described as wholly immutable, independent, absolute, non-contingent, and eternal. The model for the supreme being was much more clearly that of a rock, or even an abstraction, than a person.

Now let us consider more thoroughly the matter of God's "necessity." It goes without saying that, as *human* persons, we are born, and so depend for our existence on others. Also, we die and pass from the scene. What is more, each of us might not have come into existence at all. In short, our existence is in every respect contingent. The divine or perfect being, on the other hand, could not have merely contingent existence.

The view I am espousing insists just as much as the tradition does that God's *existence* is in no way contingent. God is unborn and undying, and God's existence as such does not depend on anything. Therefore, the terms that the traditional theology applied unconditionally to God—terms such as *absolute* or *nonrelative, independent, immutable, eternal*, and *necessary*—do apply to the divine existence. To affirm, for instance, that God's existence is necessary is to say that God must inevitably somehow exist no matter what; God cannot fail to exist. To make this point, however, is not at all to make the additional claim that God is utterly impervious to change. To say that God cannot fail to exist simply does not mean that God must be detached and unaffected by the changing lives of the creatures with whom God interacts. Our predecessors missed an important distinction which we can now see, namely, the distinction between God's bare existence and God's fuller actuality. The divine existence is but the abstract and invariant common denominator of all possible states of the changing actuality who is God at any moment.

An analogy might help us see the important distinction between God's unchanging and necessary existence and God's changing and contingent states of existence or actuality. Consider any human person throughout a lifetime. Naturally, we regard the person to be one and the same individual from childhood to old age. Granting that any of us might have failed to be conceived, and so is radically contingent, once a person exists we think of him or her as one through all the vagaries of life and as distinguishable from all others. There is an invariant individuality about this person that is usually marked by a particular name.

Nevertheless, this emphasis on the oneness or individuality of the person does not exhaust what we can and must say. As we have already been forced to remark, the "same" person undergoes many changes, and so is many different persons. We all take note of this when we encounter an old friend after many years' absence. The changes are remarkable. Something enables us to connect the person before us with the one we knew years ago, and we recognize an invariant individual. Yet what strikes us is the change. And this change is not merely surface or physical change; as we begin to catch up on the person's life, we hear of many experiences that have helped to mold this new person: marriage, children, jobs, travel, etc. This is truly as different a person as it is the same person. I recall agreeing to meet a high school friend after a hiatus of nearly 40 years. We were to meet in the lobby of a local motel, and as I sat there eagerly looking for my friend I realized that another man, to whom I had paid little attention, had also been there. Then it dawned on me that the man looked much as I remembered my friend's father looking. No doubt, when he noticed me, he thought he was seeing *my* father. So, two dramatically altered persons met again. As the evening wore on and we told our stories, it became more and more evident that the changes were far more than physical ones; we were different people than the high school friends of the '50s.

Although the accumulation of changes in another over a span of time is thus readily apparent, careful attention to our own lives discloses that each of us changes somewhat from moment to moment. To be sure, there is continuity with our past, and an active memory, together with orderly physiological functioning, helps to stabilize that continuity. But there is a difference in detail with each new experience of life. Although there may be an invariant "thatness," or individuality, the actual person that we are in each moment is different. As the Victorian hymn puts it, "New every morning is the love our wakening and uprising prove."[11] Each person is actualized anew relative to new and changing circumstances.

This distinction between the unchanging existence and the changing actuality that our human examples illustrate applies also to God. There is, to be sure, a radical difference between the two cases. In the first place, the divine existence, alone, is wholly necessary. Second, the divine actuality is related to *all*, not just to some others; it is universal and everlasting. Still, the recognition of what differentiates the divine mode of existence and actuality from all others should not obscure the fact that "existence" and "actuality" apply to all individuals. God's "existence" refers to the fact that God always is, and this is unchanging, but

God's richer "actuality" refers to the individual who is God in every moment. Each such actualization of the divine life is different from the previous actualizations; it is richer by virtue of the difference that each new detail of the world has made on it.

Finally, let us consider a problem that threatens to derail the idea of a God whose actual life changes. It is said that if a thing changes, there is no reason to suppose that it will inevitably increase or grow richer in content. In respect to what we know best, ourselves, change inevitably brings decay and, finally, death. Is there any reason to suppose, this reasoning inquires, that change must be different in principle for God? Does not the idea that God changes imply that God could diminish and finally die? Although this appears to be a serious objection, some reflection will show why it makes no sense to suppose that God could diminish or change for the worse or cease to exist.

First, if it is agreed that God's existence is necessary, this means that it is impossible that God should fail to exist. Second, every finite being that comes into existence adds something to the totality of things. Although each creature is finite, it does not erase itself or vanish into nothingness at its death; it has made its mark indelibly on the world and thus on God. Here the words of Omar Khayyam ring true:

> The moving Finger writes; and having writ,
> Moves on: nor all your Piety nor Wit
> Shall lure it back to cancel half a Line,
> Nor all your Tears wash out a Word of it.[12]

Hence, even though each creature "perishes" in the sense of having reached its finite terminus, it is not thereby annulled, canceled, or washed out. In Whitehead's words, all finite beings attain "objective immortality"; they "perish, and yet live for evermore."[13] When we ask, "Where?" the answer must be, "In the ever expanding life of God." The growing whole is the life of God. Every deed, every experience, including that of suffering, adds to the enrichment of the divine experience. Everything that occurs is "something that matters," and it matters ultimately because it matters to God; it is registered, valued, and retained everlastingly in the ongoing life of God.

SUMMARY

Let me now attempt to draw together some of what I have said in this chapter. First, God must be understood as the being who is supremely worthy of worship, the one than whom no other being can conceivably be greater even though God can surpass former states of the divine existence. If we take seriously the insight that worship, at its best, is love of God with all our heart, soul, mind, and strength, we see that we make a difference to God; we act in God's life in a significant way. Thus, God is not utterly immutable but, in fact, changes. Also, if God is the supremely loving being, God is infinitely sensitive to the needs of all creatures; God is compassionate. Again, this means that God is affected, and so changes.

The representatives of the great theological tradition quite properly wished to ascribe all perfections to God. Conditioned by a Greek bias against change and contingency, however, they declared that God was absolute, wholly necessary, eternal, independent, incapable of addition, devoid of potentiality, and immutable. And they made these claims without any qualification.

We have seen some reason for sympathizing with their intentions. Because they did not have the conceptual tools to make the required distinctions, however, they subverted the biblical faith they were trying to represent. Even so, there is no reason for us to reject the theological enterprise. Nor should we cast aside all systematic thought in favor of an irrational faith or try to replace faith with some form of rational secularism.

Taking seriously the conviction that ours is a "faith in search of understanding," I have sought and, I believe, found a mode of thought that is both adequate to our originating faith and intelligible to present-day sensibilities. Process theology enables us to see that the qualities typically ascribed to God (necessity, absoluteness, eternity, independence, immutability) properly apply only to a certain aspect of God's being, namely, God's existence. But *God*, the actual being who is the object of our faith and worship and who encompasses all reality, is contingent on all that occurs in the created world. God's life is shaped, at least in part, by what we do and think and feel. Therefore, God is temporal, relative, dependent, and mutable. God has a future as well as a past, and God actualizes new life from moment to moment. God is dependent, not for existence, but for the states of existence— God's actuality—on our decisions. God is supremely relative, which is to say that God interacts with every creature. Thus God is the ever-increasing, personal whole of which all the rest of us are parts.

Finally, and by way of adumbrating part of the next chapter, I would like to suggest a model in terms of which we may best conceive such a personal God: God as the "World Soul," the universal and supreme soul, or mind, which has the world as its body of which we may be said to be "cells." The idea of God as the World Soul is an ancient notion, although one not much utilized by Christian thinkers until recently. I suspect that the reason theologians were loath to take up this obvious image was because they thought it conflicted with the demands of divine transcendence. They construed—or misconstrued—transcendence in terms of God's separation from the world or else as a function of independence and sheer immutability. We can now see how to maintain God's transcendence more appropriately in terms of the absoluteness and necessity of God's existence and the universality, omnipresence, and all-inclusiveness of God's actual being.

Today we can make sense of the interpenetration of body and soul, the physical and mental, or, as we often say, the interaction of all components of the psycho-physical organism. If we think of the soul, or psyche, as inclusive of the body, rather than the other way around, we have, I believe, an adequate model for understanding the personal God of the Bible. And if we can understand the soul as active in the bodily cells, even as the component parts of the physical organism affect the state of the soul, we have a way of conceiving God's interactivity with the world. More of this in the following chapter.

4

God in the World; the World in God

God's activity in the world is best understood neither as a miraculous inter-vention in the ordinary course of events nor as the sole determinant of anything. Such claims run counter to the principles of natural causation, our ideas of freedom, and common sense. Rather, God's activity should be seen as a "persuasive lure" offering to every creature possibilities that enable it to actualize itself in the best possible way. As such, God is the ground of both order and freedom. Also, since all beings, in becoming actual, act beyond themselves, and are finally registered irrevocably in the ongoing life of God, God is best conceived, on the model of the human person, as the "world soul" that encompasses all being.

In both Chapters 2 and 3 I took some pains to emphasize the impor-tant distinction between the bare existence of an entity and its fuller, richer actuality. This distinction is especially important to our under-standing of God. I noted that attributes such as necessity, absoluteness, immutability, eternity, and independence, which traditional theology posited without qualification of God, should apply only to the divine existence. If we are to do justice to the biblical portrait of a personal God who is supremely worthy of worship, we must move beyond this simplistic concept to see that the contrasting attributes apply, in the supreme degree, to God's actuality. That is, God is not merely contin-gent, relative, changing, temporal, and dependent; God is contingent on *everything* that comes to be, relative to *all*, *everlastingly* mutable, *ever-lastingly* temporal or appropriately related to *all* past, present, and future, and dependent on *all* that comes to be for the content of the divine experience.

On the basis of this more nuanced understanding we are able to make sense of divine transcendence in terms of the necessary existence of God and the universal scope of divine interactivity. God is understood to be the universal agent and the recipient of all action in the world, the ultimate creator and inheritor of everything that comes to be.

GOD AND THE WORLD ORDER

Most of the positive points in Chapter 3 were worked out to re-present theologically the biblical portrait of God. But good theology must also be credible in secular terms. I believe that the mode of thought that best explains our basic experience and most adequately interprets current scientific theory is what I have called process thought. I remind the reader of the basic elements of that worldview: All ultimate actualities are interconnected occasions of experience. These are centered events that are partially the results of the actions of past events and also are causally active in the emerging world that succeeds them. The world, in fact, is an unsettled world, one of continuous becoming; it is a world in which the settled actuality of the past is always being brushed with open possibilities. Every occasion of experience that becomes does so as a free creative synthesis of the data that constitute its past and the possibilities that constitute its future. In other words, on attaining determinate status each *subject* projects itself forth as an *object* for a newly emerging subject, and the process renews itself. Thus, as I have reiterated, every occasion of experience, every instance of actuality, is something that matters. It matters for itself as a subject of experience, for others as an object to be experienced, and ultimately for the whole, since what comes to be cannot de-become; it cannot be annulled or eliminated from being.

I rehearse these points because they are germane to the question, Why introduce God into the picture at all? Or, if we concede that God somehow belongs in our view of the universe, what is God's function in the world, or how can we make sense of an "act of God"? Keep the points in the previous paragraph in mind as we proceed.

When one takes seriously the radically temporal character of the world and reflects deeply on it, it seems that nothing actual could come to be at all unless there were an interactive being of cosmic scope able to bring the infinite sea of possibilities within manageable limits. That is to say, given any situation riddled with infinite possibilities and with the risk of destruction that incompatible past actions entail, no order would ever emerge apart from the operations of a universally present orderer. Without a being able to synthesize all that occurs in the world and to envision the ideal possibility in its relevance to each actual situation, there could be nothing more than mere chaos: no order at all, no "world."

Whitehead first came to this conclusion in *Science and the Modern World* where he saw that the metaphysical situation that he had envisioned entailed a "Principle of Concretion" or a "principle of limitation" to function in place of Aristotle's "Prime Mover."[1] Even so, he quickly discerned that no "principle" could perform the activity of limiting possibilities and so, in *Religion in the Making* he expressed his insight this way: "The boundless wealth of possibility . . . would leave each creative phase still indeterminate, unable to synthesize under determinate conditions the creatures from which it springs. The definite determination which imposes ordered balance on the world requires an actual entity imposing its own unchanged consistency of character on every phase."[2]

He elaborates this intuition as follows:

> Apart from God, the remaining formative elements would fail in their functions. There would be no creatures, since apart from harmonious order the perceptive fusion would be a confusion neutralizing achieved . . . "actuality." . . . It is not the case that there is an actual world which accidentally happens to exhibit an order of nature. There is an actual world because there is an order in nature. If there were no order, there would be no world. Also, since there is a world, we know that there is an order. The ordering entity is a necessary element in the metaphysical situation presented by the actual world.[3]

These two statements, taken together, may be thought to constitute a reasonable claim for the necessity of an actual being, of cosmic scope, God, granted that there is some world at all: principles cannot effect change or bring about order, for only an actuality can act; granting the "metaphysical situation," however, which includes infinite chanciness ("the boundless wealth of possibility"), that actuality must be one of cosmic scope. This is, perhaps, a modern metaphysical rendering of the ancient principle, *ex nihilo nihil fit* ("out of nothing [actual] nothing can be produced").

But these claims demand considerable explanatory comment if they are to connect or make sense. First, keep in mind that God, as here conceived, is understood to be the *supreme* agent in shaping the world at any moment, but *never* the *sole* agent. There are always the "remaining formative elements," which are the already determinate actualities functioning as efficient causes, the possibilities or ideals functioning as final causes, and the emerging entity in question that synthesizes all this data, itself forming a new and unique emergent.[4] God's role in this creative process in every instance is to constitute God's own self anew so as to offer to the next instance of the world, in an ongoing dialogue, the most attractive way to respond. God presents to the new occasion an aim ideal for it in its historical situation.

A few more remarks are in order. When Whitehead speaks of a "harmonious order" or of an "ordered balance," he does not intend to ignore the presence of evil in the world. He never underestimates the effect of conflict. Nevertheless, the implication of the whole passage is that evil could never be so massive or out of bounds as to obliterate or thwart all creativity. Evil can never triumph; destructiveness can never reduce creation to nothingness.

On the other hand, the order that the "unchanged consistency of character" of God "imposes" on the world must not be thought of as absolute or unchanging. There could not be a static, completed order, because the inevitable presence of genuine possibilities to all emerging actualities rules this out. Nor does his phrase—the "unchanged consistency of character" of God—mean that Whitehead has slipped back into the traditional theological mold that presupposed an utterly immutable and absolute God. The point here is similar to one made in Chapter 3 about the consistency of divine will or the steadfastness of God's principles. The unchanged consistency of God is what remains steadfast amid the constantly changing intercourse with the world. It is expressed as the constant divine will that the truest, most beautiful, and best in any set of circumstances be brought about. It is that consistency of character that can absorb the worst, redeem the most antithetical elements, and then offer back to the next stage of the creative process an "aim" that is "the best for that *impasse*."[5]

It goes without saying—yet perhaps it must be said, since most of us ignore the obvious—that the best for any actual, temporal situation is not the unqualified actualization of an ideal or absolute good. It is always the best that could be brought about in a complex set of circumstances, one burdened with past decisions that inevitably make the best less than the ideal. What is more, we must keep in mind that the divine act of ordering here is a matter of providing an *aim*. It is not a matter of issuing a command or establishing a *fait accompli*.

We may now examine this divine role in the ongoing process more closely. Everything that comes to be, I have urged, is something that matters for itself, for other finite entities, and for the whole of which all are parts. The whole is understood to be the *personal whole of reality*.

It is God constituting God's self anew in each moment out of the data of the immediate past, the realm of possibilities, and God's own incomparable decision on how to synthesize all of this. Thus, when we speak of God as acting, we must understand that, in the first place, God acts to constitute God's own self in each new instance by responding to the expressed decisions of the creatures and to the possibilities with a will that the best available outcome be enacted.

By synthesizing all achieved value in one integrated personality, God minimizes the effects of conflict and disorder. Otherwise confusion would nullify any further creative synthesis, and the world long since would have unraveled. To be sure, God does not eliminate all conflict and risk, just as God does not suspend the harmful effects of natural causes. It is only in fairy tales that evil is eliminated once and for all. But between "all" and "none" there is room for an orderly and creative world.

Sometimes I imagine the divine integration of the many conflicting data of achieved reality as akin to a transformer bringing currents that are "out of phase" into phase. Or, with respect to reducing the potential confusion of the future to manageable limits, one can think of a computer searching among innumerable possibilities for those that best fit the situation. But whatever image comes to mind, the best analogy remains what we know best: the human act of self-constitution at any moment. Schubert Ogden makes the point that, by analogy with our "inner act whereby the human self as such is constituted," we can assert that "the primary meaning of God's action is the act whereby, in each new present, he constitutes himself as God by participating fully and completely in the world of his creatures, thereby laying the ground for the next stage of the creative process."[6]

This observation leads me back to a correlative point: Just as any act of creative synthesis inevitably is significant beyond its moment of achievement, so God's act of self-constitution must be expressed in the next stage of the world process; God acts back in the newly emerging world. By constituting God's self as the one who loves the world unreservedly, God offers each emerging creature an aim best for it in the given set of circumstances. And it is only because the finite entity has a relevant ideal, a goal or standard in terms of which it can organize itself, that it can achieve synthesis.

We can see, therefore, that God is the ground both of order and of novelty in the world. God lays the ground for order at every moment by integrating all past and making it available to the present. God enables the emerging world to achieve novel actuality by constituting God's self as an ideal in terms of which we should actualize ourselves.

This ideal might be perceived as a lure or an attractive goal, but it might also be perceived as a goad or even as a threat or a judgment. It has been expressed religiously as the imminence of the kingdom of God. Yet no matter how it is perceived or symbolized, the point is that God gives to the world that normative vision or subjective aim without which no new actuality could coalesce. It does indeed appear that "the ordering entity is a necessary element in the metaphysical situation presented by the actual world."

The Value of the Parts for the Whole

To this point my inspection of the processes that constitute the world has focused on the intuition that the world requires an omnipresent orderer: God as the initiator of every creative synthesis or God as creator. Continued reflection yields another insight. It is what Whitehead calls "the intuition of holiness . . . which is the foundation of all religion."[7] The intuition is that, if the things that occur make an abiding difference in the universe, they must register themselves somewhere. There must be a totality, an ever-increasing whole that contains the outcome of every creative synthesis. Thus we arrive at the idea of God as consequent upon all: God as the final recipient of everything or, in religious terms, God as redeemer.

Let us see how this intuition makes sense. In Chapter 1 I expressed the conviction that every thought, word, or deed, every experience we undergo—"the trivial round, the common task"[8]—is something that matters and that nothing can alter or annul this fact. Human experience, moreover, is a special, complex instance of experience anywhere. Everything that occurs, every event or occasion of experience or instance of actuality, is a creative synthesis of many data into one unique actuality that attains determinate status and is significant beyond itself. If we think of it, this means that every *fact* is a *value*. Everything that occurs is the attainment of some intrinsic worth as it pulls itself together. Yet it does not enjoy this value alone; it must make the private value available to the public beyond its moment of achieved value. Thus *attainment* of achieved value and *significance*, or being of instrumental value, are twin facets of every fact.

Even if we accept this position, that every fact is both an intrinsic value of some sort and an instrumental value, that it is an attainment of achieved value and yet is significant beyond itself, one might still ask: Are we not left within a world of finite reality? Does it not take a great leap or, at best, a dubious inference to get from this way of reading the facts to God? I do not think so, but to see the point more clearly, consider several passages from Whitehead that have guided my own thought on the matter. In the first place he asserts: "We are, each of us, one among others; and all of us are embraced in the unity of the whole. . . . [That is] everything has some value for itself, for others, and for the whole. . . . Also no unit can separate itself from the others, and from the whole. And yet each unit exists in its own right. . . . Everything that in any sense exists has two sides, namely, its individual self and its signification in the universe."[9]

Whitehead extends this line of thought to seek the best way of characterizing the basic stuff of experience, that which is inevitable beneath the surface of the vivid and changing details of conscious or sensory experience. His insight is summed up in three paragraphs that have had a profound effect on my own thinking:

> Our enjoyment of actuality is a realization of worth, good or bad. It is a value experience. Its basic expression is—Have a care, here is something that matters! Yes—that is the best phrase—the primary glimmering of consciousness reveals, something that matters.
>
> This experience provokes attention, dim and, all but, subconscious. Attention yields a three-fold character in the "Something that matters." "Totality," "Externality," and "Internality" are the primary characterizations of "that which matters." They are not to be conceived as clear, analytic concepts. Experience awakes with these dim presuppositions to guide its rising clarity of detailed analysis. They are presuppositions in the sense of expressing the sort of obviousness which experience exhibits. There is the totality of actual fact; there is the externality of many facts; there is the internality of this experiencing which lies within the totality.
>
> These three divisions are on a level. No one in any sense precedes the other. There is the whole fact containing within itself my fact and the other facts. Also the dim meaning of fact—or actuality—is intrinsic importance for itself, for the others, and for the whole.[10]

There are two points about this account of experience that I wish to highlight. First, fact and value cannot be torn apart, because every fact is a value in the sense of being significant for itself, for others, and for the whole. Every occasion of experience registers itself within the ongoing totality as something that matters.

Second, every experience contains within itself, however dimly, an awareness of the encompassing whole of which it, along with the others, is an important part. Thus, put in religious language, every experience is, somehow, an experience of God. As Ogden, in summing up the claim that the most elemental experience bears within itself the "sense of deity," has said: "Because at the base of whatever we say or do there is our primitive awareness of ourselves and the world as both real and important, all our experience is in its essence religious. It rests in the sense of our own existence and of being generally as embraced everlastingly in the encompassing reality of God."[11]

As with Whitehead's earlier intuition that nothing could occur apart from a universal ordering entity, this analysis has all the marks of an argument for God. Insofar as it is, keep in mind that it is an appeal to the self-evidence of experience. I am aware that many people will stoutly deny that an inspection of experience yields anything like the inseparability of fact and value, much less the sense of deity. But, as I have said, I believe that the typical attitude toward experience rests on the misguided habit of fixing on the variable, clear, and distinguishable objects of *sensory* experience rather than our most basic experiences and what all experiences have in common.[12]

In addition, our ordinary way of looking at the world divides the world into two camps: one composed of a few higher beings capable of having subjective experiences; the other, far larger part, composed of inert matter and non-sentient entities. This way of looking at the world may be useful for making our way through the daily round, but it is too crude for dealing with the microscopic world of bacteria and viruses; it fails to account for the growth of organisms or even the formation of crystals. More significantly, it begs the question whether "experience" is inapplicable to every type of actuality. If by "experience" we confine ourselves to the special, high-grade experiences of the earth's relatively few conscious beings, we will never conclude that everything that occurs is a value-experience or that every experience contains a dim sense of deity. But that is what is at issue here. My plea to those who unreflectively take this approach is to take another look: Fix on the more primitive feelings rather than on the relatively clear and distinct perceptions of sight or hearing; begin with the experience of existing from moment to moment, and see whether there is not the sense of being *one* among *others*.

In addition to this fundamentally different approach to experience, I believe we should be attentive to what physicists tell us about the liveliness and responsiveness of subatomic event-particles, or to what geneticists say about molecular inheritance and interaction, or to what ecologists teach about the vast and intricate web of life. All of these tell a different tale than does ordinary sense perception; they tell a tale that regards human experience fundamentally as on a par with others, "in a buzzing world, amid a democracy of fellow creatures."[13]

Even so, granting that any experience resolves itself into the feeling of importance for self, others, and the whole, many will doubt that "the whole," as I have been using the term, may be understood as, in any sense, personal. Is it legitimate to identify the expanding and encompassing whole with the personal God of biblical religion?

There are two responses to this question that I believe intersect and reinforce one another. From the perspective of biblical religion God is regarded, not only as supremely personal, but as necessarily existent. What this implies, however, is that the God who is experienced as personally involved in the history of Israel and in the lives of individual believers and so is always symbolized in personal images is also understood to be present to, and experienced by, every being that is actualized. Thus the God who is properly symbolized as personal is the same God who is interactive with all. It makes no difference that only a few recognize God as such; to be the interactive ground and end of all *is* to be the personal whole of which all are significant parts.

From the perspective of trying to make sense of our common experience it may fairly be claimed that the idea of being something that matters entails something like personal relations. I have in mind some remarks that Schubert Ogden once made in response to a similar question concerning the move from the ground of our confidence in the meaning and worth of existence to God as a person. He said:

> The only justification for talking about God as person or as personal is to do justice to, to account for, to make genuinely intelligible to myself and others, the experience that I actually have that my existence is worthwhile. In order to account for this, I, at least, have to use the concept "person." Worthwhileness, or significance, is in principle a relational idea. You can't say something is worth something unless it's worth something *for someone*. That's just what you mean by the idea of worth. Try to think of worth or significance except as a relational idea. I don't think you can. Now, if I say my life is worthwhile, then I have said it's worthwhile for someone. I think the idea of worth already implies the idea of a reality related to others and capable of responding to others. And I don't think it's too big a step from this to the appropriate use of personal categories to talk about God.[14]

Admittedly, none of these considerations is conclusive. But taken together they make a strong case for the claim that continued reflection on the most basic elements of our experience gives rise to the "intuition of holiness," namely, that all things make an abiding difference in the universe because, finally, they matter to the one being who is interactive with all and who embraces all other beings. This is the God whom the biblical writers symbolize in highly personal images and who is known as the redeemer of all.

GOD AS THE WORLD SOUL

In Chapter 3 I made an effort to develop the personal categories applicable to God in terms of love. And in this chapter I have tried to lay the ground for conceiving God as the personal whole of reality by showing what sense it makes to speak of God as acting in each emerging actuality and as being acted upon by every emergent actuality. In short, I have tried to make the case for understanding God as the interactive individual of cosmic scope.

Now I wish to develop this idea further by elaborating the mind-brain or the soul-body model. In what follows I shall use the terms *mind*, *soul*, and *self* more or less interchangeably. But to skeptics and persons of an especially empirical bent the question whether there is really such a thing as mind or soul occurs immediately. We can locate bodies and even brains, so this line of reasoning goes, but where is the mind or the soul? Do not these terms simply stand for brain-states, the activity of neurons in the brain, or emotional-physical states of the body?

Rather than address these questions on the grounds laid out by the truncated type of empiricism they imply, there are good reasons for shifting the perspective. In the first place, even though empiricists of this sort are reluctant to accept the reality of souls or minds and their distinction from bodies and brains, our ordinary language does, in fact, make that distinction. I believe in this case that our ordinary language reflects the deeper reality, because it is based on our experience of our selves as distinguishable from, yet interactive with, our bodies. We need to keep in mind that many things that are inseparable are, nevertheless, distinguishable, and it is important to make the distinction. I will argue, therefore, that the soul and its body, or the mind and its brain, are distinct entities even though they are coordinate and inseparable.

In addition to the clues taken from our language, bolstered by the insights provided by a "radical empiricism," as opposed to the reductive empiricism of sheer materialism, we can make an appeal to different sorts of philosophers and scientists who are convinced that a thorough analysis of the human situation precludes the thesis that all reality is nothing but matter. For instance, the philosopher Karl Popper and the neurophysiologist John Eccles have joined forces to argue in their book *The Self and Its Brain* that the mind or self is a distinct, self-conscious entity that interacts with its brain. Popper writes:

> I intend here to suggest that the brain is owned by the self, rather than the other way round. The self is almost always active. The activity of selves is, I suggest, the only genuine activity we know. The active psycho-physical self is the active programmer to the brain (which is the computer), it is the executant whose instrument is the brain. The mind is, as Plato said, the pilot. It is not, as David Hume and William James suggested, the sum total, or the bundle, or the stream of experiences; this suggests passivity. . . . [The self] is incredibly rich. Like a pilot, it observes and takes action at the same time. It is acting and suffering, recalling the past and planning and programming the future; expecting and disposing. It contains, in quick succession, or all at once, wishes, plans, hopes, decisions to act, and a vivid consciousness of being an acting self, a centre of action. And it owes this selfhood largely to interaction with other persons, other selves, and with [the products of the human mind such as stories, explanatory myths, tools, scientific theories, scientific problems, social institutions, and works of art].
>
> And all of this closely interacts with the tremendous "activity" going on in its brain.[15]

John Eccles brings a tremendous amount of scientific evidence to the support of Popper's philosophical position. Together, the philosopher and the neurophysiologist have produced a powerful tour de force for interaction between two distinct entities, the self-conscious mind and its brain.

Rather than cite Eccles, however, I wish to appeal to other eminent scientists who espouse a similar kind of interactionism or, at least, attack the habit of reducing all reality to merely physical, chemical, or biological processes. For instance, the brain surgeon and neurophysiologist Wilder Penfield writes:

> For my own part, after years of striving to explain the mind on the basis of brain action alone, I have come to the conclusion that it is simpler (and far easier to be logical) if one adopts the hypothesis that our being does consist of two fundamental elements. . . . Because it seems to me certain that it will always be quite impossible to explain the mind on the basis of neuronal actions within

the brain and because it seems to me that the mind develops and matures independently throughout an individual's life as though it were a continuing element, and because a computer (which the brain is) must be programmed and operated by an agency capable of independent understanding, I am forced to choose the proposition that our being is to be explained on the basis of two fundamental elements. This, to my mind, offers the greatest likelihood of leading us to the final understanding toward which so many stalwart scientists strive.[16]

The well-known psychobiologist Roger Sperry has taken up a similar position quite independently. While acknowledging that his view is a minority one among working scientists, he argues vigorously that "conscious awareness" must be regarded as

> a very real causal agent and rates an important place in the causal sequence and chain of control in brain events, in which it appears as an active operational force. Any model or description that leaves out conscious forces ... is bound to be sadly incomplete and unsatisfactory. The conscious mind, in this scheme, far from being put aside as a by-product, epiphenomenon, or inner aspect, is located front and center of cerebral mechanism. Mind and consciousness are put in the driver's seat, as it were: They give the orders, and they push and haul around the physiology and the physical and chemical processes as much or more than the latter processes direct them.[17]

Unlike Penfield, Sperry prefers not to speak in dualistic terms, yet he will not settle for a one-dimensional materialism that rejects all talk of a real, interdependent mind as superfluous.

I am aware that adducing several scientific and philosophic opinions does not make an airtight case for the view that would distinguish mind from brain or soul from body while demanding their interaction. What it does, however, is create an atmosphere conducive to an open and rational discussion of the issues involved.

Any productive discussion must, I believe, move us beyond the usual alternatives: a dualism that separates mind from matter and offers no intelligible way to make sense of their real interaction; and a materialism that solves the problem of causality by reducing everything to physical or chemical processes ignoring that cluster of experiences that we know best and most intimately, namely, subjective feeling, integration of feelings, contemplation of ideas, and decision-making. Process philosophy, I think, offers a better option. Recall that it views every final individual actuality as a subject essentially related to objects in its world. Thus it lays a philosophical ground for understanding the causality that science investigates as well as the subjectivity that we all experience in a way that neither dualism nor materialism can do. This viewpoint regards every fundamental unit of actuality as an occasion of experience that is partially caused by the achieved actualities of its past and partially self-caused by its own internal subjective experience. What is more, the newly emergent actuality in turn becomes an object for subsequent subjects.

It is within the purview of this genuinely "postmodern" philosophy, I believe, that we are best able to reconceive the idea of a soul and its interaction with its associated environment. Before suggesting positively how to conceive the soul in these terms, it is well to remind ourselves of how *not* to conceive the soul. In the first place, everything I have said in agreement with most recent discussions of the radically temporal character of being rejects as senseless the traditional idea of the soul as a simple, spiritual substance, if by this we mean that it is unchanging or incapable of being affected by its relations. To be an actual thing, we have seen, inevitably means to be a focus of relations, to be affected. On the other hand, I do not think it is at all helpful to think of the soul merely as the "vital principle" of a being, because principles do not act; only actualities can act. Principles are either ideals, perhaps a standard, or basic truths about actuality. But in no sense is a principle as such an actual entity.

Another tendency to be avoided is to treat each unit of actuality as if it were a particular soul. To be sure, each actuality is a *subject* or an occasion of *experience*. This point of view, which Whitehead called the "reformed subjectivist principle," namely, "that apart from the experience of subjects there is nothing, nothing, nothing, bare nothingness,"[18] was appropriated by Charles Hartshorne, who termed it "panpsychism."[19] Unfortunately, Hartshorne's term suggests that every actuality *is*, or has, a psyche or soul. I believe we are much better served by reserving the terms *psyche* and *soul* for fairly high-level individuals. A better term for expressing the reformed subjectivist view that every actual entity is an instance of subjective experience might be *omnisubjectivism* or the term that David Griffin uses, *panexperientialism.*[20]

Whatever words we use for such reformed subjectivism, the question remains: How far can it take us in the attempt to reconceive the idea of the soul in its relation to its body? In view of my rejection of the traditional ways of conceiving the soul (either as an unchanging spiritual substance or as a mere principle), and of my deep reluctance to label every basic unit of actuality a "soul," it might seem that I am at an impasse. Are we able to account for what we ordinarily term *souls* or *minds* in any distinctive way that does not reduce them to mere brain-states or simply metaphors for human behavior? In short, can we develop a position that is superior to the sheer materialism that Penfield rejects, the epiphenomenalism that Sperry rejects, or the dualism that most recent thinkers reject? I believe we can, but we must be prepared to work from the ground up and to form clear concepts, not only of the fundamental entities but also of two types of derived or secondary entities that are themselves composed of the elementary constituents. These secondary entities will be called *aggregates* and *compound individuals*.

Let us agree that ordinary bodies, including the human body, animal bodies, vegetables, and inanimate objects, are aggregates. They appear in varying degrees of complexity and some, obviously, are living, but none has the unity, integration, or self-directedness that are the marks of what we mean when we speak of a soul or mind; souls or minds are the integrating and coordinating elements of persons. To be sure, *human* bodies, so long as they are alive, seem inextricably bound to particular minds, but ordinary language insists on a distinction between the two, and it is this distinction that we are endeavoring to account for.

If we can comprehend the idea that bodies are aggregates—secondary entities—it should not be too difficult to grasp the notion of other kinds of secondary entities. These, like the aggregates, are composed of the unit actualities, and yet are vastly more unified than the aggregates. These secondary entities can be styled "individuals," although they are compound individuals. In the case of these much more complex and integrated entities we have every reason to assert that their constitutive actualities have a far greater capacity to receive and synthesize diverse data, to envision many more novel possibilities, and to actualize themselves so as to be more directive in their immediate environment than are those that make up aggregates. In short, they have high-grade, even conscious, capacity for memory, synthesis, imagination, decision, and will.

These entities are genuine individuals. They *are* the individuals whom we distinguish as this person rather than that, as "Margaret," "George," or "Raoul." In our experience such compound individuals or souls always disclose themselves as attached to particular, empirically identifiable bodies. This is so much the case that they are typically identified with their bodies. Even Whitehead, who at one point, speaking of "the unity of 'body and mind' . . . which constitutes the one human being," emphasizes the unity rather than the distinction, and so says, "No one ever says, Here I am and I have brought my body with me."[21] And yet we do speak, tellingly, of *my* body. We take for granted a distinction and a chain of command. However intimately joined the soul and the body or mind and brain are, it is always the former (soul, mind) as both Popper and Sperry insist, that dominates or guides, owns or gives orders to, the latter (body, brain). Whitehead, too, while stressing the intimacy and mutuality of mental and bodily life, sees the distinction when he says, "My brain, my heart, my bowels, my lungs, are mine with an intimacy of mutual adjustment. ... The behaviour system of the body has an element of direct relationship with the transitions of quality in personal experience. ... For this reason psychology and physiology are difficult to dissociate from each other. ... The behaviour systems of the human body and of intimate experience are closely entangled."[22] Even if we are attuned to the unity, words and phrases such as "my," "mutual adjustment," "transitions ... in personal experience," and "intimate experience" make the distinction clear.

For me one of the most illuminating statements about the relationship between soul and body, mind and brain, or the self and its body is the following by Schubert Ogden. This passage makes clear both the temporality of the self and its sociality, its being constituted by a sequence of occasions of experience that remember, synthesize, anticipate, and decide. The passage also highlights the point that the self both receives and integrates from its body and that it incarnates or expresses itself in the subsequent occasions of the body through its decisions:

> To exist as a self, as each of us does, is always to be related, first of all, to the intimate world constituted by one's own body. What I think and feel has its most direct effects on my own brain cells and central nervous system, and thence on the rest of the organism in which I as a self am incarnate. Likewise, what most directly affects me as a conscious subject is just the incredibly complex state of that same organism in which I as a self participate by immediate sympathetic feeling. By means of my body, then, I am also affected by, and in turn affect, the larger whole of things beyond myself. But whether directly or indirectly, I am really related to an encompassing society of other beings and am a self at all only by reason of that real relatedness. No less constitutive of my selfhood is its essential temporality. I know myself most

immediately only as an everchanging sequence of occasions of experience, each of which is the present integration of remembered past and anticipated future into a new whole of significance. My life history continually leads through moments of decision in which I must somehow determine what both I and those with whom I am related are to be. Selecting from the heritage of the already actual and the wealth of possibility awaiting realization, I freely fashion myself in creative interaction with the universe of others who also are not dead but alive.[23]

I believe that this idea of the soul as a temporally ordered self, distinct from, yet inevitably interactive with, the associated body, is the best for conceiving the God-world relation. Because the soul is composed of the same basic building blocks as the body, the momentary occasions of experience, it *can* interact with the body. Because it is a high-grade, compound individual, it can feel, unify, and direct the constituents that make up the body. This view, then, avoids all the problems of dualism without succumbing to reductive materialism. More than this, it clears the way to see that an "act" is not the relatively indirect activity of the body on the external world. The soul's act, in its most primary sense, is its own decision how to constitute itself anew out of the welter of impulses arising from its past decisions and those of its brain cells, and out of the possibilities confronting it. In turn, this act affects the soul's immediate future and that of its brain cells. Such an act, although clearly capable of being experienced by succeeding states of the same self, is just as clearly not empirically observable by other selves; only its consequences in its body are thus observable. Ogden sums up the matter this way: "Behind all its public acts of word and deed there are the self's own private purposes or projects, which are themselves matters of action or decision. Indeed, it is only because the self first acts to constitute itself, to respond to its world, and to decide its own inner being that it 'acts' at all in the more ordinary meaning of the word; all its outer acts of word and deed are but ways of expressing and implementing the inner decisions whereby it constitutes itself as a self."[24]

One additional question presses itself upon us when we consider this understanding of the soul-body interaction as the model for the God-world interaction. Granted that we have exposed the error of seeking for empirically verifiable "acts" of God (or of any self), is it not still the case that the soul is located within the body? If that were the case, any analogy to God would, similarly, have to locate God within the larger, encompassing universe that constitutes God's body.

To put the matter this way, however natural it may seem, is to betray an inadequate spatial model of the mind or soul. Although it is true that the soul has *temporal* relations (it remembers, decides, anticipates) so that it must be regarded as a temporal sequence of experiences, nevertheless it must be understood to be *only* temporal, and in no way spatial. To be spatial is to have externally observable relations to other entities associated with oneself in the present moment. But these relations are not causal ones. The force of the preposition *in* when we say, "the soul is in the body," is to stress the causal relationship. We say, "the soul is in the body" in the sense that each new instance of the soul acts *in* the immediately succeeding occasions of the brain, and so has its effect in the rest of the body and, consequently, in the world beyond the body. But it is equally true, and no less important, to insist that the body acts *in* the soul, since the soul is that sequence of subjects with the greatest capacity to receive and integrate into itself all the impulses of the prior occasions of the body as mediated through the brain. As the most integrative and directive sequence, the soul constitutes the organism as an individual. It is, thus, the personal whole that encompasses its body even as it acts in the body's constituent parts.

To make this point is, perhaps, to take a step toward seeing how we must conceive the analogy of God as the world soul that has the world of non-divine entities as its body. Much previous thought, to be sure, regarded the human soul as only one part within a larger whole. Therefore, it was natural to regard God, by analogy, as but a part of a larger, encompassing whole. With this way of understanding the matter, the larger universe would, in effect, be greater than God. And anyone who understands God as the greatest conceivable being would have to reject this notion.

But within the framework in which we are working, to conceive God at any moment as the world soul is not to see God as a part. Rather, it is to see God as the *encompassing whole itself*, and to take this to be personal and individual.

As with the human soul, the world soul must be temporal and social. This is the intelligible basis for our talk of God as personal and as acting personally. But whereas much uncritical talk proceeds on the assumption that bodily actions express the most primary kind of acts, we have shown that it is important to conceive any personal act primarily as the soul's act to constitute itself anew from moment to moment by responding to the creaturely decisions. The expression of this act in the next moment of the life of the world is, first, to keep the world in being and, second, to offer an appropriate subjective aim for each new creature. We cannot think of God's act as occurring in something external to God, because there is nothing external to God.

As we have already seen, this way of understanding the God-world relation enables us to articulate a genuine basis for divine transcendence: Not only is God the necessarily existent One in radical contrast to all other beings; God is here conceived as universally immanent. That is, God is the One "unto whom all hearts are open, all desires known, and from whom no secrets are hid."[25] God is the universal receiver, synthesizer, and evaluator of all creaturely decisions; and God thus actualizes God's own self anew every moment as a lure for each next occasion as it arises, the ground both of order and of freedom.

5

A Christology of Universal Redemptive Love

Schubert Ogden's insight that Jesus is the "decisive re-presentation of God for us" is unpacked in order to avoid the pitfalls of more traditional "constitutive" christologies. By asking, "Who is Jesus?" rather than "Who was Jesus?" we shift the focus from metaphysical speculation about the person of Christ to a practical-existential concern with the work of Christ, or from a "quest for the historical Jesus" to a quest for the significance of Christ-for-us-today (which is what Paul and the evangelists proclaim). The point is to show that Jesus re-presents (decisively for how we orient our lives) the same God who is already present to each creature as its loving creator and redeemer. The doctrine of the Trinity is also understood in this light.

It seems evident that the type of Christology one professes will both reflect that person's fundamental idea of God and will have a bearing on his or her understanding of Christianity and other religions.

I can put certain basic convictions about God on the table at once. The implication of these ideas for an understanding of Christianity and other religions will be seen to follow. I believe that the God affirmed throughout the Bible and in the Christian tradition is one and the same as the personal whole of reality that is suggested by a penetrating analysis of experience generally. Put otherwise, the personal God of the Bible, whom the ancient Jews and early Christians claim to have encountered as their creator and savior, is precisely the ultimate reality experienced by all creatures as their necessary ground and end. The One worshiped by Jews and Christians is, thus, worthy of worship by every human. Such

Reproduced with permission from David R. Mason, "A Christology of Universal Redemptive Love," *Dialog: A Journal of Theology*, Summer 2002 (41:2), 149.

a being is fruitfully symbolized as the supreme personal creator and redeemer of the universe and properly conceptualized as the one inter-active individual of cosmic scope.

Having made this point, however, I must be candid that the witness to the one God of all creatures is made, not simply in the name of a kind of "natural religion." Rather, it is precisely the claim of a particular historical religion, Christianity If my claim is that there is a common faith of humanity *implicit* in the acts that constitute our being human, the claim is also that this comes to *explicit* expression in the Christian witness of faith, the particular religion whose most characteristic evangelical proclamation is, "Jesus is the Christ."

This admission, then, would seem to have me hooked on the horns of a dilemma: Either I opt for a common faith for all humanity and a healthy plurality of equally valid historical religions, or I opt for the superiority of one religion that asserts that the supreme revelatory and redeeming expression of the one God is Jesus Christ. The latter option seems to entail exclusivism. Thus, we are apparently forced to choose either pluralism or exclusivism. To resolve this dilemma or begin to see beyond it, we should note that there are several traditions in Christology and then examine briefly the two major traditions.

THE EXCLUSIVIST TRADITION

There can be little doubt that for the greater part of Christian history the predominant tendency has been to promote the exclusive salvific power of Christianity, because Christ was understood to be a unique embodiment of the divine, the sole point of intersection between God and the world. The best-known and most often cited biblical expression of such exclusivism is John 14:6: "Jesus said to [Thomas], 'I am the way, and the truth, and the life. No one comes to the Father except through me.' "

One of the earlier doctrinal expressions of exclusivism comes at the hand of the third century bishop, Cyprian, who was concerned to combat the influence of the schismatics and to preserve the unity of the Catholic Church: "There is no salvation outside the Church," he said (*salus extra ecclesiam non est*).[1] This outlook was given ever more extreme expression during the Middle Ages when the church dominated the entire mindset of Europe. For instance, in 1302 Pope Boniface VIII declared: "We are obliged by the faith to believe and hold—and we do firmly believe and sincerely confess—that there is one Holy Catholic and Apostolic Church, and that outside this Church there is neither salvation nor remission of sins. . . . Furthermore we declare, state, define and pronounce that it is altogether necessary to salvation for every human creature to be subject to the Roman pontiff."[2]

Such an attitude, when joined to political power, led in the late fifteenth and early sixteenth centuries to the forced conversion, exile, or death of numerous Jews and Muslims in Spain.[3] And several decades later in Germany the ungodly consequences of this attitude spilled out in Luther's broadside against the Jews. Disappointed that his attack on Roman abuses had failed to bring about the conversion of the Jews, Luther called for the synagogues of "this damned, rejected race of Jews" to be burned, their homes destroyed, their rabbis to be forbidden to teach, and for many other cruelties to be committed against them in the name of Christ.[4] And there can be little doubt that the spirit of exclusivism that was reinforced by such utterances paved the way for the Nazi holocaust in the '30s and '40s of the twentieth century. Most present-day Christians condemn the Nazi atrocities, but the history of Christian anti-Semitism calls into question the morality of exclusivist claims and, also, the credibility of the Christology that lies at its base, namely, that Jesus Christ alone is the full disclosure of God in the world and that he is the exclusive agent of salvation for humanity.

THE TRADITION OF PLURALISTIC INCLUSIVISM

It should be noted, however, that the voice of extreme exclusivism was not the only voice of Christianity through the ages. From the earliest days a significant minority of theologians argued that allegiance to Christ committed them to an understanding that was quite different from the exclusivism of the majority. This position, which we find in the tradition going back to the New Testament, and which can be understood as a "pluralistic inclusivism,"[5] is more than an expression of toleration and goodwill; it is a genuine theological position grounded in a particular understanding of God and of the nature and function of Christ. Rather than seeing persons outside the pale of the Christian religion as excluded from God's salvation, this position understands the revelation of God in Christ to be the disclosure of God's universal redemptive love so that those who are not, in fact, baptized as Christians, but yet respond favorably to God's steadfast love, are redeemed by that love irrespective of their particular religious attachment.

This point of view has been put in a number of ways. In the New Testament both Paul and Peter give voice to it. Paul's major theme in

Romans is that the gospel is "the power of God for salvation to everyone who has faith, to the Jew first and also to the Greek" (Romans 1:16). Paul weaves this theme into many arguments but always keeps in mind that "God shows no partiality" (Romans 2:11). When he makes his famous claim that "a person is justified by faith apart from works prescribed by the law" (Romans 3:28), Paul does not reject the law but insists that it is faith in God that justifies anyone rather than obedience to the demands of a particular religion. In this way Paul counteracts what he took to be the exclusivism of the Judaism that he knew with a pluralistic inclusivism that had been disclosed to him by his encounter with Christ. Similarly, the equally famous statement in Galatians: "There is no longer Jew or Greek, there is no longer slave or free, there is no longer male and female; for you are all one in Christ Jesus" (Galatians 3:28) does not imply that now there is a superior, new religion. On the contrary, it proclaims the good news that God's redemption is not linked to culture, religion, or gender, but is, rather, available to all. That is what to be "in Christ" means to Paul.

Peter's grasp of the vision of pluralistic inclusivism is not, perhaps, as well articulated as Paul's, but it is, nevertheless, real, at least as he is portrayed in the Acts of the Apostles. Having had a vision that he must eat food that was ritually unclean, and so unfit for Jews, Peter, then, hears a voice that says, "What God has made clean, you must not call profane" (Acts 10:15). The vision and the divine command associated with it compels Peter to associate with Cornelius, a Gentile, whereupon Peter exclaims, "I truly understand that God shows no partiality, but in every nation anyone who fears him and does what is right is acceptable to him" (Acts 10:34). Despite the fact that Peter, then, baptizes Cornelius, this act is not a return to a new kind of exclusivism, but the recognition that the "Holy Spirit had been poured out even on the Gentiles" (Acts 10:45).

This New Testament perspective, however fragile, became normative for several major Christian thinkers. For instance, the second-century apologist Justin Martyr reasoned that, since everything came into being through the divine Word or Reason that "became flesh" in Jesus (John 1:14), and because this divine Reason is "the true light which enlightens everyone" (John 1:9), everyone has direct access to that divine Reason and can legitimately claim the name historically associated only with the followers of Jesus: "We have been taught," he says, "that Christ is the First-begotten of God, and previously testified that he is the Reason of which every race of man partakes. Those who lived in accordance with Reason are Christians, even though they were called godless, such as, among the Greeks, Socrates and Heraclitus and others like them; among the barbarians, Abraham ... and Elijah, and many others. ... [T]hose who lived by Reason, and those who live so now, are Christians, fearless and unperturbed."[6]

Similarly, Augustine, commenting in his later years on an earlier treatise, "Of True Religion," wrote: "[W]hat is now called the Christian religion existed of old and was never absent from the beginning of the human race until Christ came in the flesh. Then true religion which already existed began to be called Christian. ... When I said, 'This is the Christian religion in our times,' I did not mean that it had not existed in former times, but that it received that name later."[7]

Understandably, the view that one need not belong to the Christian church to lay claim to God's redemption as proclaimed by the church did not find favor among many to whom authority in the church was given. Yet it was never wholly erased. Ironically, during one of the periods of great expansion of Christianity, the nineteenth century, when Christian missionary activity was at its height, the view was revived. F. D. Maurice, an Anglican theologian writing in mid-century, made the point that the object of God's redemptive love in Christ was the world rather than Christianity. Steeped in the tradition that Justin Martyr had passed on from the Prologue to the Fourth Gospel (as distinguished from some of the anti-Jewish sentiments of that gospel) and the Epistle to the Hebrews, Maurice insists that the Christ who "took human flesh and dwelt among us" as Jesus of Nazareth was the eternal Word or Son of God whom John proclaims as the agent of all creation and the light of everyone. Thus, he writes, Christ "actually conversed with the prophets and patriarchs and made them aware of his presence" and is, in fact, "in every man, the source of all light that ever visits him, the root of all righteous thoughts and acts that he is ever able to conceive or do."[8] This Christological perspective, Maurice tells us, was not only read off the pages of scripture; it answered a deep existential need. In a letter to F. J. A. Hort Maurice confessed that he felt the need for a deliverer from "an overwhelming weight of selfishness," and that the Being able to deliver him and all creatures from such selfishness was "that Being who was exhibited in the cross of Jesus Christ." Grounded in the faith that God "in Christ [was] reconciling the world to Himself," Maurice forthrightly states his "belief that God has redeemed _mankind_, that He has chosen a family to be witnesses of that redemption, that we who are baptized into that family must claim for ourselves the title of sons of God, must witness to others that they have a claim to it as well as we."[9] Briefly put, then, Maurice claims on biblical and experiential grounds that _God_ is the redeemer, that _Jesus_, disclosed as the _Christ_, is witness to this truth, that *mankind* is the redeemed, and that *Christians* are witnesses to this fact.

Perhaps the most startling and powerful statement of the claim that the point of the Christian gospel is to witness to God's universal redemptive love comes from one who has often been charged with being a Christian exclusivist, namely, the Swiss Reformed theologian, Karl Barth. The passage I have in mind, interestingly, comes in the commentary on Chapter 3 of Romans. Speaking of the "righteousness of God" as attested by the law and the prophets, but also manifested through God's faithfulness in Jesus Christ, Barth writes:

> It is the redemption of all creation, and most particularly when the creature knows itself to be no more than a creature, and so points beyond itself. Wherever there is an impress of revelation—and does anything whatsoever lack this mark?—there is a witness to the Unknown God, even if it be no more than an ignorant and superstitious worship of the most terrible kind (Acts xvii.22,23). Where have there not been *certain of your own poets who also* have said it (Acts xvii.28)? ... We proclaim no new thing; we proclaim the essential truth in everything that is old. ... The faithfulness of God is the divine patience according to which He provides, at sundry times and at divers points in human history, occasions and possibilities and witnesses of the knowledge of His righteousness. Jesus of Nazareth is the point at which it can be seen that all the other points form one line of supreme significance. He is the point at which is perceived the crimson thread which runs through all history. Christ—the righteousness of God Himself—is the theme of this perception. ... Our discovery of the Christ in Jesus of Nazareth is authorized by the fact that every manifestation of the faithfulness of God points and bears witness to what we have actually encountered in Jesus. The hidden authority of the Law and the Prophets is the Christ who meets us in Jesus. Redemption and resurrection, the invisibility of God and a new order, constitute the meaning of every religion; and it is precisely this that compels us to stand still in the presence of Jesus. ... In Jesus we have discovered and recognized the truth that God is found everywhere and that, both before and after Jesus, men have been discovered by Him. In Him we have found the standard by which all discovery of God and all being discovered by Him is made known as such; in Him we recognize that this finding and being found is the truth of the order of eternity. Many live their lives in the light of redemption and forgiveness and resurrection; but that we have

eyes to see their manner of life we owe to the One. In His light we
see light. That it is the Christ whom we have encountered in Jesus
is guaranteed by our finding in Him the sharply defined, final
interpretation of the Word of faithfulness of God to which the
Law and the Prophets bear witness.[10]

Far from making exclusivist claims, Barth, here, gives expression to
a Christology of the revelation of God's universal redemptive love:
the God who encounters us in Jesus gives us eyes to see that the same
God is faithfully and redemptively at work in all creation. And a similar
point is made by the Roman Catholic theologian Karl Rahner in his
doctrine of "anonymous Christians." Rahner insists that in addition
to the explicit faith of Christians there is an implicit faith belonging
to all others who reach out toward God, however incomprehensibly.
For instance, he says:

> [M]an in experiencing his transcendence, his limitless openness—
> no matter how implicit and incomprehensible it always is—also
> already experiences the offer of grace. . . . But this means that the
> express revelation of the word in Christ is not something which
> comes to us from without as entirely strange, but only the explica-
> tion of what we already are by grace and what we experience at
> least incoherently in the limitlessness of our transcendence. The
> expressly Christian revelation becomes the explicit statement of
> the revelation of grace which man always experiences implicitly
> in the depths of his being. . . . [N]o matter what a man states in
> his conceptual, theoretical and religious reflection, anyone who
> does not say in his *heart*, "there is no God" (like the "fool" in the
> psalm) but testifies to him by the radical acceptance of his being,
> is a believer. But if in this way he believes in deed and in truth in
> the holy mystery of God, if he does not suppress this truth but
> leaves it free play, then the grace of this truth by which he allows
> himself to be led is always already the grace of the Father in his
> Son. And anyone who has let himself be taken hold of by this grace
> can be called with every right an "anonymous Christian."[11]

I have labeled this tradition represented by theologians from Paul to
Karl Rahner "pluralistic inclusivism" to distinguish it both from exclusivism and from a triumphalist inclusivism that regards any religion,
insofar as it is taken to be genuine, as pointing to and fulfilled in
Christianity. Admittedly, phrases such as "anonymous Christian"
appear subtly to reassert a kind of Christian triumphalism, but I believe

that an examination of the actual position discloses an alternative view; it maintains that Christ *represents* the one God who is the beginning and end of all being and so the source of grace for all persons rather than that he *constitutes* this God. And this is a great difference. Also I have given greater attention to this tradition, because I am convinced that it is truer to the heart of the Gospel than is the more common exclusivist point of view.

But this conviction depends on a particular understanding of what it means to confess, "Jesus is the Christ." Therefore, we need to examine both this confession and the specific doctrines that have been put forward to express it conceptually: what do they mean, do they make sense, and to what extent are they are consistent with the other things that can reasonably be said about God, the human condition, and the interaction between God and the world.

CONFESSION AND DOCTRINE

The doctrines about Christ, the Christologies, are so many efforts by theologians to give conceptual clarity and precision to the original, symbolic confession, "Jesus is the Christ." But there is good reason to doubt that the major Christological efforts have done that. Indeed, not only do they, in some instances, obscure the main point of the basic Christian witness of faith; they often seem to misrepresent it.

The confession, made by those who encountered Jesus as the Christ, claimed that here was the decisive manifestation of God. This confession affirmed that God, as re-presented by Jesus, is the loving creator and redeemer of every creature. At the same time, the confession challenged those who made the confession and those who received it to live their lives wholly in the light of this decisive manifestation. That is to say, the revelation of *the God of love* demands *the love of God* and of all God's creation. To confess that "Jesus is the Christ," therefore, is to proclaim the good news that God's love redeems every creature and, simultaneously, to accept the liberating news that, since God loves all beings, we, too, must love and act to promote the well-being of all. The manifestation of God in Christ is decisive because it demands a reorientation away from self and one's particular cultural or religious group toward God and God's world.

Nevertheless, the way traditional theology has talked about Jesus *as the Christ* has tended to obscure its main point. Whether taking the more orthodox approach that tries to establish the metaphysical uniqueness of Christ by embracing two utterly different "natures" in one "person" or the more recent, revisionary tack that tries to affirm the historical Jesus as a unique man of God, theologians have typically assumed that the task of Christology is to work out a doctrine of Christ or Jesus *in himself* rather than to illumine the meaning of Jesus *as* the Christ as *the symbolic re-presentation of God for us*. The more traditional, orthodox Christology tried to formulate a unique metaphysical reality; the more recent, revisionary Christology has tried to locate a unique historical reality. Both, I believe, fail, because both misrepresent the point of the confession, "Jesus is the Christ." Rather than restating, as clearly and intelligently as possible, the meaning of that confession, both try to fashion a doctrine about a being who is without peer. Consider two examples: one, a classical representative of orthodox Christology from the fifth century; the other, an instance of revisionary Christology from our own time.

A TRADITIONAL CHRISTOLOGY AND ITS PROBLEMS

The first is from the Chalcedonian Decree of 451. This definition of the person of Jesus Christ as the unique union of the divine and human natures set the standard and laid down the boundaries for most subsequent Christology until the nineteenth century:

> We all teach harmoniously that [our Lord Jesus Christ is] the same perfect in Godhead, the same perfect in manhood, truly God and truly man, the same of a reasonable soul and body; consubstantial (*homoousios*) with the Father in Godhead, and the same consubstantial with us in manhood, like us in all things except sin; begotten before ages of the Father in Godhead, the same in the last days for us; and for our salvation [born] of Mary the virgin *theotokos* in manhood, one and the same Christ, Son, Lord, unique; acknowledged in two natures, without confusion, without change, without division, without separation—the difference of the natures being by no means taken away because of the union, but rather the distinctive character of each nature being preserved, and [each] combining in one Person and *hypostasis*— not divided or separated into two Persons, but one and the same Son and only-begotten God, Word, Lord Jesus Christ.[12]

This decree clearly intends to define the "person" of Jesus Christ: He is a unique being who is said to combine two utterly different natures—"Godhead" and "manhood"—in one person such that the two natures are neither confused nor separated, each being changeless and indivisible. Happily, the theologians responsible for this definition refrained from trying to work out in detail just how such a being could be made credible. Yet there has always been some unease about it, for it gives the appearance, contrary to its intention, either of framing a hybrid entity, a unique "God-Man," or of demanding that what cannot reasonably and consistently be believed must, yet, be believed. As one careful scholar of Christian doctrine has said, "throughout the long history of attempts to present a reasoned account of Christ as both fully human and fully divine, the church has never succeeded in offering a consistent or convincing picture. Most commonly it has been the humanity of Christ that has suffered."[13]

As true as it may be that the humanity of Jesus has suffered in doctrinal and liturgical formulations, the deeper tragedy of this and every attempt to frame the Christian confession in terms of one person with two natures is that it shifts the emphasis from *faith in* God to *right belief about* a being of questionable metaphysical status. Moreover, a consequence of the demand for this particular belief has been to reinforce the exclusivist attitude: If the good news requires the belief that a unique being is the agent of salvation, then only those who so believe can be saved.

A MODERN CHRISTOLOGY AND ITS PROBLEMS

Because of the growing sense of unease with the traditional approach represented by Chalcedon, theologians have increasingly sought to develop a Christology that would do justice to the full humanity of Jesus and, simultaneously, avoid the pitfalls of illogic or outmoded metaphysics. Thus, many have tried to make a case for claiming that Jesus is the Christ by looking to the life of the historical Jesus and finding that he lived a perfect life, or was a man of utter faith, or was without sin, or claimed to be the Son of God, or some such thing. Such a claim, then, would form the basis for asserting that Jesus was the "Christ," the "Son of God."

Typical of this modern, liberal approach is the Christology of the Latin American theologian Jon Sobrino. Sobrino bases his argument for the divinity of Jesus on the perfection of Jesus's faith. He admits that there are few places in the New Testament that speak of Jesus's faith, but insists that "there are two passages in the New Testament that talk explicitly of Jesus's faith."[14] Unfortunately for Sobrino's case, neither passage is clearly or explicitly about *Jesus's* faith, but rather can be better read as referring to the faith of others. The first passage he cites is Mark 9:23. This is Jesus's response to the father of a boy possessed: "If you are able!—All things can be done for the one who believes." It strains credulity to think that Jesus is here being portrayed as speaking reflexively, that is, about his own faith, especially since the father immediately cries out, "I believe; help my unbelief." The second is Hebrews 12:2, which is a highly theological passage about Jesus perfecting our faith, not his own. So it is doubtful that the New Testament ever speaks clearly about *Jesus's* faith. And yet, on the strength of this slenderest of reeds, Sobrino leaps to the conclusion that Jesus lived his entire life as one of perfect faith. "Of prime importance," he says, "is the fact that [Jesus] himself was the one who first lived a life of faith in all its fullness. In that sense Jesus is not just an exemplar, a meritorious cause, or an object of our faith; rather, he himself is the first and foremost of believers. . . . [He] is the first to have lived as a resurrected one in history because he fully lived a life of faith."[15]

The claim that the historical Jesus lived a life of perfect faith, then, becomes in the hands of Sobrino the basis for distinguishing Jesus from "all other Christians," or for asserting "the divinity of Jesus": "The classic formulation is that Jesus possesses something by his very essence which belongs to other human beings only by grace. . . . The fundamental difference," he asserts, "is that Jesus is the one who has lived faith in all its pristine fullness, who has opened up the pathway of faith and traversed it to the very end. . . . [For] the Christian the divinity of Jesus unfolds historically in the experience of fashioning history together with Jesus. . . . [We] only know that Jesus is the Son in brotherly communion with him, in following the path of his faith."[16]

Sobrino's approach is fairly typical of several recent attempts to construct a Christology based on the life and personality of the historical Jesus. Whereas the orthodox Christology, represented by Chalcedon, affirmed that Christ is, metaphysically, God-Man, this type usually wants to claim that the historical Jesus was uniquely faithful, or sinless, or perfectly open to God's grace, and so is uniquely a man of God.

Unfortunately, this approach is as burdened with difficulties as is the more traditional one. Even assuming that the Gospels give us an accurate historical report of certain events in the life of Jesus, we have no right to generalize from a few incidents to the whole life of Jesus. The brief account we have of the public ministry of Jesus in no way warrants the claim that he always responded perfectly to God in faith or that he was inevitably sinless. Faith and sinlessness are, moreover, fundamentally matters of the interior life of a person and, so, could never simply be read off the public record even if we had a full biography. Interestingly, as we have seen, the Gospels themselves never unambiguously make claims about Jesus's faith, or sinlessness.

The last remark gets close to the heart of the problem: what we do and do not have in the Gospels. They do not claim to be empirically verifiable, historically accurate biographies of a special man, but, rather, to be proclamations of God's salvation as experienced by the disciples in their encounter with Jesus. This is made clear by the opening statement of Mark's Gospel: "The beginning of the good news of Jesus Christ, the Son of God" (Mark1:1). To change the Gospels, which are proclamations of good news, into something utterly different—whether metaphysical tracts or historical biographies—and on the basis of this metamorphosis to try to erect a Christology, is to guarantee failure. Paul Tillich made this point several decades ago about the inability of historical research to establish a foundation for belief in Jesus as the Christ. The "situation is not a matter of preliminary shortcoming of historical research which will some day be overcome," he said. "It is caused by the nature of the sources itself. The reports about Jesus of Nazareth are those of Jesus as the Christ, given by persons who had received him as the Christ."[17] Because the Gospels, no less than other New Testament writings, are witnesses of faith in Jesus as the Christ, the effort to press behind them to secure a foundation for faith on supposed facts about the historical Jesus, especially his interior life, is misconceived. An earlier "quest for the historical Jesus" as the basis for faith-claims was a failure, and inasmuch as the current quest is for the same thing, it, too, is bound to fail.

In a word, we see that the New Testament writings, including the Gospels, are not eye-witness accounts of what Jesus said and did. They are in no sense empirical-historical reportings, but are faith-statements by those whose lives had been radically reoriented by the impact of the living, resurrected Christ upon them. The evangelists, just like Paul and other New Testament writers, were not concerned with the questions about who Jesus *was*—what he *said* and what he *did*—as empirical-historical claims; their concerns, rather, were with who Jesus *is*—the meaning of Jesus as the Christ for our lives. To be sure, the Gospels take for granted that Jesus was a human being who said and did significant things. And historians are at liberty to sift through the evangelical material to try to determine a few facts about the man. But the task and the accomplishment of the various Gospels was not to record facts about the Jesus of history, but to proclaim Jesus as God's Messiah, the One who is present in worship, in preaching, and in the lives of those who attest to him in faith. This means that in story and proclamation they are witnessing to the redemptive love of God in their lives. As one New Testament scholar recently said with respect to the synoptic Gospels: "[They] are above all literary expressions of the theological convictions of their authors. . . . For far too long we modern readers of the gospels have allowed our attention to be diverted from the true intention of the gospel narratives by constantly asking the historical question, What actually happened? instead of asking the evangelical question, What is it that the gospel writer is challenging us to accept or to deny by means of this particular narrative?"[18]

There is one additional difficulty with the endeavor to reconstruct the life of Jesus as the basis for the Christian faith, and to my mind it is decisive: The attempt implicitly assumes that one can make empirical, scientifically verifiable data the criteria for making assertions about God or God-for-us. The Christian faith in Christ is a witness to the creative and redemptive love of God, as this is decisively revealed through Jesus and, at the same time, a confession of what this means for the lives of believers and for others. The attempt to make empirically based claims about the man, Jesus, the basis for assertions about God and the meaning of God for us is what might be called a "category mistake."[19] That is to say, since God, and even our experience of God's redemptive love in our lives, is never something merely thisworldly to be detected by ordinary knowledge provided by the five senses or even by a more sophisticated scientific or historical method, all attempts to justify assertions about God for us on the basis of such empirical research are mistaken in principle.

Ironically, then, it appears that many sophisticated, liberal authors, attempting to build a Christology from claims about the historical Jesus, are in the same boat as the biblical literalists who, as Tillich pointed out, treat God as an ordinary being "like any other being in the universe," thus drawing God "down to the level of that which is not ultimate, the finite and conditional."[20] The Christology purportedly based on historical research, therefore, cannot do what it claims to do. It both misrepresents the biblical witness and it is incredible inasmuch as it attempts to make empirical claims the basis for assertions about the divine.

A WAY BEYOND THE IMPASSE

Given all the problems that have plagued the various attempts to formulate a Christology, one might wonder whether it is at all possible. I believe it is, indeed, possible to develop a Christology that is both appropriate to the New Testament witness and credible. But to do so we must resist the impulse to frame the issue in terms of the nature or the "person" of Jesus Christ whether worked out metaphysically or by empirical-historical means. That impulse inevitably leads, as one recent writer said, to battles "over the precise calibration of humanity and divinity in Jesus."[21] These efforts have proved vain. Indeed, they shift the focus away from the New Testament proclamation that "God was in Christ reconciling the world to himself" (2 Corinthians 5:19) toward either right belief about a singular "metaphysical entity" of dubious credibility—a "God-Man"—or beliefs about uniqueness of the historical Jesus that are unwarranted by the New Testament and, in fact, misconstrue its message. To see our way clear to a more viable Christology let us return to some points made above, either in passing or in rehearsing the ideas of those who make up the tradition of pluralistic inclusivism.

The typical New Testament confessions, "Jesus is the Christ" or "Jesus is Lord" ("Son of God," "Son of Man," etc.), and even the mythological stories of divinely caused birth, miraculous wonder-working, and resurrection from the dead, are not made to point to Jesus-in-himself either as a "God-Man" or as a man-of-God. Rather they are so many ways of claiming that Jesus, a real human being, *re-presents* the same God who is always already present to all humans, not only as their creator and sustainer but also as their redeemer. Therefore, it may be said that the various New Testament witnesses are so many ways of confessing that Jesus, by his manner of life, his teaching, and his death, decisively reveals "the power of God for salvation to everyone who has faith, to the Jew first and also to the Greek" (Romans 1:16). This is attested by all the representatives of the tradition of pluralistic inclusivism; not only Paul, but Justin Martyr, Maurice, Barth, Rahner, Ogden, and others. We should remind ourselves, moreover, that what is thus revealed or disclosed is not so much the being of God in itself as it is God for us. That is to say, Jesus as the Christ bears witness to God working to redeem our lives or, as Paul says, God "reconciling the world to himself."

Such revelation is a manifestation of the power of God available to everyone irrespective of position in history or religious allegiance. Therefore, that "power of God for salvation" is not, and cannot be, claimed to have been located exclusively in one being. This is why I have highlighted the term "re-presents" or "presents again," which has been given currency by the contemporary theologian Schubert Ogden. For instance, Ogden writes: "The claim 'only in Jesus Christ' must be interpreted to mean, not that God acts to redeem only in the history of Jesus and in no other history, but that the only God who redeems any history—*although he in fact redeems every history*—is the God whose redemptive action is decisively re-presented in the word that Jesus speaks and is."[22]

This statement calls for comment. Ogden puts the phrase "the word that Jesus speaks and is" in the present tense for a good reason. He is referring not to the empirical, historical Jesus, a figure of the past who, presumably, taught and healed and preached and was put to death around 30 CE; he is referring to the Jesus who is experienced as alive and present to every generation of believers energizing them and redirecting their faith in God toward God. God, and God's "redemptive action" or ever-present love for all creatures, is thus "decisively re-presented" by this Jesus.

Now consider the significance and implication of the term *re-presentation* as it is used here. It means that God is always present to all persons in the same way, but is re-presented in the way that certain words or persons or events can sum up and present again ancient truths or common experiences in a wholly new way or with powerful new insight. Insofar as this is "decisive" for reordering lives, resetting priorities of values, quickening and focusing authentic existence, we can say it is a "decisive re-presentation." Thus, to say that "Jesus" is the decisive re-presentation of God's "redemptive action" in the world is, as Ogden says, "to say that in him, in his outer acts of symbolic word and deed, there is expressed *that* understanding of human existence which is, in fact, the ultimate truth about our life before God; that the ultimate reality with which we and all [people] have to do is God the sovereign Creator and Redeemer, and that in understanding ourselves in terms of the gift and demand of his love, we realize our authentic existence. . . ."[23] This is the point of the various symbolic expressions of the New Testament proclamation.

A Christology that both accurately reflects that proclamation and avoids the pitfalls of the several constitutive Christologies will, thus, be a "representational Christology." It asserts that Jesus dramatically and powerfully re-presents God's universal redemptive love. Like both the traditional Christology and its modern counterpart this Christology *assumes* that Jesus was fully, authentically human. Unlike the one, it refuses to try to meld authentic humanity with sheer divinity to produce some *tertium quid*; unlike the other, it refuses to attempt by empirical means to discover at the inner core of a particular human some sort of perfection that entitles that persons to be called God, or utterly faithful, or sinless, and thus to be followed.

Jesus is taken to be re-presentative of, but not alone constitutive of, the divine redemptive love that redeems or justifies the world's creatures. Of course, this Christology also assumes that there is an ultimate reality, whom we call God, who is internally related to every creature as the divine creative source of its being and the end of all its days—its ground and ultimate destination. And it *asserts* that this one God, known to the Jews primarily as liberator from slavery, and as the source of Torah and the word of the Prophets, which give direction and worth to life, is one and the same as the God of pure unbounded love re-presented by Jesus.

In other words, a representational Christology *assumes* both that God is the source and end of all being and that Jesus was fully human. It *asserts* that this God is decisively re-presented by Jesus as attested in the New Testament proclamation and as known to Christians in Word and Sacrament. In Jesus, as thus proclaimed, all the major religious themes of liberation from bondage, law and morality, call to repentance and new being, creation, and hope for ultimate salvation are represented, and all focus on the cross as the symbol of divine suffering love, and so of universal redemptive love.

This representational Christology rules out the sort of exclusivism that is often associated with the traditional constitutive Christology. Just as Jews, at best, understand themselves to be "chosen" only to bear witness to the nations of repentance and divine forgiveness (Jonah), so Christians are called to proclaim God's universal redemptive love. Because Jesus is re-presentative of divine love always already at work in the world, Christians are called to attest to God's redemptive love in the lives of people everywhere irrespective of their religious attachment or cultural identity. To claim, as some have done, that Christianity, or worse a part of it, is the fullest means to salvation in comparison with which other religions are seriously lacking is to miss the point of Jesus as *re-presentative* of the one God who is always already present to and redemptive of all creation. To make the additional claim that there is literally no salvation apart from the Christian church is to commit the sin that H. Richard Niebuhr called "the absolutizing of the relative," namely, "substituting religion, revelation, church, or Christian morality for God."[24]

Despite the penchant to localize deity or to "absolutize the relative" that has been the continuous thorn in the side of theology, the fundamental message of a representative Christology remains constant: That which anchors all human existence, that which is the ground and end of all meaning and value, is nothing so contingent as a particular religion, but rather that to which all religions point, the circumambient reality "in [whom] we live and move and have our being" (Acts 17:28).

6

Understanding the Trinity

The doctrine of the Trinity was, classically, a Christological doctrine, but many classical theologians made the mistake of turning the New Testament trinitarian symbols into hard and fast metaphysical concepts with the unfortunate consequence of suggesting that God is a committee. Jews and Muslims often think that Christians are "tri-theists." Several recent theologies, including some process Trinitarians, have repeated the mistakes of the past. We should take the New Testament symbols, Father, Son, and Holy Spirit, seriously as symbols but not literally as metaphysical concepts. Therefore, we must keep what metaphysics (and faith) know—there is one God interactive with all—and then "demythologize" the symbols.

We have seen that a *constitutive* Christology, giving rise to the exclusivist tradition in Christianity, misconstrues what I take to be the proclamation of Good News: that God reconciles the world to God's self through Jesus Christ, thus making each of us to be a new creation (2 Corinthians 5:17–19). At the same time the tradition that embraced constitutive Christology set Christianity apart from other religious traditions and other people, implying that the others were not only different but also somehow inferior. A *representative* Christology, on the other hand, affirms that the one God who is always already present to humans as their creator, sustainer, and redeemer is decisively represented in and through Jesus Christ, and this implies that the others, too, are embraced in the redemptive love of God.

Not only has a particular type of Christology, namely a "constitutive Christology," set Christianity apart from, and often at odds with, other religions. There is also the related doctrine that seems to follow from the experience of Jesus as the Christ, namely, that God is somehow to be characterized as "trinity." In fact it is just these two beliefs—"Jesus is the Christ" and "God is a trinity of persons"—that the sister theistic religions, Judaism and Islam, find most offensive.

For instance, Jews insist that God is "one, not three." According to Rabbi Milton Steinberg, the Jewish affirmation of divine unity is an "explicit denial of the Christian dogma of the Trinity, a total disavowal of the thesis that God, though one, is somehow at the same time three persons, 'coeternal and coequal.' " Jews regard the Trinity as a "misrepresentation of the Divine nature." Moreover, they earnestly "dissent from the notion, integral to the Trinity, of a God-man."[1]

Muslims are equally emphatic and equally negative. The Qur'an says: "O people of the Book! Commit no excesses in your religion: nor say of Allah aught but the truth. Christ Jesus the son of Mary was no more than a Messenger of Allah, and His Word, which He bestowed on Mary, and a Spirit from Him: so believe in Allah and His Messengers. Say not 'Trinity': desist: It will be better for you: for Allah is One God."[2]

Pretty strong stuff: "Say not 'Trinity': desist!" "God is one, not three!" Christ is *not* a "God-man." "Christ is "no more than a messenger of" God. Although I am convinced that both Jews and Muslims are mistaken about what Christians are bound to believe about both God and Christ, their confusion is understandable because Christians themselves have sown the seeds of confusion. As we have seen, Christians have made semi-official statements that indicate that Jesus Christ is a "God-Man" or that Christ *constitutes* the singular instance of God in the world. Moreover, as we shall see, they elevated attributes or symbols of God for us into metaphysical concepts about distinct metaphysical realities that, taken together, constitute the inner being of God.

Consider something of the genesis of the doctrine of the Trinity. It is largely agreed that the New Testament has nothing like a doctrine of the Trinity, and that trinitarian thinking emerged only as a product of Christological reflection and controversy. Thus early trinitarian *symbols* do indeed derive from the specifically Christian experience of God through Jesus Christ; they endeavor to capture and re-express the variety and complexity of the Christian experience of, and response to, the one God as that experience has been transformed, shaped, and heightened by the experience of Jesus as the Christ, the re-presentation of God for us. Their purpose, therefore, was to witness, not to the trifold being of God in itself, but to God's way of being toward us which is what moderns call the "economic trinity."[3] In the course of time, however, theologians began to believe that God's being itself could not be other than God as revealed to the world. And so something like what is now called the "essential" or the "immanent" or the "ontological" trinity began to take shape.[4]

Then subtly, and seemingly as a matter of course, the *symbols* of God for us were transmuted, under the pressure of Christological controversies and with the aid of philosophical terms such as *ousia* and *hypostasis*, into *metaphysical concepts*, concepts that were thought to mirror metaphysical realities. With these the theologians endeavored to map out the inner being of God, and to distinguish and relate individual components. The Athanasian Creed may be regarded as a typical product of this effort, and the quasi-official status that the creed held for centuries lends substance to the conviction that Christians are wedded to a strange and strained metaphysical idea of God, one that thoughtful, loyal Christians have often tried to explain away. Here is the first half of the Athanasian Creed:

> Whosoever will be saved, before all things it is necessary that he hold the Catholic Faith. Which Faith except everyone do keep whole and undefiled, without doubt he shall perish everlastingly. And the Catholic Faith is this: That we worship one God in Trinity, and Trinity in Unity, neither confounding the Persons, nor dividing the Substance. For there is one Person of the Father, another of the Son, and another of the Holy Ghost. But the Godhead of the Father, of the Son, and of the Holy Ghost, is all one, the Glory equal, the Majesty co-eternal. Such as the Father is, such is the Son, and such is the Holy Ghost. The Father uncreate, the Son uncreate, and the Holy Ghost uncreate. The Father incomprehensible, the Son incomprehensible, and the Holy Ghost incomprehensible. The Father eternal, the Son eternal, and the Holy Ghost eternal. And yet they are not three eternals, but one eternal. As also there are not three incomprehensibles, nor three uncreated, but one uncreated, and one incomprehensible. So likewise the Father is Almighty, the Son Almighty, and the Holy Ghost Almighty. And yet they are not three Almighties, but one Almighty. So the Father is God, the Son is God, and the Holy Ghost is God. And yet they are not three Gods, but one God. So likewise the Father is Lord, the Son Lord, and the Holy Ghost Lord. And yet not three Lords, but one Lord. For like as we are compelled by the Christian verity to acknowledge every Person by himself to be both God and Lord, so are we forbidden by the Catholic Religion, to say, There be three Gods, or three Lords. The Father is made of none, neither created, nor begotten.

The Son is of the Father alone, not made, nor created, but begotten. The Holy Ghost is of the Father and of the Son, neither made, nor created, nor begotten, but proceeding. So there is one Father, not three Fathers; one Son, not three Sons; one Holy Ghost, not three Holy Ghosts. And in this Trinity none is afore, or after other; none is greater, or less than another; but the whole three Persons are co-eternal together and co-equal. So that in all things, as is aforesaid, the Unity in Trinity and the Trinity in Unity is to be worshipped. He therefore that will be saved must thus think of the Trinity.[5]

Now, it is evident that the Creed is aware of the charges that might be brought against it, and so tries strenuously to avoid tritheism: "We worship one God in Trinity.... They are not three Gods, but one God.... So we are forbidden by the Catholic religion to say, there be three Gods or three Lords," etc. Even so, because the symbols have been changed into literal metaphysical concepts and then reified, the Creed is forced into a strange configuration of the inner being of God: the "persons," no longer symbols of God for us, are now individual metaphysical realities, not to be "confounded"; each person is distinct, and each has attributes attached to it: uncreate, incomprehensibility or unlimitedness, eternality, almightiness, even though there are said to be "not three eternals, but one eternal," etc. And the persons are further distinguished: "The Father is made of none, neither created nor begotten. The Son is of the Father alone, not made, nor created, but begotten. The Holy Ghost is of the Father and the Son, neither made, nor created, nor begotten, but proceeding." Yet they are "co-eternal" and "co-equal."

Most persons who try to make sense of this picture, *on its own terms*, find themselves baffled, and so exclaim, "We are in the presence of a mystery too great to comprehend," meaning that it doesn't make a bit of sense to them. The introduction of additional doctrines such as *perichoresis* or *circumincessio*—the notion that the three persons mutually indwell or interpenetrate one another—does not throw much light on the doctrine, because they still accept the fundamental supposition that the inner being of God is actually constituted by three individual realities. They only tinker with the ideas rather than question the premise that the symbols must be treated as metaphysical concepts that mirror metaphysical realities.

Many attempts to defend the doctrine of the Trinity down to the present have been satisfied merely to restate the classical doctrine without trying to reshape it. Some, however, have thought to replace the older, philosophical concepts used in the classical formulation with newer, more dynamic ones. Such has been the case with several recent "process Trinitarians" whom I want to examine. I believe that, although they utilize Whiteheadian philosophical concepts for their reconstruction, they are, in effect, simply plugging more recent philosophical concepts into the classical receptacle, and so exacerbating the predicament. Our examination of two Whiteheadian efforts to revise the doctrine of the Trinity should help to lay bare the problem of accepting the premise of the classical doctrine while endeavoring to reconstruct it in artificial ways.

Before proceeding let me set forth my guiding principle: *We are not required to accept the premise of the classical doctrine that God somehow comprises three distinct individuals each represented by a metaphysical concept. In fact, we must not. What we must do, frankly, is "demythologize" the literal metaphysical concepts that have been put into place in a way similar to that which biblical interpreters employ to interpret the myths of the Bible: When stories and myths represent themselves as scientific or historical facts, they must be interpreted as saying something not about supposedly empirical facts, but rather about God in God's relationship with the world and with humans. They are demythologized or given an existentialist interpretation. Analogously, when trinitarian terms are used to represent literal metaphysical facts about God in itself, they must be demythologized to mean symbols of God for us in a way that brings into focus the Christian understanding of God's redemptive love for the world and what Christians regard as authentic human existence.*

Metaphysics is essential to any discussion of God. Process metaphysics in particular, as I have tried to show, can tell us that God is the supreme instance of sociality and temporality, and that the one God that exists necessarily is universally interactive. But process metaphysics can no more unlock and lay bare individual constituents of the complex unity that is God than the classical metaphysics could; it cannot tell us that what is a genuine unity is composed of three distinct individuals. To see the implausibility and artificiality of such an attempt let us consider two Whiteheadian reconstructions of the doctrine of the Trinity.

TWO WHITEHEADIAN RECONSTRUCTIONS OF THE DOCTRINE OF THE TRINITY

Ford

Lewis Ford and Joseph Bracken SJ are two prominent Whiteheadian scholars. Ford has written extensively and thoroughly on Whitehead, but I believe his major contribution to what he calls "process Trinitarianism" is in an article in the *Journal of the American Academy of Religion*.[6]

In this article Ford is committed to initiating the discussion with the "economic trinity" before proceeding to the "fundamental triunity" of the being of God. But his procedure is odd. He looks first to what his reading of *Whitehead* tells him about the threefold activity of God so that he can attach the biblical/classical trinitarian symbols to the Whiteheadian concepts, as expressive of those concepts.

A clue to his approach is provided at both the beginning and the end of the article when Ford asserts that genuine trinitarian principles take their rise *only* from the Whiteheadian insight that the God-world relation involves a *double problem*: not only must we account for God's transcendence and immanence with respect to the world; we must also account for the world's transcendence and immanence with respect to God. The second part of this simply did not exist for the ancients. One set of Whitehead's antitheses frames the problem: "It is as true to say that the World is immanent in God, as that God is immanent in the World. It is as true to say that God transcends the World, as that the World transcends God."[7] It is *this* modern problem, and the Whiteheadian solution, Ford assures us, that generates the concept that demands "an ultimate triunity of principles defining the divine life."[8]

Since no one in the ancient world had so much as seen, much less formulated, this problem Ford is genuinely nonplussed that the church theologians managed to present a solution in trinitarian, rather than binitarian, terms. Indeed, he suggests that the trinitarian speculation of the fourth and fifth centuries was just that: abstract theory leaping ahead of experience for which it was later to provide a matrix of intelligibility. "Like conic sections, which had to wait nearly two thousand years for their first important application in Kepler's description of the elliptical orbits of the planets, perhaps the Trinitarian conceptuality, at least with regard to the problem of transcendence and immanence, first comes into its own in our situation."[9]

It is evident, therefore, that Ford is convinced both that the trinitarian concepts of the fourth and fifth centuries were but abstract theory, and that only the modern Whiteheadian solution to the double problem of God's and the world's transcendence and immanence with respect to each other provides a sufficient basis for producing genuine trinitarian thought. Thus armed he is prepared to show how the three biblical "symbols of Father, Word, and Spirit may be expressed in terms of the philosophy of Alfred North Whitehead, and then correlate these expressions with the threefold structure of his concept of God."[10] From within the framework of the Whiteheadian conceptuality Ford starts by working out God's relation to the world (the "economic trinity"). Naturally enough he begins with that aspect of the God-world relation that corresponds to the work of the Spirit. And he finds that the aims that prompt our own creativity—the work of the Spirit—are derived from God's "primordial nature" (Whitehead's designation), which brings about "the divine ordering of all pure possibilities."[11] At the same time he notes that the primordial nature of God is not only what we term "Spirit": "it is also pre-eminently the divine Logos."[12] So Ford finds that he has one Whiteheadian concept (the primordial nature of God) to do the work of two biblical symbols when treating God's relation to the world (the economic trinity). Even so he recognizes that the early church distinguished the work of the Spirit from that of the Logos: "While the Spirit indwells every man, at least every believer, only the Christ incarnates the Logos."[13]

With the distinction between the Spirit and the Logos established, even though both are functions of the primordial nature, Ford turns his attention to the symbol of the Father. Rather than identifying the Father with Whitehead's "consequent nature" of God, as might be expected, Ford concludes, so far as the economic trinity is concerned, that it can be expressed in Whitehedian terms this way: "The Father is constituted by the primordial nature as it expresses the nature and activity of God, the Logos as it provides emergent possibilities for the on-going creation of the world, and the Spirit as it expresses the immanence of God within every creature as its particular creative possibility."[14] Thus, so far as the economic trinity is concerned God is *one* with three modes of relating to the world.

Were this the last word on the matter we might conclude that, however problematic the project of translating biblical symbols into metaphysical concepts is, Ford had achieved some measure of success in viewing the triune relation of God to the world in Whiteheadian terms. This is not, however, his last word. There are apparently two matters that compel him to develop the doctrine further. First, there is the modern problem with which he began: God's transcendence and immanence with respect to the world and the world's transcendence and immanence with respect to God. Secondly, There is the "ancient question whether the threefoldness revealed in the economy of God's providential rule is also a revelation of the inner life of God, as he is 'in himself.' "[15]

I believe that a resolution to the modern problem has less to do with the particular "essential Trinity" that Ford posits than he claims. Seeing that there is a double problem and resolving it, no doubt demands a different understanding of God and of creatures than the ancient world envisioned, but that it demands the particular doctrine of the Trinity that he enunciates is questionable.[16] Even so, Ford posits an "essential triunity" in terms of Whitehead's metaphysics: "the divine creative act, the primordial nature, and the consequent nature," which he equates, respectively, with the Father, the Logos, and the Spirit.[17] He says that "the Logos pre-eminently symbolizes and exemplifies" the primordial nature of God; while the symbols, "Father" and "Spirit," express other aspects of God, "the Logos *is* the primordial nature" in that it is the "complete, timeless ordering of all formal structures."[18] Thus, we see that Ford has translated the symbol, "Logos," into the literal Whiteheadian concept, "the primordial nature" of God. And he does the same with the symbols, Father and Spirit; "The symbol Father is freed to point to the ultimate transcendent source of this manifest structure . . . the primordial envisagement, that nontemporal act of divine self-creation" that orders all eternal objects; it is "God's innermost subjectivity."[19]

Finally, the Spirit. Although at first Ford shrinks from making "a simple identification of the Spirit with the consequent nature," he asserts that it is "by means of our experience of successive divine aims provided by the Spirit that we have any evidence . . . for the presence of God's consequent experience."[20] And, although this is "indirect" evidence, it does bear witness to God's experience of the world that is, in Whiteheadian terms, the "consequent nature of God." "In the final analysis," Ford asserts, "we must assent to an ultimate triunity of principles defining the divine life: the divine creative act nontemporally generating the primordial nature, from which proceeds the consequent nature as implicated in the categorical conditions established by the primordial envisagement."[21]

Ford is clear, however, that this "triunity of principles . . . cannot be interpreted as implying a plurality of subjects in personal interaction within the Godhead."[22] The "natures" of God, in Whiteheadian metaphysics, he argues, are no more distinguishable "actualities" than are "persons" in classical trinitarian thought. The single "unitary actuality" is *God*, and the persons or natures are "principles or modes of functioning."[23] Thus Ford's Whiteheadian Trinitarianism would parallel "modalism" in ancient trinitarian speculation. Moreover, he rejects the supposition of some that Whitehead's one brief mention of a "superjective nature" of God is systematic and refers to a "third distinct nature" such that the *three* "natures" (i.e., "primordial," "consequent," and "superjective") constitute the "proper Whiteheadian trinity."[24]

This last comment, together with Ford's clear assumption that God is a singular entity, even though constituted by a triunity of principles, is enough to distinguish Ford's "process trinitarianism" from that of Joseph Bracken that I will examine. Even so, we must be clear that Ford has bent his entire effort toward spelling out the inner being of God in terms of Whitehead's metaphysics. One could argue that it is an ingenious effort to translate the theology of the fourth and fifth centuries into contemporary metaphysics. Because of this, however, it is not only contrived, but is misconceived. It is developed on the assumption that the biblical symbols of Father, Word, Son, Wisdom, and Holy Spirit must have exact counterpart in metaphysical concepts and that, therefore, it is the responsibility of contemporary theologians to find distinct categories or principles to replace the older ones and to reproduce the meaning of the symbols. It is, in the words of the "Articles of Religion" about another doctrine, "a fond thing, vainly invented."[25] The basic error, which Ford shares with classical theology, is the tacit assumption that the biblical, trinitarian symbols must be treated *as concepts*, and that these concepts correspond exactly with principles or "persons" that constitute the essential being of divinity or make up the inner life of God.

Bracken[26]

From the foregoing remarks about Ford's error my final appraisal of Bracken's effort will come as no surprise. In the end it is their shared assumption that is decisive: the assumption that Whiteheadian concepts must literally replace the biblical symbols and so represent metaphysical realities that constitute the being of God.

Even so, Bracken's approach to the doctrine of the Trinity is different from that of Ford, and the idea he has of God is so radically different as to cause even the casual reader to think there is something implausible about what each is doing. Bracken begins his constructive treatment of the Trinity, in contrast with Ford, with an account of the "essential" or "immanent" Trinity, the fundamental makeup of the inner being of God, from which he thinks to determine the activity of God in the world (the "economic trinity"); thus, he says we find traces of the Trinity in the created order.

It is important, at the outset, in coming to terms with Bracken's process or "neo-Whiteheadian" Trinitarianism, to be absolutely clear that he regards God as a "*community* of co-equal persons"[27] wherein "person" seems clearly to be understood in a modern sense as an individual. Thus he argues that we need to work out a "thoroughgoing process approach which begins with the premise that God is a community of three divine persons and then proceeds to show how this triune life of God is somehow continued in the process of creation as a whole, but above all in the lives of human beings redeemed by Jesus Christ."[28]

If it be objected that I have overplayed the claim that God is a "community" constituted by three distinct individuals, consider another passage that makes this even plainer. Having criticized Heribert Muehlen for "depersonalizing" the Holy Spirit, Bracken says of the "three persons of the trinity":

> Each is a separate "I"; each can address the other two persons as "Thou." Each serves as the bond of union between the other two. What makes them one God instead of three gods is the ongoing process of self-giving love which is their common nature. They constitute, in other words, a community and this community of three persons is what we really mean by the generic term *God*.[29]

"God" ... a *community*. The "persons" who constitute the community, each a *separate I* who addresses "the other two persons as 'Thou.' " Can there be any doubt that if Jews or Muslims—or any reasonable persons—were to read this they would react with the charge of "tritheism"? Bracken is not unaware of the charge, but, with the help of Josiah Royce and Ervin Lazlo, he thinks to ward off the charge by showing, first, that a community is a higher order of being than an individual and, second, that the community can be properly regarded as an agent. He says that we must conceive " 'God' as the generic term for three personally ordered societies [Whitehead's technical language for individual 'persons'] who act as a *corporate reality* both in their internal relations and vis-à-vis their creation."[30]

Lazlo, Bracken says, argues that "the properties of a group are irreducible to the properties of the individual members"[31] so that the group must be treated as a whole. Royce takes the claim further when he argues that there are two levels of "mental beings—namely, the beings that we usually call individuals, and the beings that we call communities":

> A community is not a mere collection of individuals. It is a sort of live unity that has organs as the body of an individual has organs. A community grows or decays, is healthy or diseased, is young or aged, as much as any individual member of the community possesses such characteristics. Each of the two, the community or the individual member, is as much a live creature as the other.[32]

This is not intended to be science fiction! It is thought of as sober philosophy. It seems to me, however, that Royce has been led astray by taking the metaphor of the body quite literally so as to consider the community as a unified individual, a temporally ordered self with a mind and the capacity for making decisions. Bracken, too, recognizes Royce's penchant for regarding communities as "supraindividual persons," even to the point of assigning a "mind" to the living community. But he seeks to salvage some truth to the notion of community as agent by disclosing a simple mistake in Royce's argument: "Whereas minds in the strictest sense are needed for individuals to engage in acts of interpretation," Bracken points out, "only a *mentality* or set of shared presuppositions and feelings is needed for a community to act as agent in the creation of languages, customs, religions, etc."[33] By laying bare Royce's failure to observe the difference between community and individual, specifically the appropriate criterion for understanding each as an agent, Bracken believes that he has cleared the way for conceiving God as a community of coequal and free, interrelating divine persons. Thus assured of the basic soundness of this concept of God, he believes that he has laid the groundwork for working out the doctrine of the trinity in terms of Whitehead's metaphysics.

To fix attention on "God the Father" Bracken cites various passages from *Process and Reality* in which Whitehead makes the point that every actual entity receives its "initial aim" from God. God is thus the "aboriginal condition" or the "Primal Cause," if not the sole determining cause, in every instance. Here, however, Bracken interposes his own particular trinitarian bias into Whitehead's philosophy: "God," in these passages Bracken claims, "is to be more precisely understood as *God the Father*, since even within the divine being" the Father is the "Primal Cause" even though he shares his creativity with the other two divine persons.[34]

The Son is, then, associated with the "consequent nature" of God. The Son is the one who responds affirmatively to the Father's proposals converting sheer possibility into actuality and, in turn, weaving the effects of what creatures have done with such possibilities into the ongoing life. Therefore, God the Son can be conceived as the "Primal Effect" or the "ontological center-point or source of unity for that same process at every instant and should be associated in a special way with the divine consequent nature as described by Whitehead."[35]

Finally, Bracken turns to the Holy Spirit who, he says, is "the vivifying principle of creation who is to be associated in a special way with the superjective nature of God."[36] He says that in the divine life the Spirit is that which prompts the Father to offer new possibilities of divine existence and prompts the Son to say yes to the Father's offer. Moreover, this interior activity is mirrored in the created order in that the Spirit "prompts the Father to offer initial aims to all actual occasions. . . . [The Spirit] prompts each of the occasions to say yes to the Father's initial aim for it and thus to unite its decision with that of the Son in his ongoing dialogue with the Father."[37] Pressing the point further Bracken insists that "the Spirit is the hypostatized Condition of the divine being and, by extension, of the created universe as well. Thus, more than the Father and the Son, the Spirit is responsible for the integrity of the God-world relationship from moment to moment and should be associated in a special way with the divine superjective nature."[38] It is clear, then, that especially with respect to the ontological or "essential trinity," but also with respect to the "economic trinity," Bracken equates the Father with the "primordial nature of God" in Whitehead's metaphysics, the Son with the "consequent nature," and the Holy Spirit with the "superjective nature" of God.

Let us, now, examine Bracken's attempt to make sense of the idea that a community, which he thinks God is, can have agency. Bracken claims that the agency requisite for a community to perform its tasks is "only a *mentality* or set of shared presuppositions and feelings." His own way of putting the matter, however, shows clearly that "mentality" does not have the concrete actuality, the unity, purposefulness, or decisiveness required to designate an agent—one who acts. "Mentality" does not denote a mental act. It is, rather, a term indicating the form common to a number of mental acts. Mentality is merely an abstraction and not a concrete actuality; only actualities can act. Neither Bracken, nor Lazlo, nor Royce, therefore, has given sufficient reason to regard and treat the community as an agent.[39] Moreover, while a community may, indeed, have more cohesiveness than a mere heap, one can hardly claim—beyond appealing to a metaphor—that it has the unity or integration of memory and purpose of a true individual. Lacking, therefore, both the unity and agency of true individuals, the community can hardly be regarded as of a "higher order" than its constituent parts, which are thought to be true individuals.

Bracken himself seems at times to recognize this, since "God" is typically said to be a "generic term," and it is really one of the constituents—a subordinate society within the more inclusive democratically organized society—that can be said to act (at least in the world. And I remain unconvinced that it makes any sense to speak of an intra-divine act, because that would be an "act" that has no temporal outcome). Thus, I see no alternative than to point out the obvious: Like most versions of the "social trinity," the view of God as a community of persons is not the view of One being—even a complex One—but is as close as makes little difference to tri-theism.

The major criticism directed at Ford applies all the more to Bracken. That is, from the beginning, and without any scruples, he has regarded the trinitarian symbols as concepts that spell out the being of God in itself. In addition, however, the fact that Ford and Bracken, making use of the same biblical, trinitarian symbols and the same Whiteheadian metaphysics, should arrive at such radically different pictures of the metaphysically inner life of God ought to suggest a fundamental flaw in this whole program. Remember, not only does the one take a more "modalist" approach while the other assumes a "social trinity." The correspondences they find between the symbols and the natures or aspects of God in Whitehead's scheme are also fundamentally different: Ford, who realizes that the "superjective nature" as such has no systematic standing in Whitehead's philosophy, identifies the Father with the "primordial envisagement," the Word with the "primordial nature," and the Spirit with the consequent nature"; Bracken, by contrast, identifies the Father with the "primordial nature," the Son with the "consequent nature," and the Spirit with the "superjective nature." This does not bode well for anyone seeking clarity about the details about the inner life of God by way of Whitehead's metaphysics.

Yet these dramatic differences only serve to highlight the basic error that they hold in common and that they share with much of the tradition. A misconception of the function of both the trinitarian symbols and of metaphysics has led, I believe, to the kind of inventiveness that obscures rather than illuminates. Had they allowed the biblical symbols, in all their richness and suggestiveness, to represent the variety of Christian experiences of "God for us"—God as creator, redeemer, and sustainer, as transcendent and immanent, as orderer and lure toward novel attainment, as judge and companion, for instance—they would have been free to allow Whiteheadian metaphysics to perform its proper task: to elucidate our understanding of the necessary existence and the nature of God, of the essential being of creatures, and of the general features of the God-world relation. As it is, they have posited a one-to-one correspondence between particular symbols and particular metaphysical concepts that they then reified. And this misconstrues the role of each.

I recommend, therefore, that we take the biblical, trinitarian symbols seriously *as* symbols of God for us, but not as metaphysical concepts to be translated into metaphysical facts. Wherever we find that the symbols have already been transformed into metaphysical concepts and then reified we must swiftly and surely demythologize them and see them once again as symbols of God for us. This is what good preachers instinctively do.

7

Christianity and Other Religions

Although the dominant Christian attitude for centuries was "exclusivist," epitomized by the claim that "there is no salvation outside the church," many recent theologies have accepted some form of "pluralism." This work advocates a "pluralistic inclusivism" that maintains, on biblical and rational grounds, that God is the redeemer, that Jesus disclosed as the Christ witnesses to this truth, that all humanity is redeemed, and that it is the task of Christians to witness to this truth.

One of the major contributors to the recent discussion of the relation of Christianity to other religions, Diana Eck, has said: "Our theological question is how 'we' as Christians or Jews or Muslims will think about our own faith anew in relation to the faith of our neighbors. It is true, however, that our increasing engagement with one another in civil society may well provide the context for new and transformative thinking."[1] I am quite sure that Professor Eck is right that the increasing positive engagement of persons of different religious and ethnic backgrounds with one another has had and will continue to have a transformative effect on the understanding of one's own religion and that of the others. It is regrettable, however, that the converse is also true: that attacks on the others, warfare, bitterness, etc. keep us from seeing anything good in them, and at the same time cause us to misunderstand our own ideals and fundamental beliefs. This is where we are today; this is where we have been for centuries.

Reproduced with permission from David R. Mason, "A Christian Alternative to (Christian) Racism and Antisemitism," *Journal of Ecumenical Studies*, Spring 2000 (37:2), 155–160.

Moreover, when we focus on the *Christian* self-understanding and its understanding of other religions and try to think theologically we become aware that our attitudes reflect our understanding of our Christology and our trinitarian theology. The specific self-understanding and attitude toward other religions that any Christian holds is closely linked to the particular interpretation of what he or she means by asserting, "Jesus is the Christ" and, also, that "God is a trinity." This close linkage between Christology, trinitarian thought, and the attitude of Christians to others ought to be kept in mind as we discuss "Christianity and Other Religions."

For example, as we saw in Chapter 5 a *constitutive* Christology, which understands Christ to be the sole locus or major focus of God's salvific/redemptive activity in the world, will inevitably give rise to an "exclusivist" attitude epitomized by the assertion that "there is no salvation outside the church." On the other hand a Christology that we came to understand as *representative* gives rise to the view epitomized by the New Testament statement that "God shows no partiality," namely that Jesus is re-presentative of God's "universal redemptive love," that God redeems *all* humankind, and not merely one particular group.

Likewise, the third-, fourth-, and fifth-century theology that converted the biblical symbols of God for us into metaphysical realities constitutive of the being of God was bound to alienate Christians from Jews and Muslims, because the latter understandably thought Christians were dividing up the one ultimate reality. The trinitarian view that I have advocated, which I believe is consistent with the New Testament view, holds that the various symbols (Father, Son, Holy Spirit, and others) are so many symbols of God for us. This is not inconsistent with the many symbols employed by Jews and Muslims and, for that matter, Hindus and Buddhists, to designate the relation of ultimate reality to human beings.

I have, already in Chapters 5 and 6, indicated how the predominant Christian attitude of "exclusivism" played out with respect to the Jews. Fair-minded Christians will pay close attention to that sordid history. It is not a pretty picture. Yet it is only by coming to grips with that history, I believe, that Christians can move forward. I recommend James Carroll's *Constantine's Sword: The Church and the Jews, a History*[2] as a sensitive and accurate reading of that history. To be sure, the Christian attitude toward other religions has not always been as heinous as that toward the Jews, but the attitude that "we are right and you are wrong" has been so clearly evident that it cries out for the kind of "new and transformative thinking" that Eck envisions with respect to Christianity and all religions.

As we make our way toward such transformative thinking it is well to recall what we know about religions generally and to keep several points clearly in mind. First, as Ogden has repeatedly said, "it belongs to a religion to claim to be *the* true religion" for "every religion claims implicitly or explicitly to be formally true."[3] And Ogden adds that every religion will establish norms for judging religious truth. Observe that the claim of every religion is to be "*the* true religion," but not "the *only* true religion" such that all others must be regarded as false or only partially true. There can be more than one true religion. That is to say that every religion claims, in its own way, to express the truth about the meaning of ultimate reality for us and to be able to establish the norm for evaluating the truth about itself and other religions. But what more is to be said about religion generally? Consider a few of the things I said in Chapter 1 about religion.

I noted there that religion is a complex "cultural phenomenon" comprising a number of elements such as ritual, beliefs, codes of behavior, and emotions, and that this phenomenon is both a product of the culture in which it arises and yet a producer and molder of a new cultural identity. But the point to emphasize here is that every religion is a *product*; it is historically conditioned. Each religion is "a particular cultural expression of a group's underlying faith." Even though there is an invariant faith that lies at the base of the many different religions—a "vision of something which stands beyond, behind, and within the passing flux of things" and that redeems all things—no one religion can claim itself to be the only true religion, the possessor of absolute truth. All are relative, temporal, contingent pointers toward the truth. That is why I insisted that "all religions are, in part, products of the culture in which they arise and which they represent and serve. Most of us," I said, "easily recognize this truth with respect to other religions. It is the beginning of wisdom, however, to acknowledge the truth with respect to our own. To admit the cultural relativity of our own religion, to see it as simply a special expression of 'the one true faith,' and at the same time to recognize that there is a common faith at the base of all religions is to eschew the idolatry of equating our religion with God and to take a step toward trusting the one God who creates and redeems all." And I believe that I have made it clear that Christianity's norm, which might well apply to other religions, is expressed in the "Summary of the Law," the twofold command to love God with the totality of our being and to love our neighbors as ourselves.

With this in mind we are better prepared to address the theological question of "Christianity and Other Religions." But first, let us pause and see an example of how the issue was posed and addressed in the early modern period.

LESSING'S FABLE OF THE THREE RINGS

One work of the Enlightenment brings the issue into clear relief: Gotthold Lessing's dramatic poem, *Nathan the Wise*.[4] The sensibility that now seems so widespread as to be taken for granted was then so shocking that Lessing was unable to publish the work. We are fortunate that it was published after his death, and that we still have access to this unusual "wisdom," if it is that, today.

The setting of the play is Jerusalem in the twelfth century when Muslims, Jews, and Christians were supposedly mingling. In act 3 the Fable of the Three Rings is retold by Lessing, and put to good use. In the scene in question the great Muslim Sultan, Saladin, approaches the wise Jew, Nathan, to ask for his considered opinion about which religion—Judaism, Christianity, and Islam are the ones in question— seems to him to be the best. In fact, he puts the issue even more strongly: "Of these three religions *only one can be the true one*," he says, and demands that Nathan make a clear choice among them. Although Nathan at first demurs, Saladin presses him on this issue, and so in response Nathan reproduces the Fable of the Three Rings:

> In days of yore, there dwelt a man in eastern lands who had a ring of priceless worth received from hands beloved. The stone it held, an opal, shed a hundred colors fair, and had the magic power that he who wore it, trusting its strength, was loved of God and men. No wonder therefore that this eastern man would never cease to wear it; and took pains to keep it in his household for all time. He left the ring to that one of his sons he loved the best; providing that that in turn that son bequeathed to his most favorite son the ring; and thus, regardless of his birth, the dearest son, by virtue of the ring, should be the head, the prince of all his house.

And Nathan continued:

> At last this ring, passed on from son to son, descended to a father of three sons: All three of whom were duly dutiful, all three of

whom in consequence he needs must love alike. But yet, from time to time, now this, now that one, now the third—as each might be with him alone, the other two not sharing then his overflowing heart—seemed worthiest of the ring; and so to each he promised it, in pious frailty. This lasted while it might, then came the time for dying, and the loving father finds himself embarrassed. It's a grief to him to wound two of his sons, who have relied upon his word. What's to be done? He sends in secret to a jeweler, of whom he orders two more rings, in pattern like his own, and bids him spare nor cost nor toil to make them in all points identical. The jeweler succeeds. And when he brings the rings to him, the sire himself cannot distinguish them from the original. In glee and joy he calls his sons to him, each by himself, confers on him his blessing—and his ring as well—and dies!

Now each son claimed to be the reigning prince, but argued in vain, for as Nathan said: "The genuine ring was not demonstrable—*almost as little as today the genuine faith.*"

Saladin is aghast and says that one ought not to trifle with so important a query with a story about rings: "I should think that those religions which I have named to you might be distinguished readily enough. Down to their clothing, down to their food and drink." Indeed, replies Nathan: "In all respects *except their basic grounds.*" Then Nathan adds that they are all grounded on history, traditional or written, and that each is likeliest to trust in his own forbears who from youth have given proof of their love. The adherents of each religion, he says, will, naturally and properly, trust their own history. But Nathan desires to return to the fable of the rings. The sons complained and so brought their complaints before a judge each with the claim that his father could not have been false to him. And so the perceptive judge says: "Unless you swiftly bring your father here to me, I'll bid you leave my judgment seat." And he continues,

I hear the genuine ring enjoys the magic power to make its wearer loved, beloved of God and men. That must decide! For spurious rings can surely not do that! Whom then do two of you love most? Quick, speak! You're mute? The rings' effect is only backward, not outward? Each one loves himself the most? O then you are, all three, deceived deceivers! Your rings are false, all three. The genuine ring no doubt got lost. To hide the grievous loss, to make it good, the father caused three rings to serve for one.

And so the judge, rather than issuing a verdict, gave counsel:

Accept the matter wholly as it stands. If each one from his father
has his ring, then let each one believe his ring to be the true one.
Possibly the father wished to tolerate no longer in his house the
tyranny of just one ring! And know: that you, all three, he loved,
and loved alike, since two of you he'd not humiliate to favor
one. Well then, let each aspire to emulate his father's unbeguiled,
unprejudiced affection. Let each strive to match the rest in bringing to the fore the magic of the opal in his ring! Assist that power
with all humility, with benefaction, hearty peacefulness, and with
profound submission to God's will! And when the magic powers
of the stones reveal themselves in children's children's children:
I bid you in a thousand thousand years to stand again before this
seat. For then a wiser man than I will sit as judge upon this bench,
and speak. Depart! So said the modest judge.

The widely held assumption that, among religions, "only one religion
can be the true one" is here challenged. The fable suggests that the ring
and those who wear it betoken the love of God and our fellow humans
and, in turn, love by God and our fellows. But when it turns out that
each brother loves only himself each turns out to be a "deceived
deceiver"; the ring is not authentic. For the Father could no longer "tolerate the tyranny of just one ring." And so the modest judge bid the
brothers to emulate their father's guileless, "unprejudiced affection"
and strive to match the others in bringing out the "magic" of the original
opal. A powerful fable for our own day.

A THEOLOGY OF CHRISTIANITY
AND OTHER RELIGIONS

I share William Campbell's conviction that "the key to how Christianity relates to other religions is how it perceives itself in relation to
Judaism."[5] Therefore, I will endeavor to set forth a "theology" of the
Christian self-understanding and its relation to other religions in
terms of the early Christian witness to Jesus as the Christ and that,
inevitably, in relation to the Jews.[6]

Unfortunately, when we turn to the New Testament, which contains the earliest witness to Jesus, we are confronted with a great deal
of anti-Jewish sentiment.[7] Are there any good reasons for believing
that the anti-Jewish sentiment so plainly evident in the Gospel of John,

but also a part of the other Gospels, is far from and even at odds with the fundamental principle of the Christian message? There are.

It has long been clear to New Testament scholars, even if this has not been made clear to the public at large, that none of the Gospels is an eyewitness account of the historical Jesus. Nor are the Gospels an attempt to record the biography of Jesus. All were written in the last third of the first century, and all the gospel writers were editors, not reporters. They were people who fashioned quite different accounts from stories and sayings that circulated for several generations among the earliest Christian communities. Some of the sayings circulated without any narrative framework, while other sayings and stories were found embedded in liturgies, preaching, and controversies with local Jewish congregations. The gospel writers synthesized these diverse stories and sayings into a new whole, creating sequences and situations, and even placing words in Jesus's mouth. John is the most highly theological and the least historically reliable, but all of the Gospels must be regarded as narrative theology rather than biographical record. Inevitably, all of them reflect the times and situations in which they were written. Thus, with respect to the anti-Jewish passages, which reflect the tensions between two fragile groups in the Roman Empire in the years following the Jewish revolt of 66–70 C.E., one is bound to agree with a modern Jewish commentator:

> The anti-Jewish Jesus who emerges from the gospels is thus the product of the writers who conceptualized him in the light of what had become their own anti-Jewish orientation, often a function in turn of whatever such views were current among their own constituencies . . . [It] is vital that modern readers of the gospels come to understand that the historical Jesus and the Jesus of the gospels are simply not one and the same. Reminiscent of a painting overlaid by later retouchings . . . what we have in the gospels is one Jesus-image superimposed upon another.[8]

Whether, or to what extent, anyone can penetrate the layers to attempt to form an accurate picture of the historical Jesus is still in debate. What is certain, though, is that whatever emerges from historical investigation will be fragmentary: perhaps a teacher and healer who proclaimed the imminence of God's reign and associated himself with its advent, a Jew who gathered disciples and was put to death by the Roman government.

More importantly, however, as we saw in Chapter 5 it is not the so-called historical Jesus that counts, but rather "Jesus as the Christ" proclaimed throughout the New Testament "with the authority of supreme victory."[9] That is to say, the disciples and others quickly became convinced that death had not crushed Jesus and that somehow he was among them. Thus they, and the generations following them who produced the New Testament, found their own lives quickened and oriented anew toward the only God they knew how to believe in—the God of Abraham, Isaac, and Jacob, the God of Moses and the prophets, the Redeemer of Israel and the Creator of the universe. Now, however, they were enabled to see God through the lens of Jesus. For this group Jesus decisively re-presented ultimate reality and the meaning of authentic existence for them.

It is important to emphasize my use of the term, *re-presents*, which I used throughout Chapter 5, and which I clearly borrowed from Schubert Ogden. I wish to make the same point that I believe Ogden makes: Contrary to any exclusivist or triumphalist claim for Jesus as the sole locus of divine activity in the world—a claim that on the face of it is as immoral as it is absurd—the essential witness to Jesus in the New Testament is a witness to one who for the apostolic community dramatically and decisively presents anew the pure unbounded love of the God who is always already present to every creature, not only as its creative ground but also as the redemptive love that will never abandon it. Thus, Jesus is taken to be representative of, but not alone constitutive of, the divine redemptive love that alone saves or justifies any human being.

This view maintains that the ultimate reality that is internally related to every creature as its creative source and the ultimate recipient of all its acts—its Whence and its Whither—is none other that the loving God known to the Jews decisively as their liberator from slavery in Egypt, as the source of Torah that orders the life of Israel, as the One whose steadfast love proclaimed by the prophets chastens Israel but will not let it go. This God is also the One who is there at creation and breathes spirit into humans and, so, is disclosed as the God of the nations as well as of Israel; ultimately this is the God of hope.

This same God is known to Christians decisively in Jesus. Here the major Jewish themes of liberation, law, call to repentance, creation, and hope are re-presented, and all focus on the cross as the symbol of divine suffering love. God is here presented as "the great companion, the fellow-sufferer who understands."[10] The point should be made that the crucifixion is taken neither merely as a tragic historical event nor as a divine bolt out of the blue; it is the symbol of universal divine love. As was said early in the twentieth century, "There was a cross in

the heart of God before there was one planted on the green hill outside
of Jerusalem. And . . . the one in the heart of God abides, and it will
remain so long as there is one sinful soul for whom to suffer."[11] And,
as Bonhoeffer famously said, "Only the suffering God can help."[12]
Divine suffering love, redemption, redemption for *all*, not just the special few. All this is "re-presented," as Ogden says, "in the word that
Jesus speaks and is."

If this goes to the heart of the Christian proclamation, any sort of
exclusivism or ethnocentrism is ruled out as antithetical to the first
principles of the Christian witness of faith. Just as the Jews know themselves to have been "chosen"—not for special favors but to witness to
all the world, often through their suffering, to God's steadfast love
and justice—so Christians are called to bear witness to this same God's
redemptive love for every creature in the world. The point of the
Christian faith in Jesus as "re-presentative" of God is not to get people
to join a particular religion to be saved, but to witness to the conviction
that God is creatively and redemptively at work in the lives of all people irrespective of their cultural identity, their religion, or their political or socioeconomic status. In fact, no matter how frequently
Christians may have distorted the message that God wills abundant life
for every creature and no matter that it may have been twisted into a
claim that God desires all persons to be baptized Christians or else
remain nonpersons, this *is* a distortion unworthy of the fundamental
proclamation of good news. It is a distortion, however, that is neither
uncommon nor confined to Christianity. H. Richard Niebuhr put the
distortion this way: "[The] great source of evil in life is the absolutizing
of the relative, which in Christianity takes the form of substituting religion, revelation, church or Christian morality for God."[13]

There is no evidence that there is but one true religion—much less a
superior ethnic group—such that anyone wishing to share God's
redemptive love must be initiated into that religion or be born into that
ethnic group. There is every reason to reject this as opposed not only to
common sense and the ethics of toleration but also to the deepest principles of faith—*Christian* faith and, I should think, the faith at the base of
every religion. There is no evidence that the earliest Christians thought
they constituted the one and only true religion. From the beginning the
greatest apostles of faith have directed human trust and commitment
toward God rather than toward some decisive nationality, one exclusive
sect, or one set of beliefs and rules. This, it seems evident, is the point of
Paul's discovery that salvation lies not in works of the Law, but in faith
in God. However misconceived Paul's understanding of the love of
Torah for most Jews may have been, his positive point was clear:

Devotion to a religion does not save one, but only faith in and reliance on God.

Thus, Paul urged the believers in Galatia not to sink back into sectarianism: "There is no longer Jew or Greek, there is no longer slave or free, there is no longer male and female, for all of you are one in Christ Jesus" (Galatians 3:28). Similarly, Paul, or a disciple of his, told the Colossians: "In that renewal there is no longer Greek and Jew, circumcised and uncircumcised, barbarian, Scythian, slave and free, but Christ is all and in all!" (Colossians 3:11). "Christ" in both cases is not intended in a narrow, sectarian sense, but as the God "re-presented" by Jesus. Paul's speech to the Athenians as set forth in Acts declares that the "unknown God" whom the Athenians worshiped was none other than the God known to Paul by virtue of his Jewish heritage and his faith in Jesus. Interestingly, the key phrase used to portray God and the proper human relation to God in this speech was taken from neither Jewish scripture nor any distinctive early Christian writing but from a Greek stoic poet: "In him we live and move and have our being" (Acts 17:28).[14]

Peter—who seems to have been less cosmopolitan than Paul and to have had more difficulty in grasping the notion of God's universal love—is portrayed as having gotten the point at least once when he was said to have uttered: "I truly understand that God shows no partiality, but in every nation anyone who fears him and does what is right is acceptable to him" (Acts 10:34–35).

That these particular disciples of Jesus were by no means the first to get the point that religion is not an end in itself but a means to faith in God is well attested by the wonderful story of Jonah that is read every year on the Jewish high holy day, Yom Kippur. The point of that story is to show that, despite Jonah's evasive action and bigoted sulking, God is both capable of having compassion on the wicked, non-Jewish inhabitants of Nineveh and willing and eager for their redemption. God even has compassion for the animals.

I have belabored this point because it is so easily distorted or twisted into its opposite. Christianity in particular, as practiced though the ages, can almost be read as the triumph of the negative image.[15] Yet despite the constant human tendency to reduce the divine to something familiar and manageable or, in Niebuhr's words, to "absolutize the relative," the fundamental message remains: That which anchors all human existence, that which is the ground of all meaning and value, is nothing so contingent as a particular religion or an ethnic identity, but only that to which all religions point, the circumambient reality that is the source and goal of all finite beings, the One "in whom we live and move and have our being." It is what theistic religions symbolize as "Yahweh," "God:

Father, Son, and Holy Spirit," "Allah"; others as "Brahman," "Nirvana," "the Tao," "Heaven," etc. Implicitly, it is that about the world that gives to every being the sense that it is "something that matters."

To be authentically human—human in the best way possible rather than as having fallen prey to superstition, idolatry, pride, despair, etc.—is to place one's trust utterly in this transcendent, yet universally present, reality. Such trust is what Paul calls "faith." Call it what you will, but do not confuse it with excessive zeal misdirected toward some human institution or set of ideas. Such zeal is idolatry and is the counterfeit of faith. As the seventeenth-century Cambridge Platonist Benjamin Whichcote wrote: "Nothing spoils human nature more than false zeal. The good nature of an heathen is more God-like than the furious zeal of a Christian."[16] Nor should we confuse faith with what is often called "blind faith" or "when you believe something that you know ain't true." The genuine article demands that people face their own lives and histories and the world around them honestly and with eyes wide open: "You will know the truth and the truth will make you free" (John 8:32).

Such faith is an orientation of the whole person that undergirds intellect, emotion, and will and gives these elements of personality purpose; it places what a person does in this life, and how it is done, in a larger context. Perhaps the finest religious expression of this attitude is the summary of the Jewish religion as expressed by Jesus: " 'You shall love the Lord your God with all your heart, and with all your soul, and with all your mind.' This is the greatest and first commandment. And a second is like it: 'You shall love your neighbor as yourself.' On these two commandments hang all the law and the prophets" (Matthew 22:37–40, synthesizing Deuteronomy 6:5 and Levitious 19:18). This expression of the basic attitude or orientation indicates that one's final trust must not be placed in anything finite (which would be idolatry giving rise to furious zeal) but only in that which abides. It also makes clear that this orientation is essentially love that integrates intellect, emotion, and will with the totality of one's being.

Such love, however, is not merely other-worldly in the conventional sense. To be committed to the whole is to be committed to the parts; to love God with the totality of one's being entails loving God's creatures symbolized in the summary of the law by "neighbor" and "self." Put another way, to rely wholly on God's pure unbounded love is to be committed to all that God is committed to, and that is all creation. Faith, as the Apostle Paul well understood, must issue in works of love.

Even so, as has been well said, "The one test of whether love is really present is always freedom."[17] Or, as Paul said, "Where the Spirit of the

Lord is, there is freedom" (2 Corinthians 3:17). Again, speaking sharply
to those in Galatia who had allowed themselves to be enslaved to a
certain kind of religiosity, he said, "For freedom Christ has set us free.
Stand firm, therefore, and do not submit again to a yoke of slavery"
(Galatians 5:1).

It is clear, then, that whether it is called "faith" or "authentic human
existence," whether it is framed in theistic terms as that orientation
having God at the center or simply as the unshakable confidence that
existence is worthwhile, the standard by which this fundamental attitude is judged real, its cash value, is freedom. That is, to have faith is
to exist in freedom in two senses: to be free *from* all worldly concerns
that would enslave or oppress us, and to be free *for* all others who are
in any way oppressed—to be able to respond positively to all for whom
God has compassion. To get a sense of why Christian principles disal-
low anti-Semitism, the rejection of the Other, the tyranny of just one
ring, let us unpack these two senses.

There are many things that oppress or enslave people. Not only are
persons physically and mentally limited, but they are often slaves to
their own prejudicial and narrow-minded views, prisoners to an ideology, oppressed by past decisions and anxieties about creaturely transience and the fear that one will make no real difference in the world.
Beyond the things for which anyone might be personally responsible
there are powerful social attitudes that have been inherited, political
and economic structures that both support and are supported by particular individuals. To exist faithfully in freedom is not to eliminate
any of these factors that help to frame human, historical existence,
but it is to keep them in perspective so that they are never the final
arbiters of one's existence and to change them when we can.

In terms of the issues on which I have focused, to rely on that which
transcends all finite, historical relativities is to be liberated from the
idolatry that insists that my religion or my particular set of values is
the ultimate standard by which all truth, beauty, and goodness are to
be judged. As such, faith is the beginning of freedom from any sort of
religious exclusivism, triumphalism, and the idolatry of claiming truth
to reside in only one (i.e., my) religion.

Moreover, after being liberated from such oppressors, one is bound
to seek to optimize the limits of others' freedom. The work has already
begun when one changes one's attitude, when one recognizes that
one's own way is not the only way or the only right way, when one is
able to celebrate the richness of diverse cultures and religions and to
gain the confidence that an encompassing whole can embrace and
cherish the values of all. The work of optimizing others' freedom

requires changing structures as well as attitudes, changing habits of buying, investing, living, valuing; it demands that persons be proactive in diminishing remarks, habits, and structures that demean, degrade, misrepresent, suppress, or physically harm others.

Such demons abound in our world today as they have throughout history. There is much that cries out for freedom. A return to fundamental principles, an examination of the fundamental Christian vision, however, allows us to exorcize the demons of anti-Semitism, of triumphalism, of the rejection of or patronizing of other religions so that these may be banished from Christian self-understanding. "You will know the truth and the truth will make you free."

8

The Nature of Human Persons

Chapters 3 and 4 presupposed a general understanding of persons in their discussion of God as the supreme person and world-soul. This chapter employs the basic ideas of process thought to show how the soul or psyche can be understood in a natural way. The human soul or self is seen to be continuous with all lower forms of creation, but distinguishable from them. The specific Christian mode of existing in terms of explicit faith is unpacked.

In the two chapters about God I said a fair amount about God as the supreme person with whom we have to do, and indeed, as the personal whole of which all creatures are parts. Especially in Chapter 4 I worked out something of what it is to be a person, saying that the minimal requirements are to be an individual constituted by a well-integrated series of occasions of experience having the capacity for memory, conscious planning, and decision making, and to be temporal and social (as all actual entities are). So far as we can tell the eminent way to express personhood, I have suggested, is to love. And, in trying to work out a Christology, I have said that we *assume* that Jesus was fully human even as we *proclaim* him to be the decisive re-presentation of the universal and omnipresent God for us.

In all of this I have taken for granted a good bit about what it means to be a *human* person even though I have tried to avoid equating "human" with "personal," because I wish to avoid the implication that God is *non*personal. Both God and humans are thought to be personal: God eminently so; humans merely contingently and fragmentarily so.

In this chapter I want to examine more fully and more carefully what it is to be a human person, and what our theology requires us to understand about human nature.

A WORLD OF EVENTS OR EXPERIENCES

First, let us recall what we have concluded about the world within which we have framed our understanding of persons. Ours is a radically temporal and interactive world, one in which we inevitably experience causation, anticipation, and decision, and in which we find that to be is to be related to others. Moreover, no actual being is ever static. All are partially products of their past environment, but none is wholly determined by it; every entity faces a genuine future of open possibility. And the synthesis of past and future in each is the production of a new and unique entity that adds itself to the ongoing process that is thus ever renewed. Whitehead put this succinctly in the statement quoted in Chapter 2: "The many become one, and are increased by one."[1]

Our analysis of any occasion of human experience, which we take as the starting point for understanding the rest of existence, discloses that irrespective of any particular state in which we find ourselves, there are certain constituents common to every experience. We may confront experience highly conscious, barely conscious, or unconscious. The experience may be drowsy, distracted, asleep, or alert and focusing on particular sense perceptions or consciously comparing, distinguishing, or correlating different concepts. It may be charged with any of a variety of emotions, for instance, joy or bitterness, a state of great rapture or high dudgeon. It may be an experience of satisfaction and composure, or it may be fretful and filled with anxiety. No matter what the kind of experience, a close examination of any of them yields the following common factors, elements that are invariably present:

1. All experiences are connected with, and grow out of, their immediate past; thus the past is a causal factor in the present experience.
2. No experience is wholly determined by its past or by anything else, because all are presented with genuine alternatives or real possibilities (each experience inevitably has a future).
3. Each experience, therefore, is a unique experience, having a novel perspective on the universe and being a particular synthesis of the causal data of its immediate past and the actualized potentiality that had constituted its future.
4. Every experience makes a difference in the supervening world; it is a causal agent beyond its moment of synthesis.

By the principle of the uniformity of explanation, which serves the scientist and the historian well, we are able to move from what is generally true of any *human* experience to the common elements of *any* experience whatsoever. Whenever we examine any configuration of event processes, whether they be sub-atomic processes, those of an inorganic molecule, cellular processes, animal experiences, or the highly mental, imaginative, or creative states of saints or geniuses, we find the same thing: no event, no experience, no unit of actuality, is ever found in isolation; every experience or event-process takes its rise within a context, and that context or environment makes itself felt in the occasion of experience under consideration. Every human, animal, vegetable, mineral, or even electronic state is triggered by, and grows out of, the immediately previous states or experiences that are themselves somehow ingredient in the present occasion of experience. This means that the past is present as a cause. Thus the inspection of experience discloses that any experience or unit of actuality is continuous with its immediate predecessors and partially constituted by the effect of them. The past does not vanish, dry up, or turn into nothingness; past experiences are present as data, as objects, as causal elements within the makeup of the present experience. If this were not so there could be no memory, no experience of the other, no causality at all. We would be imprisoned in what Santayana aptly called the "solipsism of the present moment."[2]

The examination of events, however, discloses more than causality alone. If that were all we found events would be wholly determined, and there would never be anything new. Whenever we inspect experience at any level we find particularity. In addition to continuity with the past experienced as causality, there is discontinuity; any experience is just this particular experience and not simply a repetition or extension of the past. There is newness in the present occasion, no matter how indiscernible it may be to the naked eye, so that every occasion of experience must be judged unique. In the first place it is just *this* particular fitting together of the many converging past data from a novel perspective. In addition, every new unit event or occasion of experience is confronted with a set of possibilities, only one of which is ever actualized. Nevertheless, one new actualized possibility, set in the context of the confluence of many past data, yields a genuinely new occasion of experience.

Every occasion of experience, therefore, every instance of actuality in this dynamic, processive universe, is a creative synthesis of the many converging data from its past and future into a new unity. Put otherwise, each new occasion of experience, in its moment of creative synthesis, is regarded as a "subject" for which its past and future are "objects." This is why Whitehead epitomized his "reformed subjectivity" with the statement, "Apart from the experience of subjects there is nothing, nothing, nothing, bare nothingness."[3]

In this review of what we find compelled to say about any occasion of experience, let us note that the process inevitably renews itself. We observe that every experience acts not only to constitute itself as a singular entity, but it acts also in the world beyond its present moment; it is causally efficacious in succeeding occasions. The use of "act" language, remember, does not mean to imply that these "subjects" are conscious. Consciousness is a high-grade mode of mental activity not sustained for long periods in even the most powerful of human minds. Decision and act mean that every actuality constitutes itself so as to make a difference for itself and in the world beyond its present. It is "something that matters ... for itself, for others, and for the whole."[4]

It is with this analysis in mind that I have claimed in previous chapters and in this one that every occasion of experience, every individual actuality, is fundamentally temporal and fundamentally social. Each occasion is a present subject whose past is an object for it and is appropriated by it, and whose future is a realm of potentiality presenting options from which that subject selects one to be actualized. Also, the subject acts in the supervening world becoming an object for a new subject. This means that every occasion is inevitably really related to the world from which it comes and into which it goes by bands of experience and causality. Not only the human world, but the entire world, is one of becoming and belonging.

My approach has been to uncover the invariant aspects of all human experiences, and to generalize these to describe all final individual actualities. The "imaginative generalization," I hope, has been controlled by coherence, logic, applicability, and adequacy.[5] Clearly, then, we can say nothing less about human persons. But can we say more, or something more specific? I think we can do so, and do it in terms of the general account I have given. But I must caution that here I move from the realm of metaphysical generality to the specificity of a special science—say, anthropology, biology, psychology, or pneumatology. It is a move, in Heidegger's words, from ontology to the ontic.

A key part of my understanding of human persons is my understanding of "the soul." If contemporary persons are distrustful of the language of soul, associating it with some ghost-like substance, I am comfortable with "psyche," "self," or "mind" (I prefer to think of an individual "person" as a particular soul associated with a particular body).

Some philosophers and many scientists have tried to reduce "mind" to "brain-states" or the firing of neurons in the brain. Similarly, many have tried to equate personal identity with bodily identity. I think there are good reasons for rejecting this approach and for articulating a well-developed understanding of the view that ordinary language bears witness to and that assumes that the soul (or mind or self) is distinguishable from brain states or the mere body even while being closely linked with the body. In Chapter 4 I appealed to the work of the neurobiologists Roger Sperry, John Eccles, and Wilder Penfield and the philosopher Karl Popper in support of the distinction and interaction between mind and brain or soul and body. The gist of their arguments is that the determinism of mere matter will never suffice to explain ideas, creativity, imagination, and the like. And I claimed that bodily identity cannot suffice to affirm *personal* identity. For instance, identical twins, even with similar outlooks, are different individuals with different experiences and so different identities. And I reported a recent experience of going to meet an old friend whom I had not seen since 1960 (and only intermittently between 1954 and 1960): We were to meet in the lobby of a motel, and as I sat looking for my friend, it dawned on me that a man walking about the lobby looked very much like my friend's father! (No doubt he may have thought he noticed my father rather than me.) So, even though sense perception failed me, I made the inference that it was, in fact, my old friend, and introduced myself. I simply could not identify the present physical appearance with the person of the young man I remembered. Only with talk, and the evocation of memory, did the personal identity begin to emerge.

These are not full-blown arguments in rejection of the Identity Thesis, but only efforts to clear the table so that we are prepared for a reasonable account that both distinguishes soul from its body and, yet, links them closely. First, let us remind ourselves that in all normal experience an individual soul is, in fact, linked intimately with a particular body. (Here I waive the interesting, but difficult, cases of "multiple personalities." Even so, in these cases the issue seems to be that of several selves or souls connected with one body, each soul being alternatively dominant and recessive. We do not have evidence for one soul skipping from body to body.) Whitehead, discussing the naive assumption that our bodies are clearly distinguishable from the external world, points out that we breathe in and out, molecules are constantly leaving our skin, and we ingest food, process and integrate it into our systems, and eliminate the waste. Nevertheless, he continues, "the unity of 'body and mind' is the obvious complex which constitutes the one human being. Our bodily experience is the basis of existence. . . . [This] is not primarily an experience of sense data . . . [since] the internal functioning of a healthy body provides singularly few sense data. . . . And yet our feeling of bodily unity is a primary experience. It is an experience so habitual and so completely a matter of course that we rarely mention it. No one ever says, Here am I, and I have brought my body with me."[6]

If, then, soul and body or mind and brain are a complex unity, how do we distinguish them? First, I want to reject a traditional notion of the soul as an unchanging spiritual substance (a *res cogitans*) that is able somehow to act in an external material environment, but is incapable of being affected by that material world. If the soul is actual, in any sense, it must, like all actualities, be interactive; it must be capable both of being acted on and of acting.

Equally, I must reject the suggestion that the soul is the "vital principle" of the body, because on my understanding principles cannot act; only actual entities can act, and principles are either ideals or truths about actuality, but not themselves actual.

Also, I want to avoid the suggestion that is sometimes derived from Charles Hartshorne's early use of the term *panpsychism* to describe or characterize all occasions of experience as subjects or organic unities.[7] Since each actual entity synthesizes itself and *completes* itself before passing into the constitution of a succeeding actual entity, to suggest that every final individual actuality is a soul will not do, because a soul or a self has extension through time from at least the birth of an individual to its death.

What, then, is the soul? Having rejected the notions that it is merely a nominal expression for neuronal activity in the brain, or the traditional idea of a static spiritual substance, or that all actualities are souls, or that soul is a principle, I must stake out my own claims in terms of the process worldview I have presented. The position I want to put forward is that the soul or mind or self is a complex macro-unity, a compound individual, composed of a tightly linked series of high-grade occasions of experience that encompasses all the occasions of experience that constitute a single human person. Whitehead has summed up this view as follows: "The soul is nothing else than the succession of my occasions of experience, extending from birth to the present moment. Now, at this instant, I am the complete person embodying all these occasions. They are mine. On the other hand it is equally true that my immediate moment is only one among the stream of occasions which constitutes my soul."[8]

As such the soul has "genetic identity" with past instances of itself, but there is not a simple or "strict" identity between the past and the present; each new instance of this stream or succession does not merely repeat the past, but it does include the past as imperishable data, as "living memory." Thus, this particular self, as distinguished from another individual soul with its own genetic identity and linked with another body, is a tightly knit company of occasions with similar environments and goals and with common characteristics that help us to determine its genetic identity.

To think in these terms is not as odd as it seems at first. Typically, we have little difficulty in conceiving the body, or any other material object, as being composed of billions of particles that turn out, on closer inspection, to be like our micro-processes: occasions of experience, energy-particles, or events. These, in bodies, are highly structured so that the particles or molecules can replicate themselves, insinuating themselves into the next moment of that body. There is no reason not to think of the soul or self similarly.

To be sure, there are differences between the sequence of occasions that constitutes a soul and the complex organization of occasions that constitutes a living organism, just as there is a difference between a living organism and an inert body. What are the differences? They are *not* metaphysical; rather, they are organizational and contingent, and often matters of more or less. Still, we can attempt to specify the differences somewhat.

Begin with the least complex and least well integrated of these entities, the inert body. A rock, for example, is an aggregate of billions of molecules and smaller particles, each of which has a greater unity and liveliness than the aggregate itself. The rock persists but has little unity except for the fact that generation after generation of similar occasions of experience transmit the same qualities on to their successors with relatively little change, few novel possibilities having been actualized.

Living organisms, by contrast, for example, plants or animal bodies, are much more complex, comprising many more closely knit and interlinked subgroups of occasions, each group with dominant and recessive characteristics. Also, by contrast with inert bodies, living organisms are made up of many occasions of experience that can respond to a wider range of possibilities and past states with greater flexibility than the corresponding occasions of inert bodies. Confronted with a greater variety of options than are the typical members of inert bodies, they can choose to enact significant change. Thus the longevity of organisms, as identifiable entities, is more fragile. Still, the larger among the inert bodies and living organisms share one common feature that also helps to distinguish both from souls or selves: They are spatially locatable and so are empirically observable.

Having made that point I should say that I feel about space as Augustine did about time. That is, if no one asks me what it is, I think I know what space is, but when someone asks me to state clearly what I think, I am at a loss. Let me simply assert that I believe spatial relations to be those that are perceived by the senses—especially sight and touch—among contemporaries. That is, they are the relations projected onto the contemporary scene by an occasion of experience that does not take account of the important temporal relations of "before" and "after."

The soul or self, by contrast, is conceived as wholly temporal and without spatial relations among its own member occasions. Because our daily lives and relations are most obviously ordered among macroscopic, spatially extended objects, and because we rely so heavily on sight, touch, and hearing to get our bearings and to order our routine, an entity that is wholly temporally ordered seems thin and wispy, neither substantial nor complex. But a few moments' reflection should dispel such a naive belief. Ideas, for instance, are real in that we have to take account of them and allow them to make a difference in our lives. Also, some among them are highly complex, containing many corollaries. But they are hardly spatially extended. We may say that they are "in the mind" or even "in the brain," but, on examination, this probably signals that spatial configurations dominate our symbols. As we will see, the preposition *in* can imply causal efficacy rather than spatial location. Where that is meant, it is legitimate to say ideas are in the mind. Moreover—taking up the thread of the argument for the reality of a wholly temporally ordered entity—memory attests to the strong bond between the occasions of the past and that of the present. This bond, while not always in the forefront of our consciousness, is never really broken.

Thus we can *feel* the soul, although we cannot see it. Therefore, it seems appropriate to conceive the self, mind, or soul as a closely knit, temporally ordered sequence of occasions of experience, each of which has an unusually great capacity to receive and integrate many diverse data from its own past and from the past of its environing body, most especially the brain. What is more, each new occasion of the soul can synthesize itself according to some aim especially ideal for it in its particular situation and can conceive novel contrasts often from a bewildering array of possibilities and contrasts with its actual world. Finally each instantiation of the self transmits itself as a significant datum into the life of that self's succeeding occasions and into the occasions of its body.

To utilize the image suggested by both Popper and Penfield, the soul at any moment is the active programmer whose computer is its brain. To alter the figure, we may say that it is the presiding officer of a well-organized company whose decisions affect the lives of even the lowliest employee. Or, we may also use the image of the soul as a "little god" to its body, reminding ourselves that we have already insisted that God is the supreme person of the universe, the "world soul" that has the universe of non-divine beings as its body, and that humans are made in the image and likeness of God. In all cases, however, we do well to remember that a god or a presiding officer or a programmer must be a well-tuned receiver and synthesizer as well as an initiator and director.

Keep in mind the extended passage by Schubert Ogden cited in Chapter 4 that made the point that the self is a fundamentally temporal and social entity that is most intimately related to its own body through the brain, and that it is "incarnate" in this body, and through the body has its relations with the larger encompassing society. I will not repeat the entire passage, but I quote the last part: "I know myself most immediately only as an ever changing sequence of occasions of experience, each of which is the present integration of remembered past and anticipated future into a new whole of significance. . . . Selecting from the heritage of the already actual and the wealth of possibility awaiting realization I freely fashion myself in creative interaction with a universe of others who also are not dead but alive."[9]

In one way or another all of these figures and descriptions emphasize that the soul is a distinct social and temporal entity that, at each moment of its life, interacts with its immediate environment. In Ogden's words, it is that "ever changing sequence of occasions" that is the "I" that most directly affects and is affected by the brain cells. Conceived as mind, it is the mind constituting itself anew at each moment by laying hold on its own past and that of the brain cells that constitute its most immediate environment, together with the wealth of possibilities available to it.

To think in these terms is to see that the soul's *act*, in the primary sense, is not the relatively indirect activity of its bodily members on the exterior world; it is its own decision how to constitute itself anew out of the welter of impulses arising from its past decisions and those of its brain cells, on the one hand, and out of the possibilities confronting it, on the other; in turn this decision affects its immediate future and that of its brain cells. Its effects, mediated by the brain and the nervous system, reverberate through the body and thence to the outer world. But the acts themselves are *not* empirically observable by other individuals; they are experienceable by ourselves, and their effects are felt by others, but the soul and its primary acts are not to be empirically observed. Neither are they merely "private," since utter privacy implies the "solipsism of the present moment" that is rejected by our basic account of actual entities. The point is that experience is much greater than sense experience, and to try to make the identity of the self and its acts dependent on empirical observation is to try to force it onto the Procrustean bed of materialism. Ogden expresses the point positively when he writes, "Behind all its public acts of word and deed there are the self's own private purposes or projects, which are themselves matters of action or decision. Indeed, it is only because the self first acts to constitute itself, to respond to its world, and to decide its own inner being that it 'acts' at all in the more ordinary meaning of the word; all its outer acts of word and deed are but ways of expressing and implementing the inner decisions whereby it constitutes itself as a self."[10]

The preceding account, I believe, presents a reasonable picture of the soul or self as a closely integrated sequence of mind-states or occasions of experience with an unusually high degree of mentality. Because each occasion is affected by its past and, in turn, affects subsequent entities, it may be said to have a kind of "physicality," too, albeit not of the empirically observable sort. Each member of the series that constitutes this particular soul remembers, integrates, decides, and acts both for itself and in others. The sequence or route of occasions as a whole is distinct from the brain cells that themselves make up its most immediate environment but, by means of each of its member occasions, the soul can be said to interact with its environment. Now, one wants to ask again: "Have we not located the soul within the brain?" We saw with respect to ideas in the mind that the preposition *in* has its significance here, but we should not force it to imply spatial location. To be spatial, I suggest, is to have an externally observable relation with other entities associated with oneself in the present moment. Even so, it is legitimate to say that the soul is "in" the body in the sense that each new instance of the soul acts in the immediately succeeding occasion of the brain, and so has its effect in the rest of the body and, mediately, in the world beyond the body. But it is equally true, and no less important, to insist that the body is *in* the soul, since the soul or self is that integrated sequence of occasions with the greatest capacity to receive and to integrate into itself all the impulses of the prior occasions of the body as mediated through the brain. The soul, therefore, is the *personal whole* that encompasses its body even as it acts in the body's constituent parts.

THE BIBLICAL PERSPECTIVE

It is well to undertake this by considering several fundamental themes about human nature that appear to be central to the biblical witness. The first thing the Bible says about humans is that they, like all creatures, are dependent on God for their existence, but that they have a special place among the created species. This is established early in Genesis: "God said: 'Let us make humankind in our image, according to our likeness; and let them have dominion over . . . [the other creatures.]' So God created humankind in his image . . . ; male and female he created them" (Genesis 1:26, 27).

Precisely what being created in the image and likeness of God entails here is not wholly clear, but at least it implies that humans are at the summit of the created order with the power of governance, control, or stewardship of the earth's goods that other creatures do not have. The theme of the superiority of humans to the rest of creation is echoed in Psalm 8. There the psalmist, marveling over the majesty of the heavens, wonders "what are human beings" that God should be mindful of them. And he answers his own question: "[God has] made them a little lower than God, and crowned them with glory and honor. You have given them dominion over the works of your hands" (Psalm 8:4, 5–6). Again, as in the Genesis creation story, the dominion that humans have over the created order is stressed, and the superiority of humans to the rest of the creatures is made by saying that humans have been created but "a little lower than God."

The psalmist in this instance does not emphasize, but rather assumes, what is elsewhere stressed—human mortality. For instance: "As for mortals their days are like grass; they flourish like a flower of the field; for the wind passes over it, and it is gone, and its place knows it no more" (Psalm 103:15–16). Or: "You sweep them away; they are like a dream, like grass that is renewed in the morning; . . . it flourishes and is renewed; in the evening it fades and withers. . . . For all our days pass away under your wrath; our years come to an end like a sigh. . . . They are soon gone, and we fly away" (Psalm 90:5–6, 9–10). And perhaps the best known and most powerful expression of human mortality, stated in stark contrast with God's everlastingness, is put by the prophet known as Second Isaiah: "All people are grass, their constancy is like the flower of the field. . . . The grass withers, the flower fades; but the word of our God will stand forever" (Isaiah 40:6, 8).

If all of these passages attest to human mortality as a balance to human dominion over the rest of creation, none of them brings out another important biblical insight that is powerfully symbolized in the Adam and Eve creation story in Genesis, namely, that humans are the creatures who have violated God's trust, destroying the right relationship with God and with God's creation by attempting to usurp the place of God. The effort to attain the kind of complete knowledge that only God can have is a bid to evade the essential creatureliness and mortality that goes with being human, or, as the serpent in the myth says, to "be like God" (Genesis 3:5). Ironically, the act that endeavors to bridge heaven and earth, so to speak, creates a vast chasm, a separation or estrangement unbridgeable by humans, by alienating humans from their divine ground and so keeping them from fulfilling their own authentic humanity (our "true selves"), and alienating humans from one another and from the rest of the nonhuman creation.

All of this is what has traditionally been designated as "original sin." Irrespective of the traditional view of the transmission of this original sin—partially worked out because of a belief that there was a *temporally* first act of disobedience—and irrespective of what we might say about specific "sins," most of us can see the main point: There is a dignity, a glory, a godlike nobility about the human species and, simultaneously, there is a tendency to distort and abuse our power, to pull apart from others, to seek fulfillment at the expense of others, to cause considerable harm by our hubris that distorts our God-given power and wrecks the balance in the scheme of things. Moreover, no amount of human striving (for example, by education, good works, social and economic programs for the well-being of all, etc.) ever seems to eradicate the wrongs and make all things right; no amount of moral teaching and living ever releases us from the tendency to corrupt whatever good we have produced. In fact, a biblical insight strongly emphasized by the Apostle Paul is that human striving in this respect is precisely the problem; it is the attempt to "be like God," and our redemption can only come from beyond us and be received by faith.

These themes—of the fundamental goodness and power and yet perversity of humans and the necessity to wait patiently for God to set things right—are attested or exemplified on nearly every page of scripture, and they form the basis of what we want to say about human nature. In a sense they are summed up by St. Augustine who says, "You have made us for yourself, and our heart is restless until it rests in you."[11] Augustine knew what he does not here say, that our "restlessness" is incurable by ourselves, that our redemption is wrought by divine grace through human faith.

This complex picture of human nature—on the one hand, of being created by God and so ultimately dependent on God, and yet as the crown of this creation having tremendous power so as to exercise dominion over the remainder of the created order; and on the other hand, being mortal (unlike God), and yet attempting to escape our essential mortality and dependence so as to "be like God," which is a fatal flaw termed "original sin"—illumines and deepens what we learned about human persons from our general philosophical analysis of experience. I do not think it is in opposition to it.

THE BIBLICAL VIEW OF PERSONS AMPLIFIED

Having attempted what seems to me to be both a credible understanding of the human person as a soul having its body as its immediate environment and one that is consonant with the biblical idea of persons as embodied, let us try to see what differentiates human persons from other creatures that may be similar, and also from God who is the supreme person. The account of the soul I have developed with the help of process philosophy finds no reason to posit souls only to humans. Aristotle, I believe, spoke of "vegetable soul" and "animal soul." I can find no good reason to speak of a vegetable soul, because vegetables seem not to have any dominant sequence that exercises a powerful influence over the whole. But equally I can find no reason to deny some kind of soul or selfhood to the higher animals. However, it is the quality of the human soul that differentiates it from whatever is like a soul in a dog.

There are many qualities that humans display that set them apart from other creatures, but I wish to emphasize four powers that humans have in a greater degree: knowledge coming to consciousness; freedom or creativity; love and the ability to fashion community; and also sin or the capacity to distort all of the higher powers.

1. Knowledge Coming to Consciousness

When the first Genesis creation story says that humans are created in the image and likeness of God, it is evident that a fundamental divine attribute that the humans mirror is knowledge. This becomes evident in the Adam and Eve story where the forbidden tree bears the fruit of "the knowledge of good and evil," and the fatal temptation is to grasp it.

Knowledge, as the saying goes, is power, and it is the vast ability that humans have to survey possibilities, to make logical connections, to see causal relations, and to investigate the relations among things—the vast array of empirical methods and principles joined with rudimentary or developed logical skills—that enables humans to have dominion over the rest of creation. In short, by comparison with other creatures, many of whom have uncanny powerful specific abilities and highly developed sensory organs, the human capacity for reason is awesome.

But it is not simply by coincidence that the Greek term *logos* signifies both "reason" and "word," because it is the human capacity for language that is the great engine for storing, sharing, communicating, extending, propelling, and applying knowledge. Apart from the ability to symbolize and articulate subtle distinctions we would hardly be able to conceptualize, to develop principles, to articulate ideals, and to apply all this to the ordering of experience. "Language," Whitehead said, "is the triumph of human ingenuity, surpassing even the intricacies of modern technology."[12] Indeed, it is the storehouse of all past accumulation of knowledge and the engine that propels technology. Moreover, language enables humans to lay down the principles for ordering their social, economic, political lives. And, as the vehicle for the arts, it allows the human spirit to soar.

As vastly superior as their knowledge is to that of other creatures, humans do not merely know. They also know that they know; they reflect on knowledge and the meaning of existence. They philosophize. Finally, they reason about their ultimate Whence and Whither, the Source and Goal of all being. Thus humans can be religious, and this, I believe, is the supreme form of knowledge.

2. Freedom or Creativity

Humans have freedom and creativity in such a vastly superior form to other creatures that many people are inclined to think humans alone have freedom or free will, whereas dumb animals, they think, have none; animals they say are merely driven or determined by instinct. As I have made clear in discussing all final individual actualities I do not think that any creature is wholly devoid of freedom. Even so I readily grant that the range of options that humans are able to entertain and the ability they have to transcend animal instincts, genetic limitations, social mores, habits—anything that limits, enslaves, or coerces us—is so much more apparent among humans as to appear to be a difference in kind rather than one of degree. I am convinced that the difference is one of degree, but, as with knowledge, it is a degree of difference that is great.

Yet even among humans the range of the degrees of freedom—physical, political, social, economic, psychological, religious—is so great as to cause us to despair. The powerful desire either to enslave others for our own short-term benefit or to allow ourselves to be enslaved for the false security it promises remains a threat to our authentic humanity.

As I have suggested above, and asserted clearly in Chapters 3 and 4, I believe that God is the source and agency for promoting more freedom, and so the best form of religion must promote freedom: "For freedom

Christ has set us free. Stand firm, therefore, and do not submit again to a yoke of slavery," Paul says (Galatians 5:1). And this ought to be a motto of the more developed religions. But, alas, religions have often been the instrument for promoting bondage of various sorts and so have devalued human existence rather than enhancing it.

3. Love and the Ability to Fashion Community

A well-developed account should say more about these qualities, as well as other distinguishing human traits, such as the aesthetic component and will power, but I turn to what I have called the greatest expression of personality—whether human or divine—namely, love. At this point I do not launch into a paean to love (see I Corinthians 13). I hope I have said a fair amount about the minimal requirements for love in Chapter 3: mutuality, reciprocity, the ability and willingness to be acted on by others, together with the desire to respond in ways that optimize others' power, freedom, and richness of life. As Erich Fromm says, mature love entails concern for the well-being of the other, respect for the integrity of the other, responsibility or the ability to respond to the needs of the other, and intimate knowledge of the other, and the intense desire for the other's growth.[13]

Love is what crowns knowledge and freedom and fruitful and able to work for the greater good of ever-widening circles of creation.

Finally, I have said that the human love of God with the totality of our being—heart, soul, mind, and strength—entails our loving God's creation: i.e., self and neighbor. Also, love of God is the essence of worship, and love of God's creation is the essence of ethics.

Sin, or the Capacity to Distort All of the Higher Powers

Alas, the powers of knowledge, freedom, and even love can and do get twisted, or distorted, or poisoned. Next to the capacity to love, perhaps, the major distinguishing human characteristic is the capacity to *sin*. Christians say that the root sin is *hubris*, or pride (although recently women have pointed out that pride is more of a male form of sin, whereas female sin is found in fear of freedom or trading freedom for security). Buddhists say that the major cause of things going awry is *tanha*, the drawing apart from the whole and clinging to self or to some fragment of reality as an authority or security. In all of these cases we have what seems to be a universal and inevitable penchant among humans to distort and pervert love, to try to enhance one's freedom and power by reducing that of others, or to enhance one's security by reducing freedom, to manipulate knowledge for the good of the few at the expense of the many.

Buddhists say the human-defeating ill can be overcome, and they propose a way to do so (the eightfold path to enlightenment). Christians say we cannot overcome sin on our own, and the more we strive to do so and to set things right, the more we increase the problem. That is, we put ourselves, rather than God, at the center of existence, and this makes things worse. Only by ceasing our efforts and by relying on God (faith) and letting God's grace lead us can authentic existence be gained. And Christians say that we have been given the effective sign of this grace and the means of participating in it: Jesus Christ and our dying and rising with Christ. But this is a message of supreme hope: "If God is for us, who is against us. . . . It is God who justifies, who is to condemn? Who shall separate us from the love of Christ? Shall tribulation, or distress, or persecution, or famine, or sword? . . . No, in all these things we are more than conquerors through him who loved us. For I am sure that neither death, nor life, nor angels, nor principalities, nor things present, nor things to come, nor powers, nor height, nor depth, nor anything in all creation will be able to separate us from the love of God in Christ Jesus our Lord." (Romans 8:31, 34, 35, 37–39).

Summary

This, in brief, is the human story: Humans are natural beings, but complex, social, and temporal, having memory, genetic identity, and agency; they are souls, or selves, intimately connected with a body, but not simply identified with the body. Humans are continuous with, but surpassing the rest of, creation by virtue of vastly superior capability for knowledge, freedom, love, and sin, and yet, with a capacity for God, that "restlessness of the heart" that can only be redeemed and validated by God's "pure unbounded love."

9

A Theology of Prayer

The belief in prayer assumes that we make a difference to God who then responds to our concerns. The classical idea of God as wholly absolute and immutable denies this as a real possibility. By unpacking the idea of God, as a personal being who is concerned for the well-being of each creature and who is affected by every act and is responsive to every need, I am able to develop a theology of prayer. Every act is a prayer in the widest sense. In its conscious, focused form, prayer is a matter of attuning our wills to what God already desires for us by establishing a conscious dialogue with the personal center of the universe. Such conscious, focused prayer also sensitizes us to the needs of our fellow creatures, and so is the conscious intensification of our being something that matters—to others and to God.

Several years ago I received the following note from a student, which, it seems to me, serves admirably as a text for reflecting on the theology of prayer:

Dear Dr. Mason: I stopped to talk with you and get my paper, but you weren't in—I am leaving today (signed ———, Modern Protestant Theology). PS. I have prayed **SO** hard for a week to get an "A" from your course, I hope you will take this into consideration. Have a nice summer.

My reactions to this were as varied as they were instant. Initially, I was amused by so transparent an attempt to manipulate the grade.

Reproduced from David R. Mason, "Reflections on 'Prayer' from a Process Perspective," *Encounter*, Autumn 1984 (45:4), 347–357, with permission from the Christian Theological Seminary.

Also, I could not help laughing at the unlikely confusion about the object of the petition—was it God or Dr. Mason? More seriously, I reflected sadly that students under stress too frequently try to escape the demands of hard study with a quick fix; in this case the effort was camouflaged, since the attempt was to substitute talk *to* God (prayer) for talk *about* God (theology). And yet I could not dismiss the note. The more I thought about it the more it seemed to raise important issues about our understanding of prayer.

On the one hand, Christians have always believed that they are to ask God for things, (e.g., "Give us this day our daily bread," or "Ask, and it shall be given you; search, and you will find; knock, and the door will be opened for you" (Matthew 6:11, 7:7). What is more, it is a staple of Christian belief that God hears our prayers, is affected by them, and responds adequately to them: "Is there anyone among you who, if your child asks for bread will give a stone? Or if the child asks for a fish, will give a snake? If you, then, who are evil, know how to give good gifts to your children, how much more will your Father in heaven give good things to those who ask him!" (Matthew 7:9–11).

THE CONFLICT OF TRADITIONAL THEOLOGY WITH RELIGION

To complicate matters the theology that Christian thinkers developed to make sense (they thought) of other deep convictions about God was such as to deny these beliefs about prayer (see Chapter 3, section one, "Some Problems with the Traditional Ideas about God"). That is to say, at the same time that Christian religion exhorted believers to pray and insisted that the being to whom prayers were addressed was personal, traditional theology cut the ground from underneath this demand. It insisted that the "personal God" who could be moved by our prayers was not only unmoved but also immovable; what is more, it said that God is totally independent of the creation. Although this apparent contradiction lay at the heart of the theology of prayer for centuries, it was ignored or glossed over.

But it can no longer be ignored. We must ask with the utmost seriousness just how any being can be said to be "personal" in any meaningful sense and yet be totally immovable and independent of its environment. An immovable and utterly independent being would be, at best, nonliving or petrified. In addition to this unwelcome implication of traditional theology God was often said to have foreseen and determined from all eternity every detail of everything that would occur in the temporal world. But what does this come to? To have determined the outcome of everything ahead of time is to have guaranteed that nothing, including the prayers of the faithful, could possibly influence or make a difference to God. And this means that the minimal requirement for being personal—the ability to enter into relations of mutuality or to be affected as well as to affect others—is denied such a deity. Unfortunately, for the theology of prayer, not to mention common sense, the "God" of traditional Christian theology was modeled far more on the philosophical concept of the Absolute—of "Being Itself"—as eternally the same, unchanging and without any real relations than it was on the Father of the Jews and of Jesus. And you can make a silk purse out of a sow's ear far more readily than you can make a personal God who responds adequately to prayers out of the classical Absolute!

THE MARK OF DIVINE PERSONALITY

So, what is to be done about this distressing state of affairs? Regrettably, many people simply dismiss the whole matter as not worth bothering about. Some, however, think it is advisable to continue praying, but avoid thinking about what is being done or about the being to whom they pray. Others would argue that the only honest response is to drop all notions of a personal deity and, with them, all forms of prayer and to rely on our wits in this world. The practical solution for many has been to live as if God doesn't exist or care about them, so that what they do or fail to do makes no difference at all, but then in a crisis to call on this Great Blank to interpose its will on their behalf; they look to God to intervene in the normal course of events and to suspend the laws of nature, or of human nature, for the benefit of a tiny fragment of the world.

Such a "practical solution" seems to me even less worthy of serious consideration than the hope of my student, which at least had the merit of being offered without guile. Nor do I think the other options bear careful scrutiny. It is important, therefore, to reexamine our understanding of God, what we can possibly mean by "prayer," and how we can understand God as responsive to our prayers and our lives.

In the first place we must affirm with Jesus and with our entire *religious* heritage—in contrast with the mainstream of theology—that God is eminently personal. But part of the problem always has been to formulate what we mean by a "person" such that we can understand

God as eminently personal without espousing absurdities. I believe that many people have worked with an inadequate or truncated idea of persons. Too often it is simply assumed that to be a person means to be biased or, at best, shortsighted. Thus, it is thought that being personal is tantamount to favoring certain persons or things that are dear to us to the neglect or harm of others. This, however, is to mistake the inevitable shortcomings of being finite and sinful for the core of personality. *Human* persons are inevitable finite; they are typically shortsighted about what is good for themselves and for others; they are biased, ideologically driven, and often emotional and unreasonable.

But if we look beyond the obvious negative aspects of human behavior and see what *all* personal activity, whether good or bad, have in common, we will see that, whatever the circumstances, being personal means being able to interact with our environment: having the power to influence and be influenced by other persons and things with whom we live, and actually employing that power. And a few moments of reflection will show that this basic characteristic need not inevitably be expressed in a finite or sinful way. To be sure, all human expressions of personality are more or less sinful, but even so we have some clues as to what the *eminent* form of personality should be like.

The greatest expression of personal activity in the human realm is *love*. To be sure, talk about love as an activity is misleading unless we see clearly that it is never merely unilateral activity. Love is the activity of one who is sensitive to the genuine needs of another; the loving person seeks to meet those needs and, in so doing, is acted on by the other. Love, thus, is an active state, yet one that *responds* to others in their concrete situation and for their good. This is not done by dominating the other. Love cannot force its way on its recipient however much the lover's vision of the good may exceed that of the beloved. Since the loving person takes the other seriously as a real center of freedom and decision making, and hence as a center of power, the loving person endeavors to increase the power and scope of living of the other. This has been well put by Erich Fromm in his discussion of "mature love" in terms of that type of giving that elicits the power of giving in the beloved. The loving person, he writes, who gives of his joy, his interest, understanding, happiness, and sadness,

> enriches the other person, he enhances the other's sense of aliveness by enhancing his own sense of aliveness. He does not give in order to receive; giving is in itself exquisite joy. But in giving he cannot help bringing something to life in the other person, and

this which is brought to life reflects back to him. Giving implies to make the other person a giver also and they both share in the joy of what they have brought to life.[1]

This type of love can only work by being constantly attentive to the other's needs, by holding a vision of truth, beauty, and goodness in general, and then offering the ideal possibilities to the other in every changing situation. But the loving person does not interfere, or try to impose her or his will, or try to evade the laws of nature and of personality. The loving person who is genuinely thoughtful and concerned for the greatest good of the beloved will realize that it would be a disaster to try to ignore the laws of nature or to interfere with the normal development of a personality. The loving person will never attempt either to evade the natural laws of cause and effect or to snuff out freedom. Rather, that person will try to elicit the best that is possible from the one loved. And the great or large-souled persons are not the ones who try to dominate a situation; they never attempt to establish their own absolute power over other persons or to control their lives. Rather, they are those who are able to evoke the creativeness in the lesser souls about them and with whom they interact and yet, at the same time, to maintain the strength of their own souls or personalities. Also, without trying to control events, they are able to see greater possibilities in these lesser beings than others of us. Inevitably, then, great-souled personalities are not immune to the influence and power of other persons and events; they are great precisely because they are capable of being influenced and enriched by a greater number of persons and a wider variety of contrasting persons and events than are persons of narrow vision and insufficient love—small, pinched souls. And they are capable of adjusting and balancing their response so that it is appropriate to each distinct being, and yet is never partial to one.

Now, it goes without saying that most of us are not large-souled persons or genuinely profound lovers. Most of us are pretty partial to our own rather narrow and fragmentary interests. Most of us, quite frankly, are extremely short-sighted when it comes to perceiving or promoting value; we seem to have little ability or desire to imagine any good but our own, and that for but a brief period. In fact, most of us are content to sacrifice the greater good for our own short-lived goods or what we, perhaps mistakenly, take to be our good. In short, compared with the great-souled personalities, most of us are brittle, selfish, myopic, unresponsive; most of us are relatively incapable of acting for the good of others or of receiving influences into our lives while sustaining our growing souls. And it is the great-souled person, the ideal lover, the expansive and empowering personality, that should be our model for God rather than the rigid, coercive, or mean-spirited types that have often been the models.

It is the capacity to receive conflicting influences, to balance them, to transform their value so as to contribute to the ongoing world while maintaining one's personal center that we attribute to God in the supreme degree. God, we claim, is universal. God is the supreme lover and the supreme person in the universe—indeed, the supreme personal center that is inclusive of everything in the universe. Hence, God is affected by every action, every desire, every prayer of every creature in the universe. God initiates activity in each new experience by responding to its past, by conceiving its best possibilities given its circumstances, and then by offering to each creature the aim ideal for it in that context. And, since God is universal, intimately related to every creature, and not short-sighted as we are, God's response is not such as to favor one part of the world to the detriment of others. Therefore, as I insisted in Chapter 3, *balanced response*, not non-response, is the mark of divine personality.[2]

GOD'S POWER AND CONTINUOUS PRAYER

If this portrait of God, as influenced by and responsive to every creature at every moment, is to be accepted, then we have the idea of one unto whom prayers properly can be addressed. Moreover, the God who is mutually related to every occasion of experience in the ongoing world is the one to whom prayers *are*, in fact, continuously being addressed by every creature in every moment of its existence. Thus, St. Paul's injunction to "pray without ceasing" (1 Thessalonians 5:17) is not a charge to become otherworldly in a bizarre way; it is, in effect, a description of what we are already engaged in whether or not we are conscious of it. The continuous commerce with the omnipresent deity is a form of continuous, silent prayer.

Now, before going directly to the matter of conscious acts of prayer, we need to make one more point about God and our relation to God clear: To say that we have a genuine influence in the life of God is not to say that we should attempt to manipulate God. There are at least two good reasons for this. First, as we have just seen, God is universal and, therefore, not partial to one part of the universe so as to be susceptible of manipulation by that part. Second, as we have also seen, it is the nature of divine power not to remove the power of a lesser creature, but to enhance it. God does not—God *cannot*—eliminate the decision-making power of the creatures, the power to determine finally what they are to be. Nor can God eliminate their power to act beyond themselves, the power to act in other creatures.

To make this point is in no way to "limit" God's power as is sometimes alleged. Rather, it is make clear that to be anything at all, whether the ultimate Creator or a finite creature, is to be partially self-creative (free) and partially creative of others (a cause), and also partially created by others (an effect). Therefore, we should never—by our prayers or for any other reason—expect God to intervene in the fabric of nature and to break the laws of nature or to overrule our freedom. God is omnipresent—omni-active and omni-receptive—but this does not mean that God is the only agent or that God can take over the task of another. God acts by offering us the aim ideal to us under our given circumstances, but it is our own decision, finally, that enacts or rejects that aim; it is not God's. God's role in the ongoing creation of the universe is to enlarge the sphere of our power and to balance the whole when conflicting powers enter the same arena. But this is as much as to say that God, acting in us, enables us to establish ourselves and to act beyond ourselves, and thus to have an effect in God's own life, to be something that matters. Or, to make the point in more traditional terms, God, the Holy Spirit, urges us to pray: "Likewise the Spirit helps us in our weakness," says Paul, "for we do not know how to pray as we ought, but that very Spirit intercedes for us with sighs too deep for words . . . according to the will of God" (Romans 8:26–27).

THE MEANING AND POINT OF CONSCIOUS PRAYER

In view of the foregoing reflections on the nature of God and of God's relations with the world, therefore, several questions regarding the nature of prayer force themselves on us. If everything that occurs in the world is closely attended to by God, if every deed is, in fact, a sacrifice and an oblation unto God, what is the point of encouraging people to enter into conscious or special acts of prayer? What is more, if, as the biblical author Jesus ben Sirach says of the craftspeople and workers who keep stable the fabric of the world: "Their prayer is in the practice of their trade" (Sirach 38:34 RSV translation) by what right do we urge people to undertake specific acts of petition, thanksgiving, praise, intercession, confession, or "centering prayer" in private or public worship. These are the kinds of questions that require us to reflect on the meaning and point of prayer.

To be sure, to call into question the meaning and point of conscious prayer is not automatically to reject it or ignore it. If for no other reason, conscious prayer must be taken seriously because all great religious geniuses in all traditions have prayed and have taught their disciples to pray. For instance, Jesus seems to have prayed frequently and to have urged us, his disciples, to pray. He taught what is called the Lord's Prayer and, as we have seen, urged his hearers to make specific requests to God, their heavenly Father. Beyond this the Psalms are filled with praise confession and petition (and complaint!). Also, the apostle Paul speaks frequently of prayer; and the church, throughout its history, is mainly known for corporate and private prayer. Still, it is important to try to understand what is going on and why.

Perhaps the first thing that ought to be said is what prayer is *not*. If all that has been said about God as intimately related to all creatures, as having been affected by all that has occurred, and as retaining all this perfectly in the divine memory is true, then it goes without saying that in prayer we do not inform God of what God is unaware of. Prayer is not a way of opening up lines of communication with a being who is otherwise absent and, therefore, uninvolved with our lives. St. Augustine made this point forcefully long ago:

> The Lord our God requires us to ask not that thereby our wish may be made known to Him, but for to him it cannot be unknown, but in order that by prayer there may be exercised in us that desire by which we may receive what He prepares to bestow. ... Hence, also when the ... Apostle says, "Let your petitions be made known to God" (Philippians iv.6), this is not to be understood as if thereby they become known to God, but in this sense, that they are to be made known to ourselves in the presence of God by patient waiting upon Him, not ostentatiously in the presence of men.[3]

Augustine's point in this passage is not wholly negative, and this should be made clear. That is, the insight that prayer is not at all a matter of making known to God what otherwise might have remained unknown also carries with it the strict implication that prayer is a way of getting ourselves oriented toward God who is already present to us. It is a matter of awakening our conscience so that it may desire "what he prepares to bestow." Thus, we may attune our sensibilities to the divine will for us so that we are able to receive what God offers to us as the best available possibility. This positive point is repeated and enlarged by Martin Luther when he says, "Our praying teaches us to recognize who we are and who God is, and to learn what we need and where we are to look for it and find it."[4] Thus, we pray not so much to instruct God as to instruct ourselves "in the presence of God." We learn thereby that God is always closer to us than we are to ourselves, and we gain a humbling awareness of our place in the universe—our relative worth—and what God desires for us.

Even so, we should not fall back into the opposite error; we should not assume that our prayers have *no* effect on God, and their *only* effect is on our own mental outlook. If the change we effect in God is not a magical or manipulative one, it is, nonetheless, real. Because every creature in everything it does makes an abiding difference in the universe and, hence, in God, we must take seriously the fact that God *takes us seriously*. In fashioning the aim ideal for us in our concrete circumstances, God takes the needs and expression of those needs into account; God weighs all the conflicting claims and measures them against the divine vision of truth, beauty, and goodness in responding adequately to each.

This point is absolutely fundamental. But there are some corollaries to our understanding of conscious prayer, and of the view that God is always actively and receptively present to each creature, that should be unpacked. If God is not only with us in every moment in an interactive way, but is so as the *personal center* of the universe, then our relationship with God should always be conceived as a personal one. Although the primary analogy for the God-world relation, perhaps, should be based on the soul-body relation, rather than on that between different individuals, there is much to be learned from our relations with individual persons, other than ourselves, whom we love. And this relation is not, finally, at odds with the soul-body relation.

Take, for example, the ongoing relationship we have with our spouses. For the most part the give and take is conducted at the symbolic, noncognitive, nonverbal level. This is what we have been taught to call "body language," such as acts, movements, looks, and sounds that communicate thought and feelings. Moreover, we do things for one another; we do various household jobs, we earn a living wage, we go places with the other person. Much of our communication—our communion—is conducted at this nonverbal, frequently almost-unconscious level. Even so, unless the relationship is freshened and enhanced with occasional, intense, conscious discussions, it likely to dissolve. If the continuous, unconscious commerce with one another is not punctuated from time to time with frank, open discussions in which complaints are aired, our hopes and fears brought to the surface, and in which we articulate what about the other specifically delights or irritates us, the relationship is subject to extinction for lack of nourishment. If, on the other hand, we do consciously focus our personal relation, we deepen it and enable the other to live more creatively and to enjoy a wider range of experience.

Just so, it seems to me, most of our relationship with God is conducted at the non-conscious level of continuous commerce, insofar as ours is a prayer "without ceasing," one that is manifest "in the practice of our trade." For the relationship to be enhanced, however, we need to change our pace occasionally and attempt to put the relationship into sharper, more conscious focus. We need, consciously, to air our needs, our desires, and our hopes for the world and for ourselves, our grievances and our delights and those things for which we are thankful. Indeed, as with any productive conversation, we need to *listen*. We need to be quiet and try to discern what God is trying to say to us. Thus, we may come "to recognize who we are and who God is, and to learn what we need and where we are to look for it and find it."

Moreover, many of us—perhaps not all, but certainly most of us— find it helpful to put these conscious, focused discussions on a regular basis, one not subject to whim or conducted under the pressure of a crisis. In precisely the same way *regular* prayer seems to be conducive to a deepening relationship with God and so with all of God's creation. Speaking for myself, I believe that this regular habit of consciously endeavoring to strengthen our personal relationship with the personal center of the universe is best organized around regular, corporate worship. Most of us do not have the self-discipline to sustain more than flights of self-indulgence on our own. Attendance at public services is more likely to become habitual than is merely private prayer, and habits that increase conscious awareness and deepen personal commitment are not all bad.

In addition, participation in corporate worship helps to make us aware of our own social nature and sensitizes us to the concrete needs of beings other than ourselves. In other words, praying with and for others stimulates a genuine and active concern for them. This was put quite strikingly by William Law, an eighteenth-century Anglican divine: "There's nothing that makes us love a man so much as praying for him; and when you can once do this sincerely for any man, you have fitted your soul for the performance of everything that is kind and civil toward him."[5] Therefore, as true as it is that "religion is what the individual does with his own solitariness," it is equally true that "the topic of religion is individuality in community" and that, ultimately, "religion is world-loyalty."[6] These three phrases from Whitehead warn us not to regard religion as something merely to be practiced alone without any regard for the community that sustains us. Taken together they suggest that we must appropriate for ourselves the religious convictions passed on to us by our tradition, but that the deepest of these convictions is that we are linked inextricably to the destiny of others and that our neighborhood is, finally, the entire world. The best sort of corporate prayers understands and fosters this attitude. I realize that there are many reasons for attending church services, not all of which are as pure as the driven snow! But whatever our motive, I doubt seriously that we can expose ourselves regularly to the prayers and praise of the faithful through the ages without being drawn out of ourselves into that life-enhancing relationship marked by the love of God and love of neighbor.

In any case, it seems to me that the more we pray—the more, that is, we focus our attention on the God who is always with us and so learn what God desires for us—the more we grow and so are enabled to see that this same God hears and responds adequately to all creatures. Therefore, prayer as personal interaction with the personal whole of reality acts to enhance our personal relations, our sensitivity to, and response to, the needs of all who contribute to God's life. This, I believe, is but the other side of a deeply held conviction expressed charmingly in the lines of Samuel Taylor Coleridge:

He prayeth well, who loveth well both man and bird and beast.
He prayeth best, who loveth best all things both great and small;
For the dear God who loveth us, He made and loveth all.[7]

SUMMARY

I believe, therefore, that the minimum that our theological perspective requires us to say about prayer is (1) that the ultimate reality with which we have to do in each moment of our lives is personal, the personal whole of which we are all parts; (2) that this personal being acts not by suspending the laws of nature on behalf of a few or by unilateral decisions that eliminate creaturely freedom, but by responding to the needs of each with the power that endures, that which enhances other lesser powers, the power of love; (3) that every decision and act on our part is a prayer, a response to this eminently personal being, a response to the Spirit sighing deep within us; (4) that we are called by this same Spirit to the state in which we consciously endeavor to deepen our personal relationship with the personal center of the universe, the God who "made and loveth all"; (5) that the only proper conclusion of this relationship with God is to attend lovingly, carefully, thoughtfully to the needs of "all things both great and small."

This belief is most nearly summed up for me in the Collect for Purity with which the Anglican tradition initiates the Eucharist: "Almighty God unto whom all hearts are open, all desires known, and from whom no secrets are hid; Cleanse the thoughts of our hearts by the inspiration of thy Holy Spirit, that we may perfectly love thee and worthily magnify thy Holy Name; through Jesus Christ our Lord."[8]

I only wish to reinforce a point made repeatedly through the book: that the perfect love of God, and the magnifying of God's name, leads ineluctably to—indeed, *means*—love of our neighbors and ourselves. Prayer is not a narcotic that makes us oblivious to the world; it is love's engine by which God's will gets carried out in this world. As such, it is eminently practical as is, in fact, the right understanding of the God to whom we pray.

10

The Last Things: A Christian Doctrine of Hope

The doctrine of the "last things" is an extension of the first principle, namely, that we are "something that matters." The Christian faith is that all creatures make a difference, not only to our fellow beings but to God, who is our ultimate environment. The Christian hope fixes on the love of God that redeems and makes of infinite worth all finite acts and experiences. Nothing that is done is either utterly trivial or lost; it is saved everlastingly in God's experience. This does not entail the hope that individuals will survive as discrete, conscious souls in a "heaven above," but rather that all will be resurrected into God's everlasting, ongoing life, and so be something that matters everlastingly.

Because hope must inevitably be grounded in faith, the doctrine of the "last things" is but an elaboration of our first principle, namely, that we live as humans only in the abiding confidence that we, and all creatures, are finally "something that matters." The Christian faith, which may be said to be a sharper, more explicit form of this common faith of humanity, holds that all creatures make a difference, not only to our fellow beings which constitute our finite environment but also to God revealed by Jesus Christ as the Father whose pure unbounded love redeems "all creatures great and small." God is the all-inclusive One "unto whom all hearts are open, all desires known, and from whom no secrets are hid." Thus the Christian hope is in the love of God that redeems and makes of everlasting value all finite acts and experiences. Nothing that occurs is either ignored or swept away; it is treasured for what it is and can be and is saved for evermore in the ongoing life of God. In God alone there is no lapse of memory, and nothing is lost or misinterpreted; in God alone the full ramifications of all deeds are felt and fully appreciated. Only in the life of God can any experience or occasion be valued adequately and with full understanding, full compassion. Only as it is "objectively immortal"[1] in God can any occasion, finally, be said to be "something that matters."

OBJECTIONS TO THIS EXPRESSION OF THE DOCTRINE OF HOPE

No sooner, however, does a person thus summarily state the basis for and meaning of Christian hope than he or she can expect to hear objections raised from two opposing sides: From the side of traditional religion comes the objection that such talk of "objective immortality" appears as but a desiccated version of the hope for a resurrected life in which the faithful live immortal lives in full, conscious relationship with God, which is the real hope of any full-blooded believer. All talk of "objective immortality," so the objection goes, implies that we are to be nothing more than a "pulse in the Eternal mind,"[2] and surely we hope for more than that.

From the other side—that of the secular critics of religion—comes the objection that all such talk is but a desperate attempt to avoid "hostile life." Is not that hope of immortality but an "illusion"? And does it not act as the "*opium* of the people" that numbs the pain of the real world even as it turns us toward that "illusory sun"?[3]

We should keep these objections in mind, and sooner or later address them, as we endeavor to work out an adequate and intelligible eschatology. Meanwhile, let us begin with aspects of "hostile life" that Christian and biblical religion knows all too well and always endeavors to respond to pastorally.

QUESTIONS RAISED FROM THE EXPERIENCE OF LIFE

One of the most insistent and challenging—not to say, troubling—questions that forces itself on any of us at one time or another is, "What is the meaning of life?" or, in reflecting on humdrum or tragic experience, "Is this *all* that life has to offer?" And implied by these questions is the even more haunting question, "What is the meaning of death—of my own death in particular?"

It is true that life has been kind to many of us who have been born in good health and into comfortable social and economic conditions that reward productivity so that we experience what we do, and what is done to us, as of real value. Even so, we, on whom fortune has smiled favorably, know something of the shocks of life, the bitter aftertaste of failure, or even the tedium that accompanies the quotidian round. Indeed, even if we have not personally experienced profound tragedy, all of us surely know those who have. For example, we can readily recount stories of the untimely death of a young person, or of the suicide of one who did not seem to fit in, or of potentially productive persons crippled by drugs. We know of children born with debilitating diseases, and of the millions born into obscene poverty, and of the slaughter of millions more. Natural disasters and preventable disease wipe out hundreds of thousands every year, and the death toll from the many wars is so massive as to stagger the imagination. The list goes on and on. And so the nagging questions forces its way into our consciousness: "What does it all come to? Is *this* the meaning of life?"

In fact, it is not only tragedy—unmerited suffering, untimely death, etc.—that presses the question. There is the less dramatic but inevitable passage of time, with the accompanying disintegration of organisms, as we move inexorably toward the particular death that awaits each of us. All of us who have passed beyond the fresh bloom of youth, having spotted an extra line about the eyes or a bit of gray, and realizing that the body does not respond with the alacrity that it once did, have shuddered at the awareness of our mortality: "*Mais où sont les neiges d'antan?*"[4] Where, indeed, are the snows of yesteryear? If we are of a mind to put it this way, we might say, with an American philosopher: "Time is the tooth that gnaws; it is the destroyer; we are born only to die and every day brings us nearer death"[5] Actually, this philosopher is only echoing Job who said: "A mortal, born of woman, [is but] few of days and full of trouble, comes up like a flower and withers, flees like a shadow and does not last" (Job 14:1–2).

With the utter realization of our transience many are compelled to reflect on the possibility that with death we perish and are obliterated from reality. Certainly, it is not only those who take a short view, or even those few who seem to be constitutionally irreligious, or even those awakened from their slumber by the shock of tragedy, who raise this possibility. Consider the ancient words of Sirach:

[There are some for whom] there is no memory; they have perished as though they had never existed; they have become as though they had never been born, they and their children after them. (Sirach 44:9)

Consider, also, the dispiriting stanza of the otherwise powerful, confident hymn, "O God our help in ages past":

> Time, like an ever-rolling stream, bears all our years away;
> They fly, forgotten, as a dream dies at the opening day.[6]

Now, if the overwhelming realization of the evanescence of existence and the threat of annihilation at death intrudes itself on all persons—whether by dint of tragedy or by the onset of age—it is just as true that religions (which, as we have seen, do not inevitably try to evade the issue) exist to give meaning to life and to answer the ultimate questions about our Whence and our Whither, the Why and Wherefore of life, its origin and goal.

THE CHRISTIAN MESSAGE OF HOPE

Before taking up what I consider to be the most adequate answer to these questions, I want to take notice of an attempt to ground our hope in immortality on supposed empirical evidence. There are some who have claimed to have gained support for a belief in a life after this life from the reports of those who seem to have experienced clinical death and both looked back on the events of this life and, at the same time, glimpsed something of what is there "on the other side." I have no way of evaluating such claims. I have not experienced what they claim to have experienced, and I would not, moreover, know whether these experiences are of something wholly beyond the self and ordinary experiences, or whether they are experiences within the brain much like the common experiences of *déjà vu* or those of night and day dreams or memory. More to the point, however, I can hardly see how claims for a soul's survival of death for a few hours could support anything like the hope for *everlasting* conscious life, the hope for "subjective immortality."[7] As clinically interesting as such reports may be, they are theologically otiose.

Are there, then, any grounds for the "Good News" proclaimed by Christianity? It is clear, I believe, that Christianity's message to the world is one of hope. It offers to all persons, everywhere, and no matter what their situation, the hope that their lives are redeemed by God. That is, no matter what tragedy may have befallen them, or how grim their prospects for even the minimal amenities of life, no matter how racked with pain, how blinded by the tears of frustration, no matter that they may be choked by poverty, crippled by disease, shut out of the marketplace of fair chance by the greedy powers of this world or simply by the passing fortunes of birth, or slaughtered—no matter: Christianity offers to all the hope of salvation. It bears witness to the confidence that our lives are not a passing whiff of insignificance, that they, indeed, have meaning and worth, not simply among the finite few with whom we ordinarily interact, but everlastingly. *Our lives are ultimately significant because they matter to God.*

This message is compelling and must be taken seriously. Yet, in taking it seriously, we are bound to reflect on its *meaning* rather than merely hearing the words and assuming that we know what they mean. In fact, it is my guess that most of us forget about the real meaning of the Christian message of hope as we concentrate our attention on the symbols by which that hope gets expressed. What is more, I suspect that this diversion of our attention away from the center to the periphery is often a result of the idolatry that tries to make *us*, rather than God, the center of existence, its be all and end all.

THE SYMBOLS OF RESURRECTION AND IMMORTALITY

Let us look first, briefly, at the way in which the Christian message of hope has traditionally been expressed. The basic message was expressed in the New Testament and in subsequent Christian litera-ture in terms of two sets of symbols or myths. These symbols were pre-Christian, and they were, in origin and expectation, quite distinct. There were those, on the one hand, that spoke of the resurrection of the body, or of the bodies of all the elect, on the last day. Other sym-bols expressed belief in the immortality of the soul taken up on the death of the individual.

Originally, expectations of resurrection came out of Persia and, at the time of the writing of the New Testament, were fairly widespread among certain groups of Jews. The beliefs in resurrection, together with various apocalyptic visions of the last times, found an especially fertile soil among a people who had been crushed by the heel of foreign powers for centu-ries, people who had previously had little concern for life after death but who were now alienated from life and power in this world. The belief was that this age, presently under the domination of powers at odds with God, would be brought to an abrupt end imminently and that the right-eous few would be raised up to meet an emissary of God, "one like a son of man" (Daniel 7:13), or, for Christians, the resurrected Christ, often as the Son of Man, who would return in glory (1 Thessalonians 4:13–18; Mark 13), and whose final reign would then commence. When, however, the destruction of this age failed to materialize, the "resurrection of the dead" was pushed back to some distant future "end of time" when all would be judged and the righteous who had died would rise to take on new bodies. The process of "demythologizing" began early.

The belief in the immortality of the soul, on the other hand, was introduced in Greek mythology and speculated about by Greek philosophers, but, at the time of the rise of Christianity, it was especially associated with a wide-ranging movement known as Gnosticism.[8] The Gnostics were thought to have secret knowledge about salvation, and some of their groups whose ideas penetrated the Christian imagination believed that when a true believer died his or her soul—which had been imprisoned in the body—was immediately released and enabled to ascend into heaven, the divine realm of light.

The belief in the "subjective immortality" of the individual soul, released immediately on the death of its body into a Heaven of similar souls where it will it interact endlessly with those souls and with God, has taken over in the popular imagination. The belief in the general resurrection at the end of time has receded somewhat, even though it is still retained in official formulations such as the Nicene Creed where it is said that the Risen-Ascended Christ "will come again in glory to judge the living and the dead, and his kingdom will have no end" so that "we look for the resurrection of the dead, and the life of the world to come."[9]

Perhaps the two mythologies, with their symbols of resurrected bodies and immortal souls, can be woven together to try to express the hope both for the significance of the individual and the destiny of the whole created order that the specifically Christian form of faith demands. Even so, we must be careful to distinguish the myths from the realities they represent or express. It is a mistake to treat the symbols and myths as themselves pointing to temporal states or observable entities that can be perceived by the senses and that empirical science should try to verify or empirical history attempt to locate. It has long since been established that the point of the biblical myths is not to give factual information about the ordinary world of things, times, and places, but rather to express our deepest human relationship with ultimate reality.[10]

This being the case, then, it will be seen that the symbols and myths pertaining to the "last things" have nothing to do with temporal events or with places ("in heaven"). Whenever we entangle ourselves in questions about what is going to happen in the future—whether *my* future immediately following my death or the *collective* future of humanity at some projected date when time comes to an end—we miss the point of the biblical symbols and myths about the last things. They always have to do with the ultimate meaning of existence at *any* moment of time. Christian hope, therefore, is primarily focused on our lives now, that is, with their present relation to God and to God's creation. Hope is only secondarily concerned with the future. To get this point we must be willing to look through the various mythical expressions to their *intention*. As Ogden has said: "Christian hope itself . . . is the criterion for judging the mythology—not the other way around." Therefore, he insists, "the language of hope must be demythologized. It must be interpreted in terms of its own intention to disclose the truth of our own existence in relation to reality as a whole," to which he adds the clarification that "the criterion of our interpretation can only be the specifically Christian understanding of man's relation to God."[11]

THE GROUND AND OBJECT OF OUR HOPE: GOD

As difficult as it may be to keep this point before our eyes, if we do so we will remind ourselves that the ground and object of our hope, as indeed of our faith and our love, is *God*; it is not ourselves, not even humanity generally. It is the eternally existing God, whose boundless love for the world continuously creates and redeems all that we are and do, who is the source and goal of all genuine hope. This is the essential message of Good News proclaimed to the world in the life and death of Jesus Christ as disclosing that even the worst cannot annul God's saving love. We may also say that the essential message of the Good News is that what is ultimately real and of final worth, and therefore the ground and end of our trust, is not merely the world or the things of the world, but *God's all-inclusive love for the world*, which love saves and redeems us.

Because we can put our final trust, our ultimate hope, in God's love for all of God's creatures, we are freed from a debilitating preoccupation with ourselves; we are liberated from anxieties about what may or may not occur to us in the future. Thus, we are enabled by God's redemptive love, and our response to it, to care for, nurture, and redeem as much of God's creation as is given into our stewardship. In other words, the object of our hope enables us to "love our neighbors as ourselves," because we can "love God with all of our heart, and all of our soul, and all of our mind." The Christian hope regards each of us as of genuine finite worth, because we are of infinite worth. We are of worth both in the present and everlastingly.

This means that Christian hope, as grounded in the creative and redemptive love of God—both "the Love that moves the sun and the other stars" (Dante) and that "tender care that nothing be lost" (Whitehead)[12]—really has two temporal foci: first and foremost is the here and now; second, however, as the myths of resurrection suggest, is the future.

As I have said, the Good News is the liberating news that God's love is for each of us *now*—wherever and however we find ourselves—and it cannot be defeated by our trials, our sufferings, or even our desire to place our final trust in such short-lived things as wealth, beauty, intelligence, or good health. We are never apart from God. Thus every thought we have, every experience we undergo, every deed we perform—for good or for ill—is shared by God's redemptive love. Every occasion of experience is taken into, and made a part of, God's ongoing life. This means that, even though we act in the finite world around us or within us, we also and at the same time act on and in God who is our ultimate and immediate environment; we etch our deeds irrevocably into the being of God: "Just as you did it to one of the least of these my brothers and sisters, you did it to me" (Matthew 25:40). Whether our thoughts, or deeds, or experiences are as they ought to be, they are redeemed by God's love, and become a part of the ongoing and everlasting life of God. As Hans Jonas, a philosopher with the soul of an artist, puts it:[13]

> In the temporal transactions of the world, whose fleeting now is ever swallowed by the past, an eternal presence grows, its countenance slowly defining itself as it is traced with the joys and sufferings, the triumphs and defeats, of divinity in the experience of time, which thus immortally survive. Not the agents, which must ever pass, but their acts enter into the becoming godhead and indelibly form his never decided image. God's own destiny, his doing and undoing, is at stake in this universe to whose unknowing dealings he committed his substance, and man has become the eminent repository of this supreme and every betrayable trust. In a sense, he holds the fate of deity in his hands.

To be sure, parts of this passage, such as the suggestion that it is possible to bring about God's "undoing," demand clarification. This means that we cause suffering in God even though we could never bring about God's literal demise. (This is acknowledged by also speaking of an "eternal presence" that "grows," and that the "acts" themselves "immortally survive.") But the point is that every deed we do, every thought we have, every moment of our lives is of infinite significance, because as it occurs it is redeemed by God and makes its mark indelibly in the divine experience. Thus, our "acts enter into the becoming godhead and indelibly form his never decided image." Our thoughts and deeds are registered, in every now, in God who continuously redeems them. They are, we may say, *resurrected* into God's life. The focus of our hope is primarily on the present.

Having said this, however, it is clear that the experience of hope inevitably bears within itself an orientation toward the future. The various expressions of hope for resurrection in the New Testament and subsequent Christian literature, and the various representations of the end time and the establishment of God's reign, all point to the future whether imminent or delayed. This means that our expectation is not only that we are significant in the present (God's as well as the world's) but that we will also be significant in the future. It is because God is ever-present yet ongoing, and our lives make their mark in God's ongoing, everlasting life, that our experiences and acts survive into the future. In the words of Jonas our experiences "immortally survive"; our acts "enter into the becoming godhead and indelibly form his never decided image." Whitehead's equally poetic prose holds the present and future in tension:[14]

> For the kingdom of heaven is with us today. . . . What is done in the world is transformed into a reality in heaven, and the reality in heaven passes back into the world. . . . God is the great companion—the fellow-sufferer who understands. We find here the final application of the doctrine of objective immortality. . . . In this way, the insistent craving is justified—the insistent craving that zest for existence be refreshed by the ever-present, unfading importance of our immediate actions, which perish and yet live for evermore.

The "kingdom of heaven" in which our actions "live for evermore" is the "consequent nature of God."[15] The ground and object of our hope, therefore, is both the present reality of God and *God's* everlasting future.

A CRITIQUE OF THE SECULARIST/ATHEIST HOPE

Having now laid out what I take to be the most adequate eschatology, and so the ground of our hope, I owe it to those who reject any belief in God, any idea of God, to consider the implications of their point of view. It is evident that the secular critics of religion, those who deny God and insist that an appeal to any sort of "immortality" is an "illusion," the "opium of the people," nevertheless themselves find reasons to believe that humans can build a world of value before being blotted out; they believe there are grounds for pursuing high ethical ideals even though the final sentence is . . . nothingness or "omnipotent matter." So, for instance, Bertrand Russell, in *A Free Man's Worship*, sounds the note of noble optimism in the teeth of "omnipotent Death," when he says: "Brief and powerless is Man's life; on him and all his race the slow, sure doom falls pitiless and dark. Blind to good and evil, reckless of destruction, omnipotent matter rolls on its relentless way; for Man, condemned to day to lose his dearest, tomorrow himself to pass through the gate of darkness, *it remains only to cherish, ere yet the blow falls, the lofty thoughts that ennoble his little day; disdaining the coward terrors of the slave of Fate, to worship at the shrine that his own hands have built* . . . the world that his own ideals have fashioned despite the trampling march of unconscious power."[16]

Russell's wholly secular optimism is echoed powerfully in Camus's "absurd hero" in *The Myth of Sisyphus*. There Sisyphus, who has been condemned to the underworld by the gods, whom he scorns, to ceaselessly pushing the rock to the top only to have it inevitably roll back again; his "whole being is exerted toward accomplishing nothing." Yet, Camus insists, Sisyphus, the Absurd Hero, "is superior to his fate. He is stronger than his rock. . . . I leave Sisyphus at the foot of the mountain! One always finds one's burden again. But Sisyphus teaches the higher fidelity that negates the gods and raises rocks. He too concludes that all is well. The universe henceforth without a master seems to him neither sterile nor futile. . . . The struggle toward the heights is enough to fill a man's heart. One must imagine Sisyphus happy."[17]

The bravado of both Russell and Camus betrays an uneasiness with the implication of their atheism. And, in fact, Camus, in one of his last essays (cited in Chapter 1), came clean about this and acknowledged the inadequacy of what was taken to be his previous view:[18]

> The absurd can be considered only as a point of departure. . . . In any case, how can one limit oneself to the idea that nothing has sense and that we must despair of everything? Without going to the bottom of the matter, one can at least observe that, in the same way that there is no absolute materialism, since merely in order to fashion this word it is already necessary to say that there is in the world something more than matter, there is no total nihilism. From the moment one says that all is nonsense, one expresses something which has sense. Refusing all meaning to the world amounts to abolishing all value judgments. . . . Anyway, what is the meaning of a literature of despair? Despair is silent. . . . A literature of despair is a contradiction in terms.

Camus had seen, finally, what Russell and contemporary atheistic ethicists fail to grasp, namely, as Whitehead put it: "Importance, limited to a finite individual occasion, ceases to be important. . . . Importance is derived from the immanence of infinitude in the finite."[19] Or, as we have insisted throughout this work, every experience of every actuality "is a realization of worth, good or bad. It is a value experience. Its basic expression is—Have a care, here is something that matters!" And to be something that matters is to be something of "intrinsic importance for itself, for the others, and for the whole." Moreover, the "whole" is the "infinite whole" of reality. Thus, Whitehead continues, "our sense of the value of the details for the totality dawns upon our consciousness. This is the intuition of holiness, the intuition of the sacred, which is the foundation of all religion."[20] A line from one of Whitehead's last public lectures sums it up: "What does haunt our imagination is that the immediate facts of present action pass into permanent significance for the Universe. The insistent notion of Right and Wrong, Achievement and Failure, depends upon this background. Otherwise every activity is merely a passing whiff of insignificance."[21]

Thus, it seems clear that to be anything of worth is to be something that matters infinitely or, what is the same, for God! On the other hand, if everything is destined to be obliterated, then nothing can be said to matter; if all comes to the same thing in the end—nothing—then everything is on a par, which is to say, it matters not a whit. I believe that the courageous proponents of living meaningful and ethical lives without any ultimate reference, that is, while simultaneously holding that our acts, and any possible acts, finally make no difference at all, do not take seriously enough the observation of Qoheleth that "all is vanity," since "time and chance happen to them all" (Ecclesiastes 1:2, 9:11).

But let us waive the logical point and grant to the optimistic secular critics of religion that human lives *may* have some meaning when they have no ultimate meaning, or that within an ultimate context of nihilism we can eke out value. Even conceding this brave hope, we should consider that much of our incredibly rich inner lives is simply lost to posterity. A vast amount of the texture of our experience—most of the nuances of our thought, our emotional experiences, and even our physical experiences—is barely perceived by others, and most of the concrete detail of it is missed entirely. What is more, much of this is effaced from conscious memory, and left to die "as a dream dies at the opening day." Large chunks of experience are simply lost. That is, they are lost *if* there is no universal and everlasting Memory, *if* there literally is no one unto whom "*all* hearts are open, *all* desires known, and from whom *no* secrets are hid."[22]

Take, for example, one's relationship with a parent. I remember my father. I have a number of cherished memories that illustrate his general character. But who could imagine that I knew his inner life at all intimately? How could I have? I only knew my father at all beginning in his 38th year. And then I only knew him on a daily basis for about 20 years, and I missed much of his concrete experience during that time. To be sure, my father told me stories of his youth, but how could I share much of that experience that was, by in large, foreign to me? How could a young boy, for that matter, share the experience of a middle-aged father, husband, and worker who was having millions of experiences from which I was, perforce, excluded? How could a young man fathom the experiences of a man in his 60s and 70s who then died? My mother, too, is dead, and my brother and sister are in much the same boat as I. Therefore, so far as the progeny, and other intimates, are concerned much—virtually all—of that rich life is lost, irrevocably lost to a merely finite world. So, in effect, the secular hope for meaning and worth in a world devoid of God is a sham.

What is genuine, however, is the religious hope. The Christian conviction, and that of religions generally, is that the finite future and the survivors in the world are *not* the ultimate repository of anyone's thoughts and deeds. We need not lament, nor even acknowledge, their utter loss. The Good News proclaimed by the life and death of Jesus of Nazareth is that God is our ultimate environment, and that God's love that energizes all being also redeems all. Therefore, although others may forget us, or slight us, or ignore us—others may simply fail to share our inner experiences—God neither fails to experience every detail nor lets any slip away. God attends to, loves, cherishes, redeems every detail of every life. Every experience we have, every act we perform, is of everlasting value, because it has its final resting place in God and in God's redemptive love for the world. Thus our hope is for the everlasting significance of our deeds and our experiences— good or bad. In other words, our hope is for their "objective immortality" in the immortal life of God and, insofar as God chooses to make them relevant, in the lives of subsequent occasions of the world.

A CRITIQUE OF THE HOPE FOR SUBJECTIVE IMMORTALITY

I have contended that the secularist/atheist lacks any solid ground for pursuing ethical ideals, since the position amounts to "abolishing all value judgments" and amounts to the confession that all our acts and experiences are but a "passing whiff of insignificance." At the same time I have tried to show that an adequate eschatology can only be one that affirms our "objective immortality" in God who alone abides.

It remains to consider the hope that I have identified as the hope for "subjective immortality." Does our faith demand the additional belief that when we die we do not really die, but that our souls are kept intact as conscious, ongoing, spiritual subjects who enjoy life everlasting in the presence of God? When we say that God "keeps us as the apple of his eye," must we mean that we go to heaven as discrete, eternal yet living souls who have ever new relationships with other souls, many of whom have "gone before," and with God? This seems to be the conventional view of an afterlife in heaven. But is it demanded by faith or the Bible or by a "reasonable, holy, and living" worship of God? I do not think so. To be sure the specific character of any ultimate existence, whether ours or God's, must remain a mystery to finite minds. And so, in the nature of the case, no definitive answer to this question can be given. Even so, there is no reason to suppose that the belief in God and in (conscious human) immortality are inextricably bound together. I do not believe that an allegiance to the Christian hope in God's redemptive love demands the express belief that discrete, conscious individuals will survive immortally in an afterlife, having what I have called "subjective immortality." The conventional idea of our subjective immortality, however, is set about with several attitudes and ideas that reinforce it. Perhaps, if we bring these to the surface and shed some light on them, the hold they have on us will diminish.

First and foremost, I believe, is what I can only call a psychological need for security and a longing to be justified. Since suffering, failure, and death make us uncomfortable, we long to be at peace and, perhaps, to have the opportunity to rectify old mistakes and to have ever-new relationships. The prospect of being cut short by death seems just too unsettling for many of us to contemplate.

But is it? I confess that the thought of my own death has not been disquieting to me. Like others, to be sure, I do not enjoy the thought of the pain that sometimes precedes death. Also like others, I would love to have my wits about me and be able to maintain a relatively sound body until I die. Anyone lucky enough to live past his or her 70s can expect diminished powers. And many can expect debilitating end-of-life diseases. But is death itself a threat? No. I recall reading Plato's *Apology* in my late teens and being persuaded then by Socrates's reasons "to hope that death is a good." He suggested two possible scenarios to follow death, the second of which anticipated our own conventional view that when we pass beyond death we will take up and enjoy relations with those who have preceded us. As Socrates says,

"What would not a man give if he might converse with Orpheus and Musaeus and Hesiod and Homer . . . or Odysseus or Sisyphus, or numberless others, men and women too! What infinite delight would there be in conversing with them and asking them questions!" This scenario seemed to me to be like the conventional view, only with no God to deal with, and it is, I suspect, what many still hope for. But I did not then find it particularly reassuring, nor do I now.

It was, however, the first scenario that struck me then as comforting, and has stuck with me since: Perhaps "death is a state of nothingness and utter unconsciousness," Socrates says. "If you suppose that there is no consciousness, but a sleep like the sleep of him who is undisturbed even by dreams, death will be an unspeakable gain. For if a person were to select the night in which his sleep was undisturbed even by dreams . . . if death be of such a nature, I say that to die is a gain; for eternity is then only a single night."[23] As I say, the realization that death could take us into sheer unconsciousness like that of a dreamless sleep appealed to me as not at all threatening. Only I have the deeper conviction that I will have been something that matters—for good and for ill—to God who alone abides. There is no psychological need for postmortem rewards and punishments nor for the consolation of a continuing, conscious, interactive life.

Another sentiment, however, that induces many to hope for our subjective survival of death in an afterlife is less preoccupied with self. It is far more other-regarding and attuned to issues of justice. It is driven by a deep concern that wrongs be righted, and it well knows that the world has produced so many whose lives were neither long nor happy; "they have perished as though they had never existed," or else, through no fault of their own and often in wretched circumstances, they have been snuffed out prematurely. As one student put it to me: "I cannot shake off the anger and the anguish I feel when I think of the *children* who were killed in the Holocaust or those slaughtered in the genocides of Rwanda and Darfur; and I cannot believe that a loving and just God would allow such unjustifiable suffering to go unredeemed." Indeed, as we have already remarked, there are many millions who have undergone immeasurable suffering in a short life and have met untimely deaths. It is natural for devout and sensitive believers to hope for some rectification of injustices in an afterlife. But it is equally natural for sensitive atheists to reply sharply that no God "worth his salt" would allow such unmerited suffering to occur in the first place. Thus many atheists believe that the existence of atrocities in this world disproves the existence of God.[24]

We can sympathize with the sentiments of both the sensitive believer and the indignant atheist. Yet they are misdirected because they are misconceived. The desire of the believer for an afterlife where wrongs are righted, as well as that of the atheist for a world where no evil occurs or else is reduced so that bad things do *not* happen to good people, rests on an idea of God and of divine power that is childish, non-biblical, and not rational.

I do not mean to be flippant by asserting that the expectations of the subjective immortalist and the atheist, in their desire that God inevitably make things right, are "childish," but they remind me of nothing so much as the sentiment of the child in A. A. Milne's poem, "If I Were King": "I often wish I were a King, and then I could do anything. . . . If I were King of anything, I'd tell the soldiers, 'I'm the King!' "[25] Children often mistakenly imagine that great power is the ability to remove obstacles, to change results, and to manipulate others—in short, to "do anything."

Likewise, the idea is non-biblical. As we saw in Chapter 3 the essential biblical portrait of God is not that of an absolute determiner of all outcomes. The God of the Bible, who is supremely worthy of worship, is the God of pure unbounded love, the personal whole of reality. "Divine love," we saw, "is not the ability to act unilaterally for our good, but the inexhaustible compassion that understands all because it is affected by all and suffers with all." To long for a world, either here or hereafter, where evil can be eradicated or where lives, once miserable and then cut short, can be remade anew, is to presuppose a God at odds with the biblical God. It is better to accept the fact that God knows, loves, and redeems our lives "just as [they are] without one plea."

The irrationality of the idea has to do mainly with the idea of "omnipotence" that it presupposes: the power to "do anything" that God might wish, to wholly determine the outcome of any event. In the first place, as Aquinas said, "nothing that implies a contradiction falls under the scope of God's omnipotence,"[26] and changing or eliminating the past that is stubborn fact, or making the free decision of another for it, or postponing the death of mortals indefinitely, may be seen as logical impossibilities and so contradictions. Moreover, as Hartshorne often maintained, the notion of one being in a universe of finite beings having a monopoly of power is a non-idea and a bad one at that. For instance, he says, "For X to have a power to prevent anything undesirable from occurring is for X to have a monopoly on decision-making. But this monopoly is itself the most undesirable thing imaginable; or rather *it is the unimaginable and indeed inconceivable absolutizing of an undesirable direction of thought.* Monopoly of decision-making is in principle undesirable."[27]

I also think it is unreasonable to suppose that righting wrongs in an afterlife would mitigate the original evils or change the fact that they occurred in the first place. Nor can a postmortem system of rewards and punishments correct anything or recompense us for the ills we have suffered. If a child has suffered and died the child has suffered and died, and God can share its suffering and love it for what it is, but God cannot revise the past out of existence.

Reasonable theists have a wholly different understanding of divine power. It is essentially the power of love: the power to create by enabling the free decisions of others within a conditioned setting; the power to redeem all that has been done; the power to suffer with the creatures in their suffering; and the power to embrace all this everlastingly.

Still, no matter how unreasonable and psychologically immature belief in our subjective immortality might be, when all is said and done does not the scripture insist that "souls go to heaven" or that we are resurrected into an afterlife, "the life of the world to come"? And doesn't this trump all appeal to psychology and reason?[28] Let us examine this claim.

There are precious few references in the Bible to souls going to heaven. The one good passage about souls and God is to be found in The Wisdom of Solomon: "But the souls of the righteous are in the hand of God, and no torment will ever touch them. . . . Their hope is full of immortality" (Wisdom 3:1, 4). This passage ought, properly, to be understood as having to do with our objective immortality in God.

Many of the references to "heaven" in the New Testament are to be found in Matthew where "the kingdom of heaven" is synonymous with "the reign or the rule of God," which refers to God's rule in this world. Even such passages as that at the end of the Beatitudes, "Rejoice and be glad, for your reward is great in heaven" (Matthew 5:12), can and should be read as the persecuted having mattered to God who suffers and yet rejoices with them who have their objective immortality in God. When, in Mark, Jesus, in an exchange with the Sadducees about the resurrection, says, "When they rise from the dead they neither marry nor are given in marriage, but are like angels in heaven" (Mark 12:25), it seems clear that he is dismissing the notion of an afterlife where life goes on much as in this world; when we rise from the dead we are with God. I believe that all talk of heaven can, and must be, demythologized. As was said earlier the language of hope must be interpreted in terms of its intention to symbolize our relation to God; we do not judge the meaning of hope by a literal rendering of the mythological symbols.

This is equally the case with the many references of "resurrection" in the New Testament. For instance, Paul's famous assertion—"If there is no resurrection of the dead, then Christ has not been raised;

and if Christ has not been raised, then our proclamation has been in vain and your faith has been in vain" (I Corinthians 15:13–14)—is followed by an elaborate argument in which he lays bare its meaning: "Christ has been raised from the dead, the first fruits of those who have died.... For he must reign until he has put all his enemies under his feet. The last enemy to be destroyed is death.... When all things are subjected to him, then the Son himself will also be subjected to the one who put all things in subjection under him, so that God may be all in all" (15: 20, 25–26, 28). This is clearly intended to show that faith in resurrection is faith in God, who is all and in all. Paul even tries to head off a literal understanding of the resurrection of the dead when he says, "What is sown is perishable, what is raised is imperishable. For it is sown in dishonor, it is raised in glory. It is sown in weakness, it is raised in power. It is sown a physical body, it is raised a spiritual body" (15:42–44).

If, then, there are no good psychological, rational, or biblical grounds for construing our hope in terms of our subjective immortality, rather than as our objective immortality in God, there is, at least, one good reason to reject it. And that reason is theological.

It seems that such a belief, however disguised or however well-intentioned, stems from an idolatrous effort to substitute our *own* ultimacy, in the form of our enjoyment of everlasting conscious life, for that which is the *true* ultimate, namely, God. In addition to implying that God must repay us for our suffering and reward us for the good we have done, the hope for our own subjective immortality seems to arise out of what is typically called "original sin." That is to say, this hope expresses the deep human desire to "be like God" (Genesis 3:5) insofar as it expresses the hope that we may escape our finitude and become immortal. Reinhold Niebuhr put it bluntly: "Man is mortal. That is his fate. Man pretends not to be mortal. That is his sin."[29] Christianity has consistently refused to endorse the belief in the soul's *pre*-existence for the reason that such a belief represents the attempt to usurp the place of deity. It ought, for the same reason, to reject the idea of our continued *post*-existence as centered, self-conscious selves. Ogden put it well when he said that our sin "Is precisely [the] refusal to acknowledge [our] dependence on God ... [so that our] faith takes the inauthentic form that Scripture speaks of as idolatry—that is, the setting up of something alongside of God's love as alone justifying [our] life by finally making it worth living.... It is this very refusal to live, finally, solely from God's love for us that I find involved in the setting up of our own subjective immortality alongside of our objective immortality in God."[30] I think this is decisive.

In addition, however, a reason for calling into question the hope for subjective immortality is the ethical objection brought forth by secular critics of Christianity from the time of Feuerbach and Marx to the present: The extreme focus on the afterlife has the real effect of depriving this life—our thought, our efforts for justice—of any genuine value. Precisely because our hope has been focused on a perfect life after this one, where "they shall hunger no more neither thirst anymore... and God will wipe away every tear from their eyes" (Revelation 7:16, 17, citing various passages from the Hebrew Bible), we have forged an "unholy alliance" with forces for exploitation and oppression of the poor and marginalized. This is not a charge that can be brought against the belief in our objective immortality.[31]

AN AFFIRMATION OF THE HOPE FOR OUR OBJECTIVE IMMORTALITY

To call subjective immortality into question is in no way to abandon hope. To live in the faith that all our lives—all experiences, deeds, and thoughts—are something that matters, are registered unfailingly in God's everlasting life where they are redeemed and made of abiding worth, is to be perfectly hopeful. Paul's resurrection hope is expressed profoundly in Romans: "If God is for us, who is against us? He who did not withhold his own Son, but gave him up for us all, will he not with him also give us everything else? ... It is God who justifies. Who is to condemn? ... Who will separate us from the love of Christ? Will hardship, or distress, or persecution, or famine, or nakedness or peril, or sword? ... No, in all these things we are more than conquerors through him who loved us. For I am convinced that neither death, nor life, nor angels, nor rulers, nor things present, nor things to come, nor powers, nor height, nor depth, nor anything else in all creation, will be able to separate us from the love of God in Christ Jesus our Lord" (Romans 8:31–39). Again Paul says, "If we live we live unto the Lord, and if we die we die unto the Lord, so then, whether we live or whether we die, we are the Lord's" (14:8).

CONCLUSION

This last chapter brings the work to a close and tries to express summarily the point of view running through it. I can think of no better summary of the whole than the opening of this chapter: "[T]he doctrine of the 'last things' is really but an elaboration of our first principle, namely, that we live as humans at all only in the abiding confidence that we, and all creatures, are finally 'something that matters.' The Christian faith, which may be said to be a sharper, more explicit, form of this common faith of humanity, holds that all creatures make a difference, not only to our fellow beings which constitute our finite environment, but to God revealed by Jesus Christ as the Father whose pure unbounded love redeems 'all creatures great and small.' God is the all-inclusive One 'unto whom all hearts are open, all desires known, and from whom no secrets are hid.' Thus, the Christian hope is in the love of God which redeems and makes of everlasting value all finite acts and experiences. Nothing that occurs is either ignored or swept away; it is treasured for what it is and can be, and is saved for evermore in the ongoing life of God. In God alone there is no lapse of memory, and nothing is lost or misinterpreted; in God alone the full ramifications of all deeds are felt and fully appreciated. Only in the life of God can any experience or occasion be valued adequately and with full understanding, full compassion. Only as it is 'objectively immortal' in God can any occasion, finally, be said to be 'something that matters.' "

This faith and its hope, we have seen, is far more firmly grounded, reasonable, and ethical than that of either atheistic secularism or traditional Christian belief. The former is not as rational as its proponents believe, and it has no grounds for faith and hope; also, it abolishes all value judgments, for all comes to nothing in the end. The latter projects an idea of God that is non-biblical, nonsensical, and for whom nothing in this world could possibly make a difference; it is a God for whom we are something that does *not* matter. By contrast, I have taken the biblical image of God seriously and have shown it to be reasonable and the ground of a reasonable and compassionate ethics. To worship God is to love God with all of our being and to love those whom God loves—all creatures great and small—unreservedly. This is the God for whom all are Something That Matters. Here, I believe, we are at the heart of the Christian proclamation of Good News.

Notes

CHAPTER 1

1. Thomas L. Friedman, "A Perfect Storm?" Op-Ed page, *New York Times*, May 18, 2001.

2. Schubert M. Ogden, *Faith and Freedom: Toward a Theology of Liberation*, revised and enlarged edition (Nashville, TN: Abingdon Press, 1989), p. 25.

3. Alfred North Whitehead, *The Aims of Education and Other Essays* (New York: The Macmillan Company, 1929), pp. 1–2.

4. The Declaration of Independence.

5. Karl Marx and Friedrich Engels, "Manifesto of the Communist Party," *Basic Writings on Politics and Philosophy*, edited by Lewis S. Feuer (Garden City, NY: Doubleday and Company, 1959), pp. 7, 29.

6. I am conscious of having paraphrased Schubert M. Ogden from *Faith and Freedom*, pp. 59–60: Having argued that many liberation theologians who are preoccupied with the urgent issues of justice fail to do their own critical theological analysis and so "perpetuate uncritically the well-known concept of God of classical metaphysics," Ogden pointedly remarks: "[The] only alternative to a good metaphysics, when one undertakes to explicate the beliefs about God implicit in the Christian witness, is a bad metaphysics; and one of the ways of virtually insuring that one's metaphysics will be bad is to take it over incidentally and uncritically instead of deliberately and reflectively." The comments of Alfred North Whitehead, respecting the death of the theoretical Greek thinker, Archimedes, at the hands of a Roman soldier, also bear noting: "[The] theoretical Greeks, with their love of abstract science, were superseded in the leadership of the European world by the practical Romans. Lord Beaconsfield, in one of his novels, has defined a practical man as a man who practises the errors of his forefathers. The Romans were a great race, but they were cursed with the sterility which

waits upon practicality. They did not improve upon the knowledge of their forefathers, and all their advances were confined to the minor technical details of engineering. They were not dreamers enough to arrive at new points of view, which could give a more fundamental control over the forces of nature. No Roman lost his life because he was absorbed in the contemplation of a mathematical diagram." Alfred North Whitehead, *An Introduction to Mathematics* (New York: Oxford University Press, 1958), p. 26. The comments, *mutatis mutandis*, apply to "practical" Christians!

7. Stephen Prothero, scrambling to dissociate himself from teaching theology, says: "Theology and religious studies ... are two very different things—as different as art and art history. While theologians *do* religion, religious studies scholars *study* religion." Stephen Prothero, *Religious Literacy: What Every American Needs to Know—and Doesn't* (New York: HarperCollins, 2007), p. 8.

8. See Paul Tillich, *Dynamics of Faith* (New York: Harper and Row, 1957), pp. 1ff.

9. I have seen this statement used by both Mark Twain and William James. See William James, *The Will to Believe: And Other Essays in Popular Philosophy* and *Human Immortality: Two Supposed Objections to the Doctrine* (New York: Dover Publications, Inc., 1956), p. 29.

10. St. Anselm, *Proslogium; Monologium; An Appendix in Behalf of the Fool by Gaunilon; and Cur Deus Homo*, translated by Sidney Norton Deane, BA (LaSalle, IL: The Open Court Publishing Company, 1958), p. 2.

11. Alfred North Whitehead, *Modes of Thought* (New York: The Free Press, 1966), p. 116. I have obviously borrowed this phrase for the title of this work, and because I think it is so important for expressing succinctly everything I want to say, I should quote the entire passage from which it is taken: "What is our primary experience which lies below and gives its meaning to our conscious analysis of qualitative detail? In our analysis of detail we are presupposing a background which supplies a meaning. These vivid accidents accentuate something which is already there. We require to describe that factor in our experience which, being a matter of course, does not enter prominently into conversation. ... *Our enjoyment of actuality is a realization of worth, good or bad. It is a value experience. Its basic expression is—Have a care, here is something that matters!*" (my emphasis). Anyone would be richly repaid for reading Lecture Six of these Wellesley Lectures, especially sections 3–9.

12. Schubert M. Ogden, *The Reality of God and Other Essays* (New York: Harper and Row, 1966), pp. 34, 37.

13. Albert Camus, "The Riddle," *Atlantic* (June 1963), p. 85.

14. Whitehead, *Modes of Thought*, p. 116.

15. Clifford Geertz, *The Interpretation of Cultures* (New York: Basic Books, 1973), p. 90.

16. Alfred North Whitehead, *Science and the Modern World* (New York: The Macmillan Co., 1925), pp. 267–68.

17. M. Scott Peck, MD, *The Road Less Traveled: A New Psychology of Love, Traditional Values and Spiritual Growth* (New York: Simon and Schuster, 1978), p. 223.

18. Alfred North Whitehead, *Religion in the Making: Lowell lectures, 1926*, Introduction by Judith A. Jones, Glossary by Randall E. Auxier (New York: Fordham University Press, 1996), pp. 145–46.

CHAPTER 2

1. Alfred North Whitehead, *Modes of Thought* (The Free Press: New York, 1966), p. 6.

2. Alfred North Whitehead, *Process and Reality: An Essay in Cosmology*, Corrected Edition, edited by David Ray Griffin and Donald W. Sherburne (New York: The Free Press, 1978), pp. 346, 351, and 346.

3. Ibid., p. 343. Also, see Alfred North Whitehead, *Adventures of Ideas* (New York: The Macmillan Company, 1933), p. 214, where he speaks of "the life of Christ as a revelation of the nature of God and of his agency in the world."

4. *Modes of Thought*, pp. 114, 159–64.

5. Anselm, *Proslogium*, pp. 7, 8.

6. Charles Hartshorne, *Man's Vision of God and the Logic of Theism* (New York: Harper and Row, 1941). See Chapter 9, "The Necessarily Existent," and especially pp. 312–15.

7. Charles Hartshorne, *The Divine Relativity: A Social Conception of God* (New Haven: Yale University Press, 1948), p. 20.

8. Whitehead, *Modes of Thought*, Lecture Six, "Civilized Universe," especially pp. 110–11 and 115–16. Also, see the passage in which he maintains that it is the "unity in the universe, enjoying value and (by its immanence) sharing value" that can account for the value of particular facts, so that "our sense of the value of the details for the totality . . . is the intuition of holiness, the intuition of the sacred, which is the foundation of all religion" (p. 120).

9. Whitehead, *Process and Reality*, p. xi.

10. Ibid., p. 267.

11. Ibid., pp. 81 and 158. For the reference in Santayana, see George Santayana, *Scepticism and Animal Faith: Introduction to a System of Philosophy* (New York: Dover Publications, 1955), pp. 15–16.

12. Whitehead, *Process and Reality*, Chapter 1, "Speculative Philosophy."

13. Ibid., p. 5.

14. Schubert M. Ogden, *Faith and Freedom: Toward a Theology of Liberation*, Revised and Enlarged edition (Nashville, TN: Abingdon Press, 1989), p. 62.

15. Alfred North Whitehead, *The Concept of Nature* (Cambridge: Cambridge University Press, 1964), p. 68.

16. Whitehead, *Process and Reality*, p. 21.

17. Ogden, *Faith and Freedom*, pp. 59–60.

CHAPTER 3

1. See, for instance, St. Thomas Aquinas, *Basic Writings: Volume One*, *"Summa Theologica*, Part I,"* edited and annotated, with an introduction by Anton C. Pegis (New York: Random House, 1944), pp. 22–23, 32–36, 70–71. Even the modern theologian, Paul Tillich, who endeavors to move beyond the tradition, says that the only nonsymbolic statement we can make about God is "that God is being-itself or the absolute" and "only that which is unconditional can be the expression of unconditional concern. A conditioned God is no God." *Systematic Theology: Volume I* (Chicago: University of Chicago Press, 1951), pp. 239, 248.

2. Tillich, *Dynamics of Faith*, p. 52, puts this effectively: "The presupposition of such literalism is that God is a being, acting in time and space, dwelling in a special place, affecting the course of events and being affected by them like any other being in the universe. Literalism deprives God of his ultimacy and, religiously speaking, of his majesty. It draws him down to the level of that which is not ultimate, the finite and conditional. . . . Faith, if it takes its symbols literally, becomes idolatrous."

3. Rabbi Harold S. Kushner, in *When Bad Things Happen to Good People* (New York: Avon Books, 1981) has treated this problem sensitively and with an almost intuitive grasp of the principles of "process theology" as set forth in this book.

4. St. Anselm, *Proslogium*, p. 7.

5. Charles Hartshorne, *Reality as Social Process: Studies in Metaphysics and Religion*, Forward by William Ernest Hocking (Boston: Beacon Press, 1953), p. 112.

6. Dietrich Bonhoeffer, *Letters and Papers from Prison: The Enlarged Edition*, edited by Eberhard Bethge (London: SCM Press LTD, 1971), p. 361.

7. Whitehead, *Process and Reality*, p. 351.

8. Anselm, *Proslogium*, pp. 13–14.

9. James Russell Lowell, "Once to Every Man and Nation," *The Hymnal, 1940: According to the Use of the Episcopal Church* (New York: The Church Hymnal Corporation, 1940), # 519.

10. Charles Hartshorne, *The Logic of Perfection and Other Essays in Neoclassical Metaphysics* (La Salle, IL: Open Court Publishing Co., 1962), p. 135.

11. John Keble, *The Episcopal Hymnal, 1940*, #155.

12. *The Rubaiyat of Omar Khayyam*, translated by Edward FitzGerald, Stanza 71.

13. Whitehead, *Process and Reality*, pp. xiii et passim, 351.

CHAPTER 4

1. Whitehead, *Science and the Modern World*, pp. 243, 249.

2. Whitehead, *Religion in the Making*, p. 94.

3. Ibid., p. 104.

4. Strictly speaking these "formative elements" are slightly different from those enumerated by Whitehead, but the point is the same. Cf. *Religion in the Making*, p. 90.

5. Whitehead, *Process and Reality*, p. 244.

6. Ogden, *The Reality of God*, p. 177.

7. Whitehead, *Modes of Thought*, p. 120.

8. John Keble, "New Every Morning Is the Love," *Episcopal Hymnal: 1940*, #155.

9. Whitehead, *Modes of Thought*, pp. 110–11.

10. Ibid., pp. 116–17.

11. Schubert M. Ogden, "Present Prospects for Empirical Theology," *The Future of Empirical Theology*, edited by Bernard M. Meland (Chicago: University of Chicago Press, 1969), p. 86.

12. I made this point in the last part of Chapter 2, "Some Final Reflections on Experience."

13. Whitehead, *Process and Reality*, p. 50.

14. Schubert M. Ogden and Charles Hartshorne, *Theology in Crisis: A Colloquium on the Credibility of God* (New Concord, OH: Muskingum College, 1967), p. 53.

15. Karl R. Popper and John C. Eccles, *The Self and Its Brain* (London: Springer-Verlag, 1977), p. 120.

16. Wilder Penfield, "The Mind-Brain Question," *Harper's Magazine*, December 1975, p. 6.

17. Roger Sperry, "Mind, Brain, and Humanist Values," in *New Views of the Nature of Man*, edited by John R. Platt (Chicago: University of Chicago Press, 1965), p. 78.

18. Whitehead, *Process and Reality*, p. 167.

19. See, among several of his earlier works, *Reality as Social Process*, pp. 69–84.

20. David Ray Griffin, "Some Whiteheadian Comments on the Discussion," in *Mind in Nature: Essays on the Interface of Science and Philosophy* (Washington: University Press of America, 1977), pp. 97–98, and David Ray Griffin, "Charles Hartshorne's Postmodern Philosophy," in *Hartshorne, Process Philosophy, and Theology*, edited by Robert Kane and Stephen H. Phillips (Albany: State University of New York Press, 1989), p. 6. For Hartshorne's acceptance of the term *panexperientialism* see p. 181.

21. Whitehead, *Modes of Thought*, p. 114.

22. Ibid., p. 72.

23. Ogden, *The Reality of God*, p. 58.

24. Ibid., p. 177.

25. *The Book of Common Prayer and Administration of the Sacraments and Other Rites and Ceremonies of the Church Together with the Psalter or Psalms of David: According to the Use of the Episcopal Church* (New York: The Seabury Press, 1977), p. 323.

CHAPTER 5

1. Cited in J. N. D. Kelly, *Early Christian Doctrines* (London: Adam and Charles Black, 1958), p. 206.

2. Boniface, "Unam Sanctum," in *Documents of the Christian Church* selected and edited by Henry Bettenson (New York: Oxford University Press, 1947), pp. 161, 163. Also, see the statement of the Council of Florence: "[N]o one remaining outside the Catholic Church, not just pagans, but also Jews or heretics or schismatics, can become partakers of eternal life; but they will go to 'everlasting fire which was prepared for the devil and his angels,' unless before the end of life they are joined to the Church." Cited in John Hick, *God Has Many Names* (Philadelphia: Westminster Press, 1982), p. 30.

3. Kenneth Scott Latourette, *A History of Christianity, Volume I: to A.D. 1500* (San Francisco: Harper SanFrancisco, 1975), pp. 657–58.

4. Martin Luther, *Concerning the Jews and Their Lies*, cited in Mary Christine Athans, "Antisemitism? or Anti-Judaism?" *Introduction to Jewish-Christian Relations*, edited by Michael Sermis and Arthur E. Zannoni (New York: Paulist Press, 1991), pp. 127, 128. Cf. Heiko Oberman, *Luther: Man between God and the Devil* (New York: Doubleday Image Books, 1992), pp. 289–92, who points out that Luther's ferocity against the Jews was of a piece with his attitude toward the papists and the peasants.

5. I have borrowed this phrase from Schubert M. Ogden, *Is There Only One True Religion or Are There Many?* (Dallas: Southern Methodist University Press, 1992), pp. x–xi.

6. Justin Martyr, "The First Apology of Justin, the Martyr," *Early Christian Fathers*, translated and edited by Cyril C. Richardson (Philadelphia: Westminster Press, 1953), p. 272.

7. Augustine, "Review of 'De Vera Religione': Retractations I, xiii," *Augustine: Earlier Writings*, selected and translated with Introductions by John H. S. Burleigh (Philadelphia: The Westminster Press, 1953), pp. 218–19.

8. Frederick Denison Maurice, *Theological Essays*, with an Introduction by Edward F. Carpenter (London: James Clarke & Co. LTD, 1957), p. 60.

9. Frederick Maurice, ed., *The Life of Frederick Denison Maurice: Chiefly Told in His Own Letters*, Vol. 2 (New York: Charles Scribner's Sons, 1884), pp. 15, 16.

10. Karl Barth, *The Epistle to the Romans*, translated from the Sixth Edition by Edwyn C. Hoskyns (Oxford: Oxford University Press, 1933), pp. 95–97.

11. Karl Rahner, S. J., *Theological Investigations Vol. VI: Concerning Vatican Council II* (London: Darton, Longmans and Todd, 1969), pp. 394–95.

12. "The Chalcedonian Decree," *Christology of the Later Fathers*, edited by Edward Rochie Hardy, PhD in collaboration with Cyril C. Richardson, ThD, DD (Philadelphia: Westminster Press, 1954), p. 373.

13. Maurice Wiles, "Christianity without Incarnation?" in *The Myth of God Incarnate*, edited by John Hick (London: SCM Press Ltd, 1977), p. 4.

14. Jon Sobrino, S. J., *Christology at the Crossroads: A Latin American Approach*, translated by John Drury (Maryknoll, NY: Orbis Books, 1978), p. 88.

15. Ibid., p. 89.

16. Ibid., pp. 107–8.

17. Paul Tillich, *Systematic Theology, Volume II: Existence and the Christ* (Chicago: University of Chicago Press, 1957), p. 102.

18. Norman Perrin, *The Resurrection According to Matthew, Mark, and Luke* (Philadelphia: Fortress Press, 1977), pp. 5–6.

19. This phrase was coined by the philosopher Gilbert Ryle to express the kind of "big mistake" that represents certain facts "as if they belonged to one logical type or category...when they actually belong to another." See Gilbert Ryle, *The Concept of Mind* (New York: Barnes and Noble, 1949), p. 16.

20. Tillich, *Dynamics of Faith* (New York: Harper Torchbooks, 1957), p. 52.

21. Charlotte Allen, *The Human Christ: The Search for the Historical Jesus* (New York: Free Press, 1998), p. 59.

22. Schubert M. Ogden, *The Reality of God and Other Essays* (Dallas: Southern Methodist University Press, 1992), p. 173.

23. Ibid., p. 186.

24. H. Richard Niebuhr, *The Meaning of Revelation* (New York: Macmillan Company, 1962), pp. viii–ix.

CHAPTER 6

1. Milton Steinberg, *Basic Judaism* (New York: Harcourt, 1947), p. 45.

2. *The Meaning of the Holy Qur'an*, a New Edition with Revised Translation and Commentary by Abdullah Yusuf Ali (Beltsville, MD: Amana Publications, 1989), Surah 4:171.

3. See J. P. Mackey, "Trinity, Doctrine of the," *The Westminster Dictionary of Christian Theology* edited by Alan Richardson and John Bowden (Philadelphia: Westminster Press, 1983), p. 581: "The doctrine of the Trinity is primarily a christological doctrine and its most widely accepted form is a product mainly of the fourth century A.D. It was the christological concerns of the early Christian centuries which persistently motivated and which finally fashioned most of the classical trinitarian doctrine, and in modern

times the declared purpose of that doctrine still is to point to the presence and action of God in this world in Jesus the Christ (economic trinity)."

4. Mackey, "Essential Trinity," *Westminster Dictionary of Christian Theology*, pp. 186–87: "As a term, essential or immanent Trinity is intended to convey the conviction that God is triune in God's inner essence or being and not just in creative or salvific outreach to the world. So expressed a distinction tends to emerge between essential and economic Trinity which was almost certainly absent during the formative centuries of Trinitarian theology, and which once it has more recently emerged, invites those calls for identity of economic and immanent Trinity... From that more ancient point of view it seems best to say that trinities (or binities) primarily, to the extent that they are or were at all successful, point to God's being in outreach to us and as such suggest some self-differentiation in God which, however, we are quite unable to describe."

5. *The Book of Common Prayer*, pp. 864–65.

6. Lewis Ford, "Process Trinitarianism," *Journal of the American Academy of Religion* XLIII, No. 2 (June 1975), pp. 199–213.

7. *Process and Reality*, p. 348, cited in Ibid., p. 212.

8. Ibid., p. 213.

9. Ibid., p. 200. Ford's comments about conic sections as merely theoretical speculation only finding their application years later in Kepler's description of the elliptical orbit of the planets are taken from Whitehead's little book from 1911. See Alfred North Whitehead, *An Introduction to Mathematics* (New York: Oxford University Press, 1948), Chapter 10, "Conic Sections," pp. 100ff.

10. Ibid., p. 200.

11. Ibid., p. 201.

12. Ibid., p. 201.

13. Ibid., p, 203.

14. Ibid., p. 205.

15. Ibid., p. 205.

16. Ford himself sees that the peculiarly modern aspect of the problem is how to account for *the world's transcendence and immanence with respect to God*. But he has already provided the groundwork for answering this in his discussion of God's work as Spirit. He has argued that every creature, being a creative unification of the conditions and possibilities presented to it, is "radically free" and so transcends all other actualities including God. Similarly, he makes the point that every actuality, once it has become a "past event," is a cause immanent in its effect. The additional Whiteheadian point, that the religious intuition that we are something that matters infinitely, entails the view that God, as consequent on the world, is the one Effect in which all finite causes are immanent. Therefore, while the problem, together with its Whiteheadian solution, is genuine enough, it does not itself require a "triad of principles." See Ford, Ibid., pp. 201, 200, 205.

17. Ibid., p. 205.

18. Ibid., pp. 205, 206.

19. Ibid., p. 206.

20. Ibid., p. 206.

21. Ibid., p. 213.

22. Ibid., p. 207.

23. Ibid., p. 207.

24. Ibid., pp. 207–8, footnote 16. The equation of the Spirit with the "superjective nature" is, as we will see, precisely what Bracken does.

25. Article XXII, *Book of Common Prayer*.

26. Joseph Bracken, S.J., has written extensively about the trinity. At least three books, *What Are They Saying about the Trinity, The Triune Symbol: Persons, Process, and Community*, and *God: Three Who Are One*, are wholly given to Trinitarian theology. Two sets of two-part articles, one in the *Heythrop Journal* and the other in *Process Studies* treat the doctrine from a perspective deeply informed by Whiteheadian categories and ideas. For my purpose it will be sufficient to inspect mainly the *Process Studies* pieces supplemented by some crucial remarks in *What Are They Saying about the Trinity* and *God: Three Who Are One*.

27. "Process Philosophy and Trinitarianism," *Process Studies*, No. 8 (1978), p. 221.

28. *What Are They Saying about the Trinity* (New York: Paulist Press, 1979), p. 33.

29. Ibid., pp. 50–51.

30. "Process Philosophy and Trinitarians-II," *Process Studies*, No. 11 (1981), p. 83.

31. Cited in "Process Philosophy and Trinitarian Theology," *Process Studies*, No. 8, p. 225.

32. Cited in Ibid., p. 225.

33. Ibid., p. 225.

34. "Process Philosophy and Trinitarian Thought—II," p. 86. My italics.

35. Ibid., p. 88.

36. Ibid., p. 89.

37. Ibid., p. 89.

38. Ibid., p. 91.

39. The majority opinion in the Supreme Court's "Citizens United" case seem to me to have rested on a similar misconception—that corporations are *individual agents* having "free speech." Just as the common parlance suggests that "Congress acted," as if "Congress" were an individual who can act, the majority apparently believed that corporations are individuals with the ability (and right) to speak freely. The British are more careful in their use of language. They typically say "Parliament *have* done thus and such," indicating that Parliament is a group whose individual members make the decisions.

CHAPTER 7

1. Diana L. Eck, "Preface 2003" to *Encountering God: A Spiritual Journey from Boseman to Banaras* (Boston: Beacon Press, 2003), p. xi. There are many important contributors to the current discussion. Among them are John Hick, *God Has Many Names* (Philadelphia: Westminster Press, 1982), Paul F. Knitter, *No Other Name? A Critical Review of Christian Attitudes toward the World Religions* (Maryknoll, NY: Orbis Books, 1985), John Hick and Paul F. Knitter, eds., *The Myth of Christian Uniqueness: Toward a Pluralistic Theology of Religions* (Maryknoll, NY: Orbis Books, 1987), Congregation for the Doctrine of the Faith, *Dominus Iesus; On the Unicity and Salvific Universality of Jesus Christ and the Church*, August 6, 2000; and Schubert M. Ogden, *Is There Only One True Religion or Are There Many* (Dallas: Southern Methodist University Press, 1992).

2. James Carroll, *Constantine's Sword: The Church and the Jews, a History* (New York: Houghton Mifflin Company, 2001).

3. Ogden, *Is There Only One True Religion or Are There Many?* pp. 13, 100. Ogden adds to the second passage (what he had made clear throughout Chapter 1, "The Challenge of Pluralism"): "The adherents of any religion are bound to employ what it, in turn, specifies as formally normative as exactly that in judging all claims to religious truth."

4. Gotthold Ephraim Lessing, *Nathan the Wise: A Dramatic Poem*, ed. George Alexander Kohut, tr. Patrick Maxwell, 2nd ed. (New York: Block Publishing Co., 1923).

5. William S. Campbell, "The Challenge of Peace and Reconciliation for Christian Self-Understanding and Contemporary Interreligious Relations," being the Walter and Mary Tuohy lectures at John Carroll University, Spring 2011. The lectures have not been published, but the quote is from the prospectus for the first lecture, "Christian Triumphalism and the Creator God."

6. Most of what follows reproduces the second half of my article, "A Christian Alternative to (Christian) Racism and Antisemitism," *The Journal of Ecumenical Studies* (37:2, Spring 2000), pp. 151–60.

7. I have provided plenty of examples of this in the first half of the article: e.g., the Synoptic gospels setting Jesus over against Pharisees and leaders of the Jews, the "Woes" against the Pharisees, the portrayal of Pilate as an innocent stooge of the wicked Jewish leaders, and above all, the many hostile references to "the Jews" in the Gospel of John.

8. Michael Cook, "The New Testament: Confronting Its Impact on Jewish-Christian Relations," in Michael Shermis and Arthur E. Zannoni, eds., *Introduction to Jewish-Christian Relations* (Mahwah, NJ, and New York: Paulist Press, 1991), p. 55.

9. Alfred North Whitehead, *Adventures of Ideas* (New York: The Macmillan Co., 1933), p. 214.

10. Whitehead, *Process and Reality*, p. 351.

11. Charles Allen Dinsmore, *Atonement in Literature and Life* (Boston: Houghton, Mifflin and Co., 1906), pp. 232–33.

12. Dietrich Bonhoeffer, "Letter to Eberhard Bethge," 16 July 1944 in *Letters and Papers from Prison: The Enlarged Edition*, edited by Eberhard Bethge, translated by Reginald Fuller, Frank Clarke, John Bowden, and others (London: SCM Press, 1971), p. 361.

13. *The Meaning of Revelation*, pp. viii–ix.

14. I am well aware that Acts is not a reliable history but is more of a "historical novel" or even a dramatic theological narrative written by the author of "Luke-Acts" in which stories, events, and speeches are created to make the Christian movement look good to Roman officials. Thus the speeches of both Paul and Peter are probably not real speeches by the "historical Paul" and the "historical Peter." But they represent a powerful point of view widespread in the early Christian community.

15. I first became fully conscious of this—and how Christians are perceived by others—when I read Walter Kaufmann's Prologue to Martin Buber's *I and Thou*. There, speaking of the unmediated "return to God," Kaufmann writes: "Christianity in particular is founded upon its implicit denial. The Jewish doctrine holds that a man can at any time return and be accepted by God. That is all" (Martin Buber, *I and Thou, A New Translation* with a Prologue "I and You" and Notes by Walter Kaufmann [New York: Charles Scribner's Sons, 1970], p. 36). Then, rehearsing the story of Jonah and the "return" of the Ninevites, he continues: "This conception of return has been and is at the very heart of Judaism, and it is for the sake of this idea that Jonah is always read on the highest holiday of the year. But the theology of Paul in the New Testament is founded on the implicit denial of this doctrine, and so are the Roman Catholic and the Greek Orthodox churches, Lutheranism and Calvinism. Paul's elaborate argument concerning the impossibility of salvation under the Torah ('the Law') and for the necessity of Christ's redemptive death presupposes that God cannot simply forgive anyone who returns" (Ibid., p. 37). It goes without saying that I am sure that Kaufmann is quite wrong about Paul and wholly misunderstands his approach, but it is equally likely that Paul misunderstood the Judaism of his day that he felt to be so constricting. It is also true that much Christianity has misunderstood Paul—and Jesus, for that matter.

16. Benjamin Whichcote, "Moral and Religious Aphorisms," in Gerald R. Cragg, ed., *The Cambridge Platonists* (New York: Oxford University Press, 1968), p. 424.

17. Ogden, *Faith and Freedom: Toward a Theology of Liberation*, pp. 54–55.

CHAPTER 8

1. Whitehead, *Process and Reality*, p. 21.

2. George Santayana, *Scepticism and Animal Faith: Introduction to a System of Philosophy* (New York: Dover Publications, 1955), p. 15.

3. Whitehead, *Process and Reality*, p. 167.

4. Whitehead, *Modes of Thought*, pp. 116–17.

5. These are the criteria that Whitehead invokes by which to evaluate a metaphysical scheme. See *Process and Reality*, p. 3.

6. Whitehead, *Modes of Thought*, p. 114.

7. See, for instance, Hartshorne, *Reality as Social Process*, pp. 69–84.

8. Whitehead, *Modes of Thought*, p. 163.

9. Ogden, *The Reality of God*, p. 58.

10. Ogden, *The Reality of God*, p. 177.

11. St. Augustine, *The Confessions of St. Augustine*, translated, with an Introduction and Notes by John K. Ryan (New York: Doubleday, 1960), p. 43.

12. Whitehead, *Modes of Thought*, pp. 31–32.

13. Erich Fromm, *The Art of Loving* (New York: Bantam Books, 1956), pp. 22–27.

CHAPTER 9

1. Erich Fromm, *The Art of Loving* (New York: Bantam Books, 1963), pp. 20–21.

2. In Chapter 3 I quoted Hartshorne from *The Logic of Perfection* where making an analogy to God as "supremely worshipful," he said: "A 'good' man is not, compared to a bad or inferior one, any less relative or contingent; but rather, he is far more adequately related to other things and richer and more harmonious in his accidental qualities. . . . The wise person balances the stimuli of the moment against the background of past stimuli and past decisions of his own. Balanced appropriateness in one's relativity to other things or persons, not non-relativity, is the mark of wisdom and goodness. The non-relative or merely inflexible person, who will not be influenced, who will not or cannot adjust to the actual situation sensitively and quickly, need not be especially admired."

3. Augustine, "Epistle CXXX" in *An Augustine Synthesis*, arranged by Erich Przywara (New York: Harper Torchbooks, 1958), pp. 383–84.

4. Cited in Ogden, *The Reality of God*, p. 67, n. 105.

5. William Law, *A Serious Call to a Devout and Holy Life* and *The Spirit of Love* edited from the first editions by Paul G. Stanwood; Introduction by Austin Warren and Paul Stanwood; Preface by John Booty (London: SPCK, 1978), p. 302.

6. Whitehead, *Religion in the Making*, pp. 16, 59, and 86.

7. Samuel Taylor Coleridge, "The Rime of the Ancient Mariner," in *Immortal Poems of the English Language*, edited by Oscar Williams (New York: Washington Square Press, 1952), lines 612–17.

8. *The Book of Common Prayer*, p. 323.

CHAPTER 10

1. The phrase is Whitehead's, and it stands for the doctrine that every actuality or occasion of experience, as it attains determinate status in the temporal world, becomes significant beyond itself, and finally is registered everlastingly and attains "unfading importance" in the life of God. See *Process and Reality*, pp. xiii–xiv, 45, 351 and throughout the text.

2. Rupert Brooke, "The Soldier," *Norton Anthology of English Literature: Sixth Edition, Volume 2*, M. H. Abrams, General Editor (New York: W.W. Norton, 1993), p. 1827.

3. The critical phrases are the well-known ones of Freud and Marx. See Sigmund Freud, *The Future of an Illusion*, translated and edited by James Strachey, with a biographical Introduction by Peter Gay (New York: W.W. Norton, 1961), pp. 38–71; esp. p. 63, and Karl Marx, "Toward the Critique of Hegel's Philosophy of Right," *Basic Writings on Politics and Philosophy; Karl Marx and Friedrich Engels*, edited by Lewis S. Feuer (Garden City, NY: Doubleday & Co. 1959), p. 263.

4. François Villon, "Le Grand Testament. Ballade des Dames du Temps Jadis," *Familiar Quotations: A Collection of Passages, Phrases and Proverbs Traced to Their Sources in Ancient and Modern Literature*. Sixteenth Edition, John Bartlett, Justin Kaplan, General Editor (Boston: Little, Brown and Co., 1992), p, 134.

5. John Dewey, "Time and Individuality," *On Experience, Nature, and Freedom* (Indianapolis: Bobbs-Merrill Co., 1960), p. 225.

6. Isaac Watts, *The Hymnal 1982 According to the Use of The Episcopal Church*, # 680 (New York: The Church Hymnal Corporation, 1985). The hymn, including the stanza quoted, is a paraphrase of Psalm 90:1–5.

7. I use this phrase to convey the conventional view that conscious individual souls survive death forever in an afterlife or heaven. It is used this way by both David Ray Griffin and Schubert Ogden. See, for example, David Ray Griffin and Huston Smith, *Primordial Truth and Postmodern Theology* (Albany: State University of New York Press, 1989), pp. 4, 25, 130, and Schubert M. Ogden, *The Reality of God*, pp. 36, 225, 229, 230, and in "The Meaning of Christian Hope," in *Religious Experience and Process Theology: The Pastoral Implications of a Major Modern Movement*, edited by Harry James Cargas and Bernard Lee (New York: Paulist Press, 1976), pp. 199, 206, 207, 210.

8. See Hans Jonas, *The Gnostic Religion: The Message of the Alien God and the Beginning of Christianity* (Boston: Beacon Press, 1958).

9. "The Nicene Creed," *The Book of Common Prayer*, p. 359.

10. It was precisely with respect to eschatological symbols that Reinhold Niebuhr famously said: "[I]t is important to take Biblical symbols seriously but not literally. If they are taken literally the Biblical conception of a dialectical relationship between history and superhistory is imperiled." Reinhold Niebuhr, *The Nature and Destiny of Man: Volume II. Human*

Destiny (New York: Charles Scribner's Sons, 1954), p. 50. The best and clearest understanding of the point of myth, however, and what biblical myths intend and why they must, therefore, be "demythologized" is given by Bultmann: "The real point of myth is not to give an objective world picture; what is expressed in it, rather, is how we human beings understand ourselves in our world. Thus, myth does not want to be interpreted in cosmological terms but . . . in existentialist terms. Myth talks about the power or the powers that we think we experience as the ground and limit of our world and of our own action and passion. It talks about these powers in such a way, to be sure, as to bring them within the circle of the familiar world. . . . Myth talks about the unworldly as worldly, the gods as human" (Here Bultmann adds in a note: "That mode of representation is mythology in which what is unworldly and divine appears as what is worldly and human or what is transcendent appears as what is immanent . . . ")

"What is expressed in myth is the faith that the familiar and disposable world in which we live does not have its ground and aim in itself but that its ground and limit lie beyond all that is familiar and disposable and that this is all constantly threatened and controlled by the uncanny powers that are its ground and limit. In unity with this myth also gives expression to the knowledge that we are not lords of ourselves, that we are not only dependent within the familiar world but that we are especially dependent upon the powers that hold sway beyond all that is familiar, and that it is precisely in dependence on them that we can become free from the familiar powers."

"Therefore, the motive for criticizing myth, that is, its objectifying representations, is present in myth itself, insofar as its real intention to talk about a transcendent power to which both we and the world are subject is hampered and obscured by the objectifying character of its assertions." Rudolf Bultmann, *New Testament and Mythology: and Other Basic Writings*, Selected, edited, and translated by Schubert M. Ogden (Philadelphia: Fortress Press, 1984), pp. 9–10, 42.

11. Ogden, "The Meaning of Christian Hope," p. 203.

12. Dante Alighieri, *The Divine Comedy of Dante Alighieri: Paradiso*, A Verse Translation with an Introduction by Allen Mandelbaum (New York: Bantam Books, 1984), p 303; Whitehead, *Process and Reality*, p. 346.

13. Hans Jonas, "Immortality and the Modern Temper," *The Phenomenon of Life: Toward a Philosophical Biology* (New York: Harper and Row, 1966), p. 274.

14. *Process and Reality*, p. 351.

15. *Process and Reality*, p. 350.

16. Bertrand Russell, *Mysticism and Logic: And Other Essays* (Totowa, NJ: Barnes and Noble Books, 1981), pp. 46, 47. My italics.

17. Albert Camus, *The Myth of Sisyphus and Other Essays* (New York: Vintage Books, 1955), pp. 89, 91.

18. Camus, "The Riddle," *The Atlantic Monthly*, Vol. 211, 1963, p. 85.

19. Alfred North Whitehead, *Modes of Thought* (Cambridge: Cambridge University Press, 1956), p. 28.

20. *Modes of Thought*, pp. 159, 164.

21. Alfred North Whitehead, "Immortality," *The Philosophy of Alfred North Whitehead*, edited by Paul Arthur Schillp (New York: Tudor Publishing Company, 1941), p. 698.

22. The phrase is from the Collect for Purity in *The Book of Common Prayer*, p. 323 (cited above and at the end of Chapter 4). Hartshorne, in his essay "Time, Death, and Everlasting Life," argues persuasively that Divine Memory as utter omniscience is the only adequate registry of all acts. Having first likened our lives to a book that is continuously written from day one to the final hour, and which can neither be effaced from reality nor written continuously anew in a postmortem state, he says: "Our adequate immortality can only be God's omniscience of us. He to whom all hearts are open remains evermore open to any heart that ever has been apparent to Him. What we once were to Him, less than that we never can be, for otherwise He Himself as knowing us would lose something of His own reality; and this loss of something that has been must be final, since, if deity cannot furnish the abiding reality of events, there is, as we have seen, no other way, intelligible to us at least, in which it can be furnished. Now the meaning of omniscience is a knowledge which is coextensive with reality, which can be taken as the measure of reality. Hence, if we can never be less than we have been to God, we can in reality never be less than we have been. Omniscience and the indestructibility of every reality are correlative aspects of one truth. Death cannot mean the destruction or even the fading, of the book of one's life; it can mean only the fixing of its concluding page. Death writes 'The End' upon the last page, but nothing further happens to the book, by way of either addition or subtraction." *The Logic of Perfection*, pp. 252–53.

23. Plato, *Apology, Crito, Phaedo, Symposium, Republic*. Translated by B. Jowett. Edited, with Introduction, by Louise Ropes Loomis (New York: Walter J. Black, 1942), pp. 59–60.

24. This is the gravamen of Sam Harris's argument in his little book, *Letter to a Christian Nation* (New York: Alfred A. Knopf, 2006). See, for instance, pages 51–55, where he claims that "the entirety of atheism is contained in" the response to the many atrocities the world experiences: "An atheist is a person who believes that the murder of a single little girl— even once in a million years—casts doubt upon the idea of a benevolent God. ... If God exists, either He can do nothing to stop the most egregious calamities, or He does not care to. God, therefore, is either impotent or evil. ... There is another possibility, of course, and it is both the most reasonable and least odious: the biblical God is a fiction ... "

25. A. A. Milne, *The World of Christopher Robin: The Complete When We Were Very Young and Now We Are Six* (New York: E.P. Dutton & Co., 1958), p. 111.

26. *Summa Theologica*, I, Q. 25, a. 4 (p. 265).

27. Charles Hartshorne, "A New Look at the Problem of Evil," *Current Philosophical Issues: Essays in Honor of Curt John Ducasse*, edited by Frederick C. Dommeyer (Springfield, IL: Charles C. Thomas Publishers, 1966), p. 202. With respect to the "problem of evil" Hartshorne says (pp. 207–8): "(a) it is a pseudoproblem due to a pseudoconcept of omnipotence or divine power; evil springs from creaturely freedom, and without such freedom there could be no world at all; (b) creaturely freedom capable of producing evil, at least in the form of suffering, is universal to the creation, not confined to man or rational animals or even to animals; (c) God's supremacy consists, not in his making the creatures' decisions for them, but in his setting abstract limits of law to creaturely decisions, and in his ideally free evaluations of the results so that they acquire permanent meaning; finally, (d) God shares in all suffering since he cherishes all creatures, so that he may be seen as the ideal companion in sorrow as well as joy. God would be masochistic as well as sadistic if it were true that he deliberately caused us to suffer. But he is neither, for no concrete evil is divinely decided, whether as punishment, means of spiritual education, or in view of any other end. God sets the creatures free, within limits, because there is no other way to have creatures or any world. The risks of freedom are inseparable from freedom, and the price of its opportunities. Without freedom there could be nothing, whether good or evil."

28. We are much too ready to assert that "The Bible says . . . " Consider, for instance, the running "church signs" debate that is being passed around by e-mail: A Catholic Church: "All dogs go to heaven." A Presbyterian Church: "Only humans go to heaven. Read the Bible." Catholic: "God loves all His creations, dogs included." Presbyterian: "Dogs don't have souls. This is not open to debate." Catholic: "Catholic dogs go to heaven. Presbyterian dogs can talk to their pastor." Presbyterian: "Converting to Catholicism does not magically grant your dog a soul." Catholic: "Free dog souls with conversion." Presbyterian: "Dogs are animals. There aren't any rocks in heaven either." Catholic: "All rocks go to Heaven." The Catholics have the better sense of humor here. And, if they are willing to demythologize "going to heaven" to mean being embraced everlastingly by God, the Catholics have the better of it. But if they both take Heaven literally as an afterlife where conscious souls go to have an extended, developing life, both are demanding "subjective immortality" that the Bible may not demand.

29. Reinhold Niebuhr, *Beyond Tragedy: Essays on the Christian Interpretation of History* (New York: Charles Scribner's Sons, 1937), p. 28.

30. Ogden, "The Meaning of Christian Hope," p. 209.

31. So Ogden argues: "by focusing our ultimate hope on our subjective existence beyond death, Christianity appears to many of our contemporaries to belittle the urgent problems of a humanity struggling for greater justice and enlightenment and to provide at least a negative sanction for the social and political status quo. And this appears all the more certain to them

because, with its virtual abandonment of apocalypticism as expressing a truly collective hope, much of modern Christianity has, in fact, focused man's ultimate expectations on the existence beyond death of the individual persons. Thus it has been widely taught in modern Churches that all that finally counts is the other-worldly salvation of individuals, with the result that efforts for the fulfillment and humanization of this world have been deprived of any ultimate significance." Ibid., pp. 210–11.

Index

About the Author

DAVID R. MASON is an Episcopal priest and professor of religious studies at John Carroll University. He is the author of *Time and Providence: An Essay Based on an Analysis of the Concept of Time in Whitehead and Heidegger* (University Press of America, 1982) and editor of *Talking about God: Doing Theology in the Context of Modern Pluralism* by David Tracy and John B. Cobb Jr. (Seabury Press, 1983). He is also known through his speaking engagements on Alfred North Whitehead, process thought, God, atheism, St. Paul, Christian anti-Semitism, and other topics for church, synagogue, and civic groups.

Mason has written many articles for *The Journal of Religion*, *Process Studies*, and *Zygon*. He received his MA and PhD from the University of Chicago and his MDiv from The General Theological Seminary. He lives in Cleveland Heights, Ohio.